AN INTRODUCTION TO
VULGAR LATIN

ALSO FROM TIGER XENOPHON
& TIGER OF THE STRIPE

Benjamin Hall Kennedy, Revised by Gerrish Gray
Kennedy's New Latin Primer (UK edn)
264 pp., paperback, ISBN 978-1-904799-18-4

Benjamin Hall Kennedy, Revised by Gerrish Gray
Kennedy's New Latin Primer (US edn)
264 pp., paperback, ISBN 978-1-904799-19-1

Charles H. Grandgent
*From Latin to Italian: An Historical Outline of the
Phonology and Morphology of the Italian Language*
200 pp., paperback, ISBN 978-1-904799-23-8

Charles H. Grandgent
*An Outline of the Phonology and Morphology
of Old Provençal*
176 pp, paperback, ISBN 978-1-904799-27-6

Joseph Anglade
Grammaire Elémentaire de l'Ancien Français
240 pp., paperback, ISBN 978-1-904799-20-7

Edward Maunde Thompson
An Introduction to Greek and Latin Palæography
616 pp., hardback, ISBN 978-1-904799-30-6

Edward Maunde Thompson
The History of English Handwriting A.D. 700–1400
80 pp., paperback, ISBN 978-1-904799-10-8

AN INTRODUCTION TO
VULGAR LATIN

C. H. GRANDGENT
*Former Professor of Romance Languages
at Harvard University*

Richmond
TIGER XENOPHON
MMIX

This edition first published
in 2009 by
Tiger Xenophon
50 Albert Road
Richmond
Surrey TW10 6DP
United Kingdom

© 2009 Tiger Xenophon
All rights reserved

Tiger Xenophon is an imprint of
Tiger of the Stripe

ISBN 978-1-904799-43-6

Printed in the US and UK by
Lightning Source

PREFACE.

WHILE this book is intended primarily for students of Romance Philology, it will, I hope, be of some interest to Classical scholars as well. Although it has been long in the making, I have endeavored to keep it, at every stage, abreast of current scholarship. I have tried, furthermore, to treat all portions of the subject, not exhaustively, but with even fulness; I fear, however, that the Syntax — perhaps unavoidably — is somewhat scanty as compared with the other parts. It will be seen that I have continually furnished abundant references for the guidance of those who wish to look further into special topics. My principal authorities are listed in the Bibliography; others are cited in the appropriate places in the text.

C. H. GRANDGENT.

TABLE OF CONTENTS.

	PAGES
MAPS	x, xi
The Roman Empire	x
The Neo-Latin Territory in Europe	xi
BIBLIOGRAPHY, with Abbreviations	xiii–xvi
PHONETIC ALPHABET and Other Symbols	xvii
INTRODUCTION	1–5
VOCABULARY	6–29
Words and Their Meanings	6–12
Words used alike in Classic and in Vulgar Latin	6
Words used differently in Classic and in Vulgar Latin	7–8
Sense Restricted	7
Sense Extended	7–8
Words used in Classic but not in Vulgar Latin	8–9
Synonyms	9
Substitutes	9–10
Particles	10
Words used in Vulgar but not in Classic Latin	10–12
Native Words	11–12
Foreign Words	12
Derivation	13–29
Post-Verbal Nouns	13
Prefixes	13–16
Prefixes used with Nouns, Adjectives, and Pronouns	13–14
Prefixes used with Verbs	14–16
Suffixes	16–28
Suffixes for Verbs	16–17
Suffixes for Nouns	18–23
Suffixes for Adjectives	23–25
Suffixes for Adverbs	25–26
Change of Suffix	27–28

TABLE OF CONTENTS.

	PAGES
Compounds	28–29
Nouns	28
Adjectives	28
Pronouns	28
Verbs	28
Adverbs	28–29
Prepositions	29
Conjunctions	29
SYNTAX	30–59
ORDER OF WORDS	30–32
USE OF WORDS	32–41
Nouns and Adjectives	32–34
Comparison	33
Numerals	33–34
Pronouns	34–38
Personal and Possessive Pronouns	34
Demonstratives	35–36
Interrogatives and Relatives	36–37
Indefinite Pronouns	37–38
Verbs	38
Adverbs	38–39
Prepositions	39–41
Conjunctions	41
USE OF INFLECTIONS	42–59
Cases	42–48
Locative	42–43
Vocative	43
Genitive	43–44
Dative	44–45
Ablative	45–47
Accusative	48
Fall of Declension	48
Verb-Forms	48
Impersonal Parts	48–51
Supine	48–49
Gerund	49
Gerundive	49
Future Active Participle	49

	PAGES
Present Participle	50
Perfect Participle	50
Infinitive	50–51
Voice	51–52
Mood	52–54
Imperative	52
Subjunctive	52–54
Tense	54–59
The Perfect Tenses	54–56
Future and Conditional	56–59
PHONOLOGY	60–143
SYLLABICATION	60–61
ACCENT	61–68
Primary Stress	61–66
Vowels in Hiatus	61–62
Compound Verbs	62–63
Illac, Illic	63
Ficatum	63
Numerals	64
Greek Words	64–66
Greek Oxytones	64
Greek Paroxytones	64–65
Greek Proparoxytones	65–66
Other Foreign Words	66
Secondary Stress	66–67
Unstressed Words	67–68
QUANTITY	68–77
Position	68–70
Vowel Quantity	71–77
Vowels in Hiatus	72–73
Lengthening before Consonants	73–75
Disappearance of the Old Quantity	75–76
Development of a New Quantity	76–77
VOWELS	77–104
Greek Vowels	78–82
Accented Vowels	82–91
Single Vowels	82–87
a	82–83

TABLE OF CONTENTS.

	PAGES
ē	83–84
ĕ	84
ī	84
ĭ	84–85
ō	85–86
ŏ	86
ū	86–87
ŭ	87
Diphthongs	88–90
æ	88–89
au	89–90
eu	90
œ	90
ui	90
Influence of Labials	91
Clerical Latin	91
Unaccented Vowels	91–104
Unaccented Vowels in Hiatus	93–96
Initial Syllable	96–98
Intertonic Syllable	98–99
Penult	99–102
Final Syllable	102–104
CONSONANTS	104–143
Latin Consonants	106–137
Aspirate	106–107
Gutturals	107–114
C and G *before Front Vowels*	109–112
C and G *before Back Vowels*	112
C and G *Final and before Consonants*	112–114
Palatals	114–118
Dentals	118–121
Liquids	121–124
L	121–123
R	123–124
Sibilants	124–126
Nasals	127–132
Labials	132–137
P	132–133

	PAGES
B	133–135
F	135
V	135–137
U	137
Greek Consonants	137–141
Β, Γ, Δ	138
Κ, Π, Τ	138
Θ, Φ, Χ	138–139
Liquids, Nasals, and Sibilants	140
Ζ	140–141
Germanic Consonants	141–143
MORPHOLOGY	144–187
NOUNS AND ADJECTIVES	144–161
Gender	144–147
Masculine and Feminine	144
Masculine and Neuter	145–146
Feminine and Neuter	146–147
Declension of Nouns	147–156
First Declension	149–151
Second Declension	151–152
Third Declension	152–156
Loss of Declension	156
Declension of Adjectives	157–158
Comparison	158–159
Numerals	159–161
PRONOUNS AND PRONOMINAL ADJECTIVES	161–165
Personal Pronouns	161–162
Possessives	162–163
Demonstratives	163–164
Interrogative and Relative Pronouns	165
Indefinite Pronouns and Adjectives	165
VERBS	166–187
The Four Conjugations	166–170
First Conjugation	166–167
Second Conjugation	167
Third Conjugation	167–170
Fourth Conjugation	170
Fundamental Changes in Inflection	170–173

	PAGES
Inchoative Verbs	173–174
Present Stems	174–176
Imperfect	176–177
Perfect	177–182
Weak Perfects	177–180
Strong Perfects	180–182
Pluperfect and Future Perfect	183
Perfect Participle	183–185
Personal Endings	186–187
INDEX	189–219

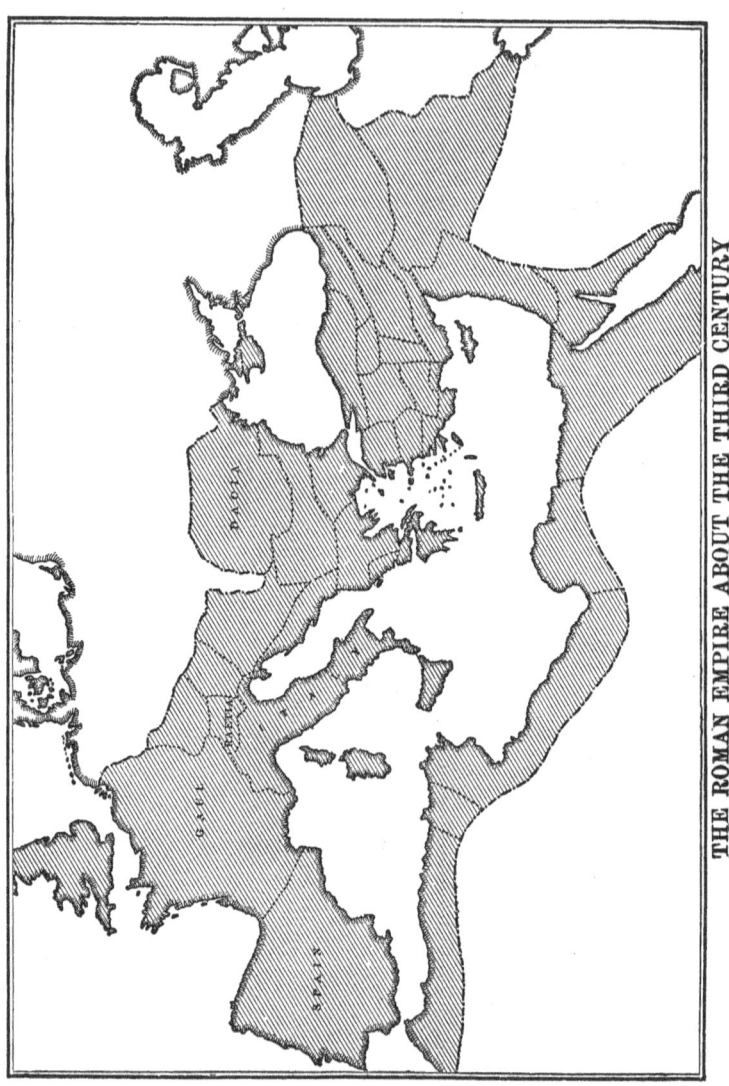

THE ROMAN EMPIRE ABOUT THE THIRD CENTURY

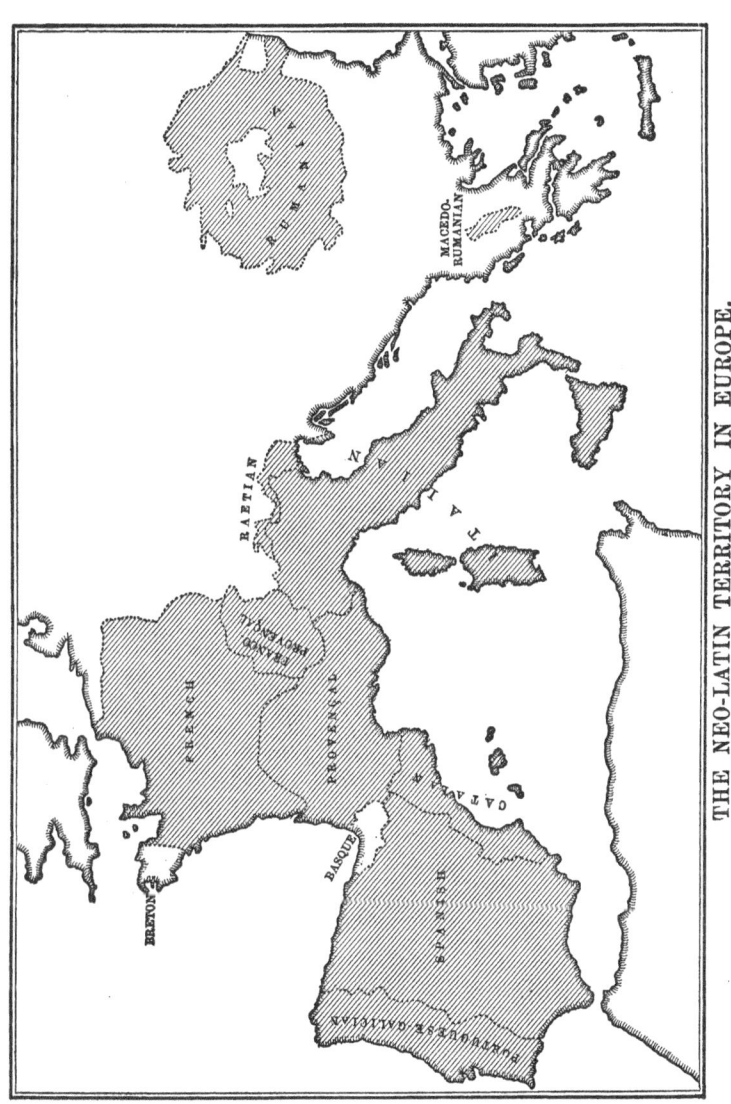

THE NEO-LATIN TERRITORY IN EUROPE.

BIBLIOGRAPHY
WITH ABBREVIATIONS.

App. Pr.: *Die Appendix Probi*, ed. W. Heræus, 1899. A Latin list of correct and incorrect spellings, possibly as early as the third century. Cf. *Mélanges Renier* 301-309; *Mélanges Boissier* 5-9; *Wiener Studien* XIV, 278 ff.; *Romanische Forschungen* VII, 145 ff.

Archiv: *Archiv für lateinische Lexicographie und Grammatik mit Einschluss des älteren Mittellateins.* Quarterly, Leipzig.

Audollent: A. Audollent, *Defixionum Tabellae*, 1904.

Bausteine: *Bausteine zur romanischen Philologie*, 1905. A volume of miscellaneous studies issued in honor of A. Mussafia.

Bayard: L. Bayard, *Le latin de saint Cyprien*, 1902.

Bechtel: E. A. Bechtel, *S. Silviae Peregrinatio, The Text and a Study of the Latinity*, 1902. Cf. Per.

Bon.: M. Bonnet, *Le latin de Grégoire de Tours*, 1890.

Buck: C. D. Buck, *A Grammar of Oscan and Umbrian*, 1904.

Carnoy: A. Carnoy, *Le latin d'Espagne d'après les inscriptions*, 2d ed., 1906.

Chronologie: F. G. Mohl, *Introduction à la chronologie du latin vulgaire*, 1899.

C. I. L.: *Corpus Inscriptionum Latinarum*, 1863—. New ed. (Vol. I, Part 1), 1893 —.

Claussen: T. Claussen, *Die griechischen Wörter im Französischen*, in *Romanische Forschungen* XV, 774.

C. G. L.: G. Goetz, *Corpus Glossariorum Latinorum*, Vol. IV, *Codex Vaticanus 3321.*

Cohn: G. Cohn, *Die Suffixwandlungen im Vulgärlatein und im vorlitterarischen Französisch nach ihren Spuren im Neufranzösischen*, 1891.

Cooper: F. T. Cooper, *Word Formation in the Roman Sermo Plebeius*, 1895.

Corssen: W. Corssen, *Ueber Aussprache, Vocalismus und Betonung der lateinischen Sprache*, 2d ed., 1868-70.

D'Arbois: H. d'Arbois de Jubainville, *La déclinaison en Gaule à l'époque mérovingienne*, 1872.

Densusianu: O. Densusianu, *Histoire de la langue roumaine*, Vol. I, 1901.

Dottin: G. Dottin, *Manuel pour servir à l'étude de l'antiquité celtique*, 1906.

BIBLIOGRAPHY.

Draeger: A. Draeger, *Historische Syntax der lateinischen Sprache*, 2ᵈ ed., 1878.
Dubois: A. Dubois, *La latinité d'Ennodius*, 1903.
Eckinger: T. Eckinger, *Die Orthographie lateinischer Wörter in griechischen Inschriften*, 1892.
Edon: G. Édon, *Écriture et prononciation du latin savant et du latin populaire*, 1882.
Einf.: W. Meyer-Lübke, *Einführung in das Studium der romanischen Sprachwissenschaft*, 2ᵈ ed., 1909.
Ernoult: A. Ernoult, *Les éléments dialectaux du vocabulaire latin*, 1909.
Facere: G. Rydberg, *Le développement de* facere *dans les langues romanes*, 1893. Reviewed by G. Paris in *Rom.* XXII, 569.
Franz: W. Franz, *Die lateinisch-romanischen Elemente im Althochdeutschen*, 1883.
Franz. ə: G. Rydberg, *Zur Geschichte des französischen ə*, 1896 —.
Futurum: P. Thielmann, *Habere mit dem Infinitiv und die Entstehung des romanischen Futurums*, in *Archiv* II, 48, 157.
G.: H. Goelzer, *Étude lexicographique et grammaticale de la latinité de saint Jérome*, 1884.
Gl. Cassel: *Kasseler Glossen* in *Altfranzösisches Uebungsbuch*, W. Foerster and E. Koschwitz, 2ᵈ ed., 1902. Made, probably in France, in the eighth or ninth century. Cf. *Zs.* XXVI, 521 ff.
Gl. Reich: *Reichenauer Glossen* in *Altfranzösisches Uebungsbuch*, W. Foerster and E. Koschwitz, 2ᵈ ed., 1902. Made in France in the eighth century. Cf. P. Marchot in *Romanische Forschungen* XII, 641 ff.; K. Hetzer, *Die Reichenauer Glossen* in *Zs.*, Beiheft 7; J. Stalzer, *Die Reichenauer Glossen der Handschrift Karlsruhe 115* in *Sitzungsberichte der philosophisch-historischen Klasse der Kaiserlichen Akademie der Wissenschaften* CLII, Vienna, 1906 (see W. Foerster in *Zs.* XXXI, 513, XXXVI, 47).
Gram.: W. Meyer-Lübke, *Grammaire des langues romanes*, 3 vols., 1890–1900.
Grundriss: G. Gröber, *Grundriss der romanischen Philologie*, 2 vols., 1888–1902; 2ᵈ ed. of Vol. I, 1904 —.
Haag: O. Haag, *Die Latinität Fredegars*, 1898.
Hammer: M. Hammer, *Die locale Verbreitung frühester romanischer Lautwandlungen im alten Italien*, 1894.
Hoppe: H. Hoppe, *Syntax und Stil des Tertullian*, 1903.
Keil: H. Keil, *Grammatici Latini*, 1857–1880.

BIBLIOGRAPHY.

Kluge: F. Kluge, *Romanen und Germanen in ihren Wechselbeziehungen*, in *Grundriss*, I², 498.
Körting: G. Körting, *Lateinisch-romanisches Wörterbuch*, 3d ed. 1907.
Koffmane: G. Koffmane, *Entstehung und Entwickelung des Kirchenlateins*, 1879.
Lat. Spr.: W. Meyer-Lübke, *Die lateinische Sprache in den romanischen Ländern*, in *Grundriss*, I², 451.
Lebreton: J. Lebreton, *Études sur la langue et la grammaire de Cicéron*, 1901.
Lexique: F. G. Mohl, *Études sur le lexique du latin vulgaire*, 1900.
Lindsay: W. M. Lindsay, *The Latin Language*, 1894.
Löfstedt: E. Löfstedt, *Beiträge zur Kenntniss der späteren Latinität*, 1907.
Loth: J. Loth, *Les mots latins dans les langues brittoniques*, 1892.
Ltblt.: *Literaturblatt für germanische und romanische Philologie*. Monthly, Leipzig.
Mulomedicina: E. Oder, *Claudii Hermeri Mulomedicina Chironis*, 1901.
Neue: F. Neue, *Formenlehre der lateinischen Sprache*, 3d ed., 1892–1902.
Neumann: Franz Neumann, *Verzeichniss der auf Aussprache und Rechtschreibung bezüglichen Eigenthümlichkeiten in den Inschriften aus Gallia Narbonensis*, 1857. *Fortsetzung*, 1898.
Olcott: G. N. Olcott, *Studies in the Word Formation of the Latin Inscriptions; Substantives and Adjectives, with special reference to the Latin Sermo Vulgaris*, 1898.
Oliver: A. Oliver, *Observations on the Use of Certain Prepositions in Petronius with special reference to the Roman Sermo Plebeius*, 1899.
Part. Perf.: P. Thielmann, *Habere mit dem Part. Perf. Pass.*, in *Archiv* II, 372, 509.
Per.: *Peregrinatio ad loca sancta*, ed. P. Geyer, in *Itinera hierosolymitana sæculi iiii–viii*, 1898. Written probably in the latter part of the fourth century by an ignorant nun, perhaps from Spain. See **Bechtel.** Cf. J. T. Gamurrini, *S. Hilarii Tractatus de Mysteriis et Hymni et S. Silviæ Aquitanæ Peregrinatio ad loca sancta*, 1887, and *S. Silviæ Aquitanæ Peregrinatio ad loca sancta*, 1888; M. Férotin, *Le véritable auteur de la Peregrinatio Silviæ* in *Revue des questions historiques* LXXIV (N.S.XXX), 367 ff.; J. Anglade, *De latinitate libelli qui inscriptus est Peregrinatio ad loca sancta*, 1905; W. Heræus, *Silviæ vel potius Ætheriæ Peregrinatio ad loca sancta*, 1908; E. Löfstedt, *Philologischer Kommentar zur Peregrinatio Ætheriæ*, 1911. Cf. E. Wölfflin in *Archiv* IV, 259; P. Geyer in *Archiv* XV, 233; D. D. de Bruyne in *Revue Bénédictine*, 1909, 481; K. Meister in *Rheinisches*

BIBLIOGRAPHY.

Museum für Philologie LXIV, 368; J. Deconinck in *Revue Biblique*, 1910, 432.

Phon. : P. Marchot, *Petite phonétique du français prélittéraire*, 1901.

Pirson : J. Pirson, *La langue des inscriptions de la Gaule*, 1901.

Planta : R. von Planta, *Grammatik der oskisch-umbrischen Dialekte*, 1892-97.

Pogatscher : A. Pogatscher, *Zur Lautlehre der griechischen, lateinischen und romanischen Lehnworte im Altenglischen: II. Teil, Vokalismus der Tonsilben*, 1888.

Pr. Pers. Pl. : F. G. Mohl, *La première personne du pluriel en gallo-roman*, 1900.

Quillacq : J. A. Quillacq, *Quomodo lingua latina usus sit S. Hilarius*, 1903.

R. : H. Rönsch, *Itala und Vulgata*, 1869.

Regnier : A. Regnier, *De la latinité des Sermons de saint Augustin*, 1886.

Richter : Elise Richter, *Zur Entwicklung der romanischen Wortstellung aus der lateinischen*, 1903.

Rom. : *Romania*. Quarterly, Paris.

S. : E. Seelmann, *Die Aussprache des Latein nach physiologisch-historischen Grundsätzen*, 1885.

Sepulcri : A. Sepulcri, *Le alterazioni fonetiche e morfologiche nel latino di Gregorio Magno e del suo tempo*, in *Studi Medievali* I, 171.

Sic. : N. Maccarrone, *Il latino delle iscrizioni di Sicilia*, 1910.

Sittl : K. Sittl, *Die lokalen Verschiedenheiten der lateinischen Sprache*, 1882.

Sommer : F. Sommer, *Lateinische Laut- und Formenlehre*, 1902.

Stolz : F. Stolz, *Historische Grammatik der lateinischen Sprache*, Vol. I, 1894.

Substrate : G. Gröber, *Vulgärlateinische Substrate romanischer Wörter*, in *Archiv* I, 204, 539; II, 100, 276, 424; III, 138, 264, 507; IV, 116, 422; V, 125, 234, 453; VI, 117, 377; VII, 25.

Suchier : H. Suchier, *Die französische und provenzalische Sprache und ihre Mundarten*, in *Grundriss* I[2], 371.

Thurot : *Notices et Extraits des Manuscrits de la Bibliothèque nationale et autres bibliothèques* : Vol. XII, Paris, 1868, Charles Thurot, *Notices et Extraits de divers manuscrits latins pour servir à l'histoire des doctrines grammaticales au moyen âge*.

Tiktin : H. Tiktin, *Die rumänische Sprache*, in *Grundriss*, I[2], 564.

Travaglio : C. Travaglio, *La scrittura latina volgare nei papiri dei primi cinque secoli dopo Cristo* in *Atti della R. Accademia delle Scienze di Torino* XLIII, 525.

BIBLIOGRAPHY.

Urbat: R. Urbat, *Beiträge zu einer Darstellung der romanischen Elemente im Latein der Historia Francorum des Gregor v. Tours*, 1890.
Vok.: H. Schuchardt, *Der Vokalismus des Vulgärlateins*, 3 vols., 1866–68.
Walde: A. Walde, *Lateinisches etymologisches Wörterbuch*, 1906.
Waters: W. E. Waters, *Petronius, Cena Trimalchionis*, 1902.
Wick: F. C. Wick, *La fonetica delle iscrizioni parietarie pompeiane*, 1905.
Windisch: E. Windisch, *Die keltische Sprache*, in *Grundriss* I^2, 371.
Wölfflin: E. Wölfflin, *Lateinische und romanische Comparation*, 1879.
Zauner: A. Zauner, *Romanische Sprachwissenschaft*, 1900.
Zs.: *Zeitschrift für romanische Philologie*. Four to six numbers a year. Halle.
Zs. fr. Spr.: *Zeitschrift für französische Sprache und Litteratur*. Quarterly, Chemnitz and Leipzig.

Works to which only occasional reference is made are cited in full in the text.

PHONETIC ALPHABET
AND OTHER SYMBOLS.

β = bilabial *v*, the sound of Spanish *v* and *b*.
ð = the sound of *th* in English *this*.
ə = the sound of *e* in French *me*.
ŋ = the sound of *ng* in English *long*.
ö = rounded *e*, the sound of German *ö*.
þ = the sound of *th* in English *thin*.
ü = rounded *i*, the sound of German *ü*.
χ = the sound of *ch* in German *ach*.

- ・ (a dot) under a vowel letter shows that the vowel is close.
- ␎ (a hook) under a vowel letter shows that the vowel is open.
- ⌢ (a semicircle) under a vowel letter shows that the vowel is not syllabic.
- ´ (an acute accent) after a consonant letter shows that the consonant is palatal.
- * (an asterisk) before a word shows that the form is conjectural, not attested.
- > indicates derivation, the *source* standing at the *open* end of the figure, whichever way it be turned.
- SMALL CAPITALS mean that the forms so printed occur in inscriptions (but this indication is used only when for some special reason it seems desirable).

The other marks and abbreviations employed are so generally accepted as to need no explanation.

AN INTRODUCTION TO VULGAR LATIN.

1. The extent of the Roman Empire is shown by the map on p. x. Throughout this territory the official language was Latin, originally the speech of Latium, a little district on the Tiber. The Latin tongue was thus extended to many peoples, representing different races, civilizations, and linguistic habits. In central Italy it was adopted by Etruscans and by various Italic tribes, in northern Italy by Ligurians, Celts, and Illyrians, in southeastern and southwestern Italy respectively by Illyrians and Greeks; beyond the peninsula it spread among Iberians, Ligurians, Celts, Aquitanians, Semites, Germanic tribes, and others still. The Latinization of these peoples was the work of several centuries[1]: by 272 B. C. all Italy was subdued south of the Macra and the Rubicon; Sicily became a province in 241, Sardinia and Corsica in 238; Venetia cast her lot with Rome in 215; Spain was made a province in 197; Illyria was absorbed after 167, Africa after the fall of Carthage in 146, southern Gaul in 120; the Cimbri and Teutones were destroyed in 102-1; northern Gaul was a province in 50, Rætia in 15; Dacia was colonized in 107 A. D., forsaken in the third century, and quite cut off from the rest of the Latin-speaking world in the sixth. The Latin language never gained a foothold in Greece; political changes drove it from Great Britain, the Orient, and Africa; in the rest of the Empire it has remained, for the most part,

---

[1] See Mohl, *Chronologie;* also Meyer-Lübke, *Lat. Spr.*, pp. 451–455.

until the present day, and has been carried thence to America, Africa, and Asia. The map on p. xi marks the parts of Europe where Latin in its modern forms is now spoken.

2. The Latin tongue, like every living language, has always been in an unstable condition. The evidence of inscriptions and of grammarians indicates that from the beginning to the end of Roman history speech was constantly changing, the alteration being most rapid in the earliest and the latest periods. Furthermore, there were at all times, but especially before the Social War, considerable local divergences. The Latin-speaking peoples were not homogeneous, and their speech reflected their varied origin. In Italy the language of Latium was adopted by tribes using, in the main, kindred languages. At first there was sturdy resistance; until the conflict of 90–89 B. C. all southern Italy was under Oscan influence, and Oscan was used in inscriptions until the first century of our era.[1] When Latin conquered, it blended more or less with the native idioms; the resulting geographical discrepancies are manifest in early monuments. The Social War, however, had a levelling effect, and speech in Italy became more uniform; but there doubtless were still noticeable differences in pronunciation and even in vocabulary.[2] In the outlying provinces, and to some degree in the peninsula, Latin was simply substituted for foreign tongues, and there was little or no mixture; nevertheless a few native words were kept, and there must have been a variety of accent. It should be remembered, moreover, that the language carried

---

[1] See *Chronologie* 133 and 116–120. Oscan forms are *ligud* for *lēge*, *pru* for *pro*, *ni* for *nē*, etc.

[2] The S. Italian *nn* for *nd*, *i* for *ē*, and *u* for *ō* may be Oscan. *Pomex*, *ēlex* for *pūmex*, *īlex* are perhaps Umbrian: *Lat. Spr.* 445, 464. The Italian word *zavorra* is possibly Etruscan: *Chronologie* 98–99.

§ 3] AN INTRODUCTION TO VULGAR LATIN. 3

to the several provinces was not identical: it represented different chronological stages and different local dialects of Italic Latin; the earlier acquisitions received a more popular, the later colonies a more official speech. Administration and military service tended to obliterate distinctions; under the Empire the variations probably came to be no greater than those now to be found in the English of the British Empire. We may say in general that the Roman territory, excepting Greece and the East, was completely Latinized by the fourth century after Christ.

3. With the beginnings of culture and literature there came inevitably a divergence between the language of the upper and that of the lower classes, and also between city and country speech. Literary influence is conservative and refining, while popular usage tends to quick change. In late Republican and early Imperial times educated speech became highly artificial, drawing away from the everyday language; on the other hand, the common idiom, throughout the Republic and the Empire, was constantly developing away from the archaic standard of elegant parlance.[1] What we call Vulgar Latin is the speech of the middle classes, as it grew out of early Classic Latin. It is not an independent offshoot of Old Latin: it continues the Classic, not the primitive, vowel system.[2] Neither is it the dialect of the slums or of the fields: grammarians tell us of not a few urban and rustic vulgarisms that are not perpetuated in the Romance tongues. It is distinct from the consciously polite utterance of cultivated society, from the brogue of the country, and from the slang of the lowest quarters of the city, though affected by all of these.[3] Vulgar Latin naturally developed differently in

[1] Cf. J. Marouzeau, *Notes sur la fixation du latin classique* in *Mémoires de la Société de Linguistique de Paris*, XVII, 266.
[2] Cf. *Lat. Spr.* 463-464.   [3] Cf. Cooper XV-XXX; W. Konjetzny in *Archiv* XV, 297

various localities, as far as the levelling influence or school and army permitted; the universal inclination of language to diverge was reinforced by the original habits of the diverse speakers and by such peculiarities of native accent as had survived.[1] The differentiation progressed, being accelerated when schools decayed and military was replaced by ecclesiastical organization, until the dialects of distant localities became mutually unintelligible. At this point we may say that Vulgar Latin stops and the Romance languages begin. Although any definite date must be arbitrary, we may put it, roughly speaking, in the sixth or seventh century of our era. The Vulgar Latin period lasts, then, from about 200 B. C. to about 600 A. D.; it is most sharply differentiated from Classic Latin in the last few centuries of this epoch.[2]

4. If we compare Classic and Vulgar Latin, we shall see that the latter was always tending to become more flexible and more explicit. We note an enormous development of modifying and determining words, such as articles and prepositions, and an abundant use of prefixes and suffixes. We find also a great simplification of inflections, due partly to phonetic but mainly to syntactic causes. Furthermore, we observe certain changes in pronunciation, some of which can be ascribed to an inclination to discard those parts of words that are not necessary for their identification (as when *viridis*, *vetulus* become *virdis*, *veclus*), some to a tendency to assimilate unlike adjacent sounds (so *ipse* is spoken *isse*, and the diphthong *ai* is reduced to *e*), some to a desire for differentiation (which lowers i̯ to e̯ to make it more remote from i̯), some to unknown reasons. Why, for instance, ai almost

---
[1] Cf. Sittl and Hammer; Pirson and Carnoy; also, for African Latin, B. Kübler in *Archiv* VIII, 161.

[2] For a history of the Latin language, see *Lat. Spr.* 492-497.

universally became ẹ, while au did not in Latin generally become ọ, is a problem as yet unsolved.

5. Our sources of information[1] concerning the current spoken Latin are : the statements of grammarians[2]; the non-Classic forms occurring in inscriptions and early manuscripts[3]; the occasional lapses in cultivated authors, early and late; a few texts written by persons of scanty education; some glossaries and lists of incorrect forms; and, most important of all, the subsequent developments of the Romance languages.[4] All of these are to be used with caution. Of especial value are the *Peregrinatio ad loca sancta*, a considerable fragment of a description of travel in the East, by an uneducated woman (probably a Spanish nun) of the latter part of the fourth century[5]; the *Appendix Probi*, a list of good and bad forms, possibly as early as the third century[6]; the veterinary treatise known as *Mulomedicina Chironis*[7]; the so-called *Glossary of Reichenau*, made in France in the eighth century.[8] There is an interesting collection of curses by A. Audollent, — *Defixionum Tabellæ*, 1904.

---

[1] Cf. Meyer-Lübke, *Lat. Spr.* 455-461; G. Gröber, *Sprachquellen und Wortquellen des lateinischen Wörterbuchs* in *Archiv* I, 35.

[2] Utilized by E. Seelmann, *Aussprache des Latein*, 1885. For a brief account of the Latin grammarians, see Stolz, 55-67.

[3] Used by H. Schuchardt, *Vokalismus des Vulgärlateins*, 1866-68. For papyri see Travaglio. For coins see M. Prou in *Mélanges de philologie romane et d'histoire littéraire offerts à M. Maurice Wilmotte*, 1910, 523. This volume contains on p. 485 *Pamphlets bas-latins du VIIe siècle* by J. Pirson.

[4] For the chronology of developments, the distinction of learned and popular words, and the establishment of unattested Vulgar Latin words, see G. Gröber, in *Archiv* I, 204 ff., and VII, 25 ff. Something can be learned from the charters and laws of the barbarians: cf. F. Schramm, *Sprachliches zur Lex Salica*, 1911.

[5] See Bibliography: Bechtel and *Per.*; note E. Wölfflin, *Ueber die Latinität der Peregrinatio ad loca sancta* in *Archiv* IV, 259.

[6] See W. Heræus, *Die Appendix Probi*, 1899, *Zur Appendix Probi* in *Archiv* XI, 61, *Die Appendix Probi* in *Archiv* XI, 301; G. Paris in *Mélanges Renier* 301, *Mélanges Boissier* 5; W. Fœrster in *Wiener Studien* XIV, 278.

[7] See Bibliography; E. Lommatzsch, *Zur Mulomedicina Chironis* in *Archiv* XII, 401, 551, and W. Heræus, *Zur Sprache der Mulomedicina Chironis* in *Archiv* XIV, 119.

[8] See Bibliography.

I. VOCABULARY.[1]

A. WORDS AND THEIR MEANINGS.

6. It is natural that the speech of the literary and fashionable classes should differ from that of the common people; so it is in all civilized communities. Literature inclines to extend the senses of words, popular use tends to restrict them. The polite language, too, has many poetic figures and many abstract terms unknown to the crowd. On the other hand, the vulgar idiom has homely metaphors of its own and numerous specific, technical words not found in literature.

1. WORDS USED ALIKE IN CLASSIC AND VULGAR LATIN.

7. This class includes a great mass of words, forming, so to speak, the nucleus of the language. Examples are: *canis, filius, mater, panis, pater, puteus, vacca; altus, bonus, longus, viridis; amare, audire, dicere, vendere; bene, male; quando, si; in.*

---

[1] See A. Hatzfeld, A. Darmesteter, and A. Thomas, *Dictionnaire général de la langue française*, II, *Traité de la formation de la langue française;* Densusianu, 185-203; W. Heræus, *Die römische Soldatensprache* in *Archiv* XII, 255, *Die Sprache der römischen Kinderstube* in *Archiv* XIII, 149; J. G. Kempf, *Romanorum sermo castrensis quid sit quibusque e fontibus quaque via ac ratione eius reliquiæ hauriantur* in *Jahrbücher für classische Philologie*, Suppl. XXVI, 342. For an approximately complete vocabulary, reconstructed out of Romance words, see G. Körting, *Lateinish-romanisches Wörterbuch*, 1907. For a thorough discussion of reconstructed forms, see G. Gröber, *Vulgärlateinische Substrate romanischer Wörter* in *Archiv:* I, 233 ff. (*abbreviare — buttis*), 539 ff. (*caccubus — curbus*); II, 100 ff. (*damnum — dui*), 276 ff. (*eber — fiticum*), 424 ff. (*flagrare — gutta*); III, 138 ff. (*hædus — ilicem*), 264 ff. (*ille — lamma*), 507 ff. (*lacusta — mille*); IV, 116 ff. (*minaciæ — nutrire*), 422 ff. (*obedire — putidus*); V, 125 ff. (*quadraginta — rasculare*), 234 ff. (*reburrus — runcare*), 453 ff. (*sabanum — suus*); VI, 117 ff. (*tabanus — zirulare*), 377 ff. (supplement.)

2. WORDS USED DIFFERENTLY IN CLASSIC AND IN VULGAR LATIN.

8. Very many Classic words are used in Vulgar Latin with a different sense: *comparare* = 'buy', *focus* = 'fire', *paganus* = 'pagan', *viaticum* = 'journey'. *Capit* assumed the meaning of *fieri potest:* R. 351-352, *non capit prophetam perire*, etc.; Hoppe 48, *hæc æstimare non capit, non capit utique videri Deus*. Most of the examples can be classified under the heads of restriction or extension of meaning.

a. SENSE RESTRICTED.

9. This happens frequently, a word assuming a more definite or concrete signification: *cognatus* = 'brother-in-law'; *collocare* = 'put to bed' (*se collocare* = 'go to bed', Bon. 286); *dominicus* = *divinus*; *ingenium* = 'trick', Bon. 283; *lectio* = 'text'; *machinari* = 'grind'; *mulier* = 'wife'; *necare* = 'drown', Bon. 286, Dubois 220; *orbus* = 'blind'; *tractatus* = 'treatise'. Many words kept their literal but lost their metaphorical sense: *captio* = 'act of taking', G. 243, not 'sophism' nor 'deceit'; *robur* = 'oak', not 'strength', 'authority', nor 'best part'.

b. SENSE EXTENDED.[1]

10. The general use of a word in an extended sense is not common, but there are some examples: *fortis* = 'strong' in all senses, Bayard 105; *infans* = 'child', Pirson 257-258; *parentes* = 'relatives', Pirson 260-262; *se plicare* = 'go', *Per.* 46,11, etc.; *villa* = 'town', G. 272.

Many words, however, assume a new meaning in addition to the old one: *ambulare* = 'march', *Archiv* XII, 269-270, Bechtel 137, etc., and also 'continue', Regnier 24, perhaps

---

[1] Cf. Bayard 63-202, Bon. 235-328, Dubois 185-225, Quillacq 54-79.

'go'; *facere* = 'pass (time)', Regnier 27 (*quadraginta dies fecit*), *Per.* 66, 11 (*fecimus ibi biduum*), etc.; *fascia* means a measure of land, Pirson 255; *habet* is used like the French *il y a* (Old French *a*), G. 422 (*in arca Noe . . . habuit serpentes*), Regnier 29 (*in carne paucas habet virgines sanctimoniales*), Bechtel 127 (*habebat de eo loco forsitan quattuor milia*, etc.), *Per.* 37, 13, etc.; *homo* has the sense of French *on*, Regnier 20, Dubois 218; *ille* = 'the' and 'he', Bechtel 144, Bon. 258 ff.; *populus minutus* = 'common people', Waters Ch. 44; *replicare* = 'reply', Dubois, 204; *res* is used of persons, Waters Ch. 58 (*bella res*); *satis* = 'much', Bayard 83, *Per.* 38, 25, etc.; *unus* = 'a', Bechtel 144; *virtutes* = 'miracles' (in imitation of the Greek), Bayard 94.

So various prepositions and conjunctions (as *ad*, *apud*, *cum*, *de*, *per*, and *quasi*, *quia*, *quod*, *quomodo*) assumed new functions. *Unde* came to mean 'and so', Bon. 328.

3. WORDS USED IN CLASSIC BUT NOT IN VULGAR LATIN.

11. Numerous Classic Latin words either were not employed at all in the vulgar speech or went out of use before the earliest monuments of the Romance languages: so *funus*, *jubere*, *proles*. Very many adverbs and conjunctions disappeared: *an*, *at*, *autem*, *diu*, *donec*, *enim*, *ergo*, *etiam*, *haud*, *igitur*, *ita*, *nam*, *postquam*, *quidem*, *quin*, *quippe*, *quoad*, *quoque*, *saltem*, *sed*, *sive*, *ut*, *utrum*, *vel*, etc.; *tamen* must have been moribund, although it is common in the *Peregrinatio*. Poetic terms and some abstract nouns were not needed: *aurora*, *frondifer*, *horrescere*, *fletus*. Ecclesiastical Latin, to be sure, is very rich in abstract nouns (G. 391–397, Dubois 301–308), but most of them are new formations. When lost terms were needed for literary or other purposes, they were either borrowed from Classic or clerical Latin (as *nobilis*) or replaced by new constructions (as *carrica for *onus*).

a. SYNONYMS.

12. When Latin had two words nearly synonymous, one often crowded out the other: *atrium* gave way to *cors;* *cur* to *quare;* *equus* to *caballus*, R. 472; *ferre* to *portare*, Dubois 220; *ludus* to *jocus;* *magnus* to *grandis;* *os* to *bucca*, R. 472; *parentes* to *genitores*, Olcott XXV; *senex* to *vetulus*.

Sometimes the survivor was far from a synonym in Classic Latin: *discere* was displaced by *apprendere;* *domus* by *casa*, *mansio*, *hospitale*[1]; *emere* by *comparare;* *humerus* by *spatula*, R. 324; *ignis* by *focus*, R. 313; *nunc* by *hora;* *omnes* by *toti*, R. 338, Zs. XXXIII, 143; *quot, tot* by *quanti, tanti*, R. 336, 337; *urbs* by *civitas*, Dubois 209, and by *villa*, G. 272.

b. SUBSTITUTES.

13. Sometimes a term was replaced by a word not found in Classic Latin at all: *anser* was driven out by *auca (< *avica, diminutive of *avis*); *noverca* by **matraster;* *privignus* by **filiaster;* *vitrĭcus* mostly by *patraster*. Occasionally the substitute was apparently a slang word: *aliquis* yielded in part to *res nata*, R. 345; *caput* to *testa*[2]; *crus* gave way to *gamba;* *edere* in the main to *manducare*, Bechtel 140; *gena* to *gabata*.

Some words were replaced by diminutives, some nouns by derivative adjectives: *avis* by *aucellus;* *avus* by **aviolus;* *sol*

---

[1] According to Olcott XVIII, *casa* occurs only in Italian inscriptions, *mansio* (= 'dwelling') only in Roman. For *mansio*, cf. R. 472, Dubois 212. Among the Romance languages, Rumanian, Rætian, Italian, Spanish, Portuguese prefer *casa*, French and Provençal *mansio* and *hospitale*. Cf. Zauner 41–42.

[2] *Caput* (or rather *capum) is preserved by Rumanian, Rætian, Italian, Provençal, French; *testa* by Italian, Provençal, French; *capitia (< *caput*) by Spanish and Portuguese. Cf. Zauner 41–42.

in part by *soliculus; vetus* for most part by *vetulus; dies* largely by *diurnus, Gl. Reich.; hiems* by *hibernum*, R. 472; *mane* extensively by *matutinum*. Diminutives were extremely common in late Latin: G. 121-130 (*cereolus, schedula*, etc.), Olcott 250-263 (*gemelli, mammula* = 'grandmother', *naucella, neptilla*, etc.), Dubois 147 (*novellus*). Adjectives used as nouns were frequent also: R. 100-107 (*arida, infernus*, etc.), G. 108-121 (*brevis, credens, infernus*, etc.).

Occasionally, too, words were replaced by phrases: *diu* by *longum tempus* (Bon. 201, *paucum tempus* for *haud diu*); *ver* by *vernum tempus*, Bon. 203, and other phrases.

c. PARTICLES.

14. Many prepositions, conjunctions, and adverbs were lost by subsitution.

Ab was made unnecessary by *de* and *per; apud* was partially supplanted by *ad; cum*, in Gaul, yielded to *apud; ex* gave way to *de*, R. 395-396; *ob* to *pro* and *per*. *Pro*, doubtless under the influence of *per*, became *por, which replaced *per* and *pro* in Spain and to a considerable extent in northern Gaul; southern Gaul, Italy, and Dacia preferred *per*. *Cis, erga, præ, propter* were displaced by other words.

The functions of *an, ne, utrum* were assumed by *si;* the place of *cum* was taken by *quando* and other conjunctions; *quando, quod, quoniam* were often replaced by *quomodo*, R. 403. *Autem, ergo, etiam, etsi, igitur, sed, tamen, ut* were ousted by various substitutes. Cf. Densusianu, 184-185.

4. WORDS USED IN VULGAR BUT NOT IN CLASSIC LATIN.

15. Vulgar Latin evidently had many words that do not appear in Classic texts. Some of these were probably old native terms that do not happen to occur in the works preserved, some were late creations, some were borrowed from other languages.

a. NATIVE WORDS.

16. Some native words are rarely attested, although they were doubtless in common use: *amma*, *Archiv* XIII, 154; *atta*, *Archiv* XIII, 154; *baro* = 'athlete', Waters Ch. 53, Ch. 63; *battalia*, *Archiv* XII, 270-271; *branca*, Densusianu 196; *circare* = 'hunt', *Archiv* VIII, 186; *cloppus*, Densusianu 196; *drappus*, *Substrate* II, 106, Körting (found in the 6th century); *ficatum*, Densusianu 190; *gavia* (used by Pliny); *mamma*, *Archiv* XIII, 151-152; *nonna, nonnus*, *Archiv* XIII, 156-157; *pa(p)pa*, *Archiv* XIII, 158, Bayard 179 (applied by St. Cyprian to the bishop of Carthage); *pappus* = 'grandfather', Pirson 243; *serutinus*, Audollent 199; *tata, tatus*, Pirson 244, *Archiv* XIII, 151-153; *trepalium, Rom.* XVII, 421.

17. A few that must have existed are not attested at all: *refusare, *Substrate* V, 234; *retina = 'rein', *Substrate* V, 237; so not improbably the original of the Romance words meaning 'touch', and perhaps those of the words meaning 'find', 'gape', and 'go' (cf. § 405). Likewise words made by onomatopœa, as **miaulare;* cf. M. Grammont, *Onomatopées et mots expressifs* in *Revue des langues romanes* XLIV, 97.

Some of the unattested words were obviously late developments: *finis, adj. (Fr., Pr. *fin;* It. *fine fino*), from the noun *finis* in such phrases as *honorum finis, pudoris finis*, etc. (so, e. g., *finis honoris* > *fins onors*, etc.), E. Herzog in *Bausteine* 484; *gentis, adj. (Fr., Pr. *gent*, It. *gente*), apparently a cross between *genĭtus* and *gentīlis; prode*, then m. and f. *prodis, adj., detached from *prodest* (cf. *potis est* = *potest*, Neue II, 176-177), R. 468-469 (*quid enim prode est homini, sed non fuit prode illis, hoc enim prode fit vobis*, etc.).

18. Late Latin was rich in derivatives, some of popular creation, some made by Christian writers. According to Olcott XIX, African Latin was freest in word formation. This subject will be discussed at length in the following chapter, but a few examples may be given here: post-verbal *dolus* < *dolere*, Regnier VIII; **abbellire;* **ausare; carricare, Gl. Reich.; confessor* = 'martyr'; **coraticum; dulcor,* *dulcior = 'sweetness'; *follia;* **man(u)aria; modernus,* Dubois 144; **nivicare;* **soliculus; vict(u)alia;* **vir(i)dura.*

b. FOREIGN WORDS.

19. A few Celtic terms were adopted, such as *alauda, vertragus*. More Germanic words (cf. *Gram.*, Introduction) found their way into Latin: *bannus,* Bon. 226; *hapja; haribergum, Gl. Reich.* (cf. *alberca,* Pirson 236); *haunjan; watan; wërra.*

We find a large number of Greek words, a few of them apparently borrowed by popular speech: *amygdalum; cata,* a distributive preposition, verging on the sense of 'every', R. 247 (*cata mane mane*), Bechtel 95 (*cata mansiones, cata pascha*), cf. § 71; *colaphus; dactylus,* Bon. 211; *sagma.* More came in through the Christian vocabulary: *angelus; baptizare; blasphemare;* etc. Some were introduced by fashionable society, which affected familiarity with Greek; there are many Greek words in Petronius: *hepatia,* Waters Ch. 66; *schema,* Waters Ch. 44.

Very many Greek terms used by ecclesiastical writers never became popular. Cf. G. 205–226: *anathema, prophetare, zelare;* numerous verbs in *–izare,* as *allegorizare, anathematizare, catechizare, colaphizare, evangelizare, eunuchizare, Judaizare, prophetizare, sabbatizare, scandalizare, thesaurizare;* and not a few new derivatives, as *baptizatio, diaconissa,* G. 225, 224.

B. DERIVATION.

20. Vulgar Latin is very rich in derivatives and compounds; it has many affectionate diminutives, some of them made with new suffixes (as *-icca, -itta*).[1] Petronius shows a fondness for long derivatives, such as *gaudimonium* (Waters Ch. 61). Late writings almost all abound in abstract nouns (Cooper 1-2). In strictly Classic texts there seem to be few really living suffixes[2]; but the facility of word formation, which the literary language lost, popular speech preserved and increased.[3] This freedom of formation was abused by African authors, who were especially addicted to prepositional compounds with *con-, in-, sub-,* etc.[4] We shall consider first post-verbal nouns (i. e., substantives taken from the roots of verbs), then prefixes, next suffixes, and finally composite words.

1. POST-VERBAL NOUNS.

21. After the model of *cantus — cantare, saltus — saltare,* etc. (pairs in which the derivative verb seemed to come from the noun, whereas in reality both come from a primitive verb, as *canere, salire*), a fictitious primitive noun was derived from a number of verbs in Vulgar Latin and in the Romance languages: so *dolus* from *dolere*, *Vok.* I, 35, 98, Bon. 367, Regnier VII (blamed by St. Augustine).

2. PREFIXES.[5]

a. PREFIXES USED WITH NOUNS, ADJECTIVES, AND PRONOUNS.

22. *Bis-* or *bi-* was used with some adjectives and apparently with a few nouns: *bimaritus*, G. 130; *bisacutus*, G. 170; *bisaccium*, Petronius.

---

[1] See *Gram.* II, 430-693; Densusianu 156-173.   [2] Cooper XXXIV.
[3] Cooper XXX ff   [4] Cooper XXXVI, XLVI, 246-247.   [5] Cooper 246-297

23. *Ad–, con–, de–, dis–, ex–, in–, re–* and some others were occasionally used to form adjectives: **adaptus; commixtius,* G. 160; *defamatus;* **disfactus; exsūcus; inanimatus;* **replēnus.* Cf. G. 160 ff.

24. *Ac–, atque–, ecce–, eccu–, met–* were used as demonstrative prefixes to pronominal adjectives and to adverbs. *Eccu–* is *eccum,* i.e., *ecce hum;* its origin being forgotten, it was used in late Vulgar Latin as a synonym of *ecce. Met,* primarily a suffix, came to be used as a prefix through such combinations as *semet ipsum,* understood as *se metipsum.* In archaic writings such reinforced demonstratives as *eccum, eccam, eccos, eccas, ecca, eccillum, eccillam, eccillud, eccistam* are not uncommon; in Classic texts they are rare. Vulgar Latin examples are: *ac sic; atque ille; ecce hic;* * *eccu iste;* * *eccu sic,* Substrate VI, 385; *met ipse.* Cf. A. Köhler, *Die Partikel ecce* in *Archiv* V, 16. See §§ 65, 66.

b. PREFIXES USED WITH VERBS.

25. *Ad–, con–, de–, dis–, ex–, in–, re–* were freely used, *dis–* being mainly a Vulgar Latin prefix: *abbreviare,* G. 179; * *ad-cap(i)tare; adgenuculari,* R. 181; *adpretiare,* R. 181, G. 180; *adpropiare,* R. 181, G. 180; *adunare,* R. 182; *confortare,* R. 185, G. 181; **cominitiare; complacere,* R. 184; *deaurare,* G. 182; **disjejunare; exaltare,* G. 183; *excoriare,* G. 182; *impinguare,* G. 183; **infurcare; recapitulare,* G. 185; **requærere. Ad–, con–, de–* lost their special significance; *ad–* was particularly favored in Spain, *con–* in Italy. Cf. *Lat. Spr.* 487. Occasionally there was a change of prefix: *aspectare* was used with the sense of *expectare,* *convitare sometimes took the place of *invitare; dis–* was often substituted for *ex–*.

26. *Ab–, contra–, per–, sub–, super supra–, tra trans–* were

§ 31]   AN INTRODUCTION TO VULGAR LATIN.   15

used occasionally: *aboculare; *contrafacere; *perdonare; subaudire, G. 185; *subcludere; subsannare, R. 199, G. 187; superabundare, G. 187; *super-*suprafacere; *trabuccare; *transannare; transplantare, G. 188.

27. *Extra–* was sometimes used in Italy and Dacia, *infra–* and *intra–* in Italy: *extrabuccare; *infraponere; *intratenere.

28. *Abs–, e–, ob–, præ–, pre–, pro–, retro–* were apparently not used to form new verbs in the popular spoken language, although some of them are occasionally so employed by late writers: opprobrare, G. 184; prædestinare, G. 184 (cf. Livy); prolongare, G. 184. *Ob–* is sometimes replaced by *ad–:* obdormire > addormire.

29. *Foris* and *minus* came to be used as prefixes in some regions: *forisfacere; *minuscredere. *Foris* was confounded in Gaul with the Frankish *fir–* (= *ver–*) : verslahen = Old Fr. forbatre. See G. Baist, *Fränkisches* fir– *im ältesten Französischen* in *Romanische Forschungen* XII, 650; cf. *Rom.* XXX, 633. For this use of *minus*, compare the phrase *minus est =deest*, Regnier 109 : caritas in quantum adest . . . in quantum autem minus est. Cf. § 245.

30. Some verbs take a double prefix : adimplere; coexcitare, R. 207 (cf. Quintilian, coexercitatus); deexacerbare, R. 207 ; *deexcitare; *exeligere.

31. Recomposition, i.e., the restoration of the full form of the primitive verb, was a regular process in Vulgar Latin (cf. §139): *aspargo* for *aspergo* is blamed by Velius Longus, Édon 127, and is used by St. Cyprian, Bayard 3; *commando* is, according to Velius Longus, the usual form, rather than *commendo*, S. 60, Édon 131 ; *consacrati* etc. occur in inscriptions, S. 60 ; *crededit,* Bon. 490 ; *reddedit,* Bon. 490 ; *retenere*, Bon. 489 ;

tradedit, Bon. 490. Cf. S. 58-64, Bon. 486-493. *Cómpŭto, cólligo, cóllŏco, cónsto, cónsŭo, érĭgo, éxĕo, ínflo, prǽsto* seem to have been regarded as simple verbs: S. 64.

32. Late writers were in the habit of restoring the full, primitive form of prefixes; but this was doubtless merely a matter of spelling, and did not indicate the common pronunciation. In Tertullian, Cyprian, and some others there is generally no assimilation of the prefix; other writers, such as Gregory of Tours, apparently used both assimilated and unassimilated forms. Bayard 12-15: *adpetere, conpendium, inprobus, obfero, subplanto*. Bon. 178-188: *adtonitus, conmittere, inlatus, obprimere, subcumbere*.

3. SUFFIXES.

a. SUFFIXES FOR VERBS.[1]

33. Verbs *from nouns*[2] generally end in *-are;* occasionally in *-iare* or *-ire;* sometimes in *-icare*, which was eventually supplanted in Italy and in Gaul by *-izare* (for pronunciation see § 339). This last ending came from Greek -ιζειν through borrowed words, such as *baptizare*. For a list of Greek verbs in -ιζειν adopted by Christian writers, see R. 248-249 (cf. § 19 above); some new formations were used, as *catechizare*. In early Latin this same ending appears as *-issare* (*atticisso, rhetorisso*): see A. Funck, *Die Verba auf issare und izare* in *Archiv* III, 398.

Examples: *oculare; pectinare; plantare; potionare;* **trepaliare;* — *plagiare;* — *ignire;* — *carricare; follicare;* **nivicare;* — **dom'nizare;* *werrizare.

---

[1] Cf. Cooper 205-245, Dubois 151-162, Quillacq 41-46, Bonnet 471-474.
[2] Cf. R. 154-162.

§ 36]   AN INTRODUCTION TO VULGAR LATIN.   17

34. Verbs *from adjectives and perfect participles* end in *-are*, *-iare*, *-ire;* also in *-icare* (cf. *albicare*), *-itare* (cf. *debilitare*, *visitare*), *-ēscere* and *-īscere* (cf. *canescere, mollescere*); possibly in *-izare: angustare;* **ausare; captivare; confortare; falsare; gravare; levare;* **oblītare; rŭtare; ūsare;* — *alleviare;* **altiare;* **captiare; humiliare;* — **abbellire; unire;* — *amaricare;* — **vanitare;* — *fortescere; lætiscere; vilescere;* — **blankizare?*

Many verbs from perfect participles (frequentatives, etc.) replace the original verbs: *adjuvare > adjutare; audere > ausare; canere > cantare; uti > usare*. The endings –(*i*)*tare*, *–escere* lost their frequentative or inchoative sense: *adparescere*, Dubois 157; *ostentare*, Dubois 156.

35. Verbs *from other verbs* end in *-icare* (cf. *fodicare < fodere*), *-itare* (cf. *clamitare < clamare*); also in *-ēscere, -īscere* (cf. *florescere, dormiscere*), which lost its inchoative force: **bullicare < bullire;* — *crocitare;* — *apparescere;* **finiscere; stupescere*. Vulgar Latin has many old frequentive verbs: G. 178–179, Cooper 205. There are some late diminutives in *-aculare, -ĭculare, -ŭculare*, through diminutive nouns or adjectives (cf. *periculari < periculum*): *saltīculare. We find also some miscellaneous imitative formations: *expaventare (and some others) apparently after the analogy of *præsentare;* *misculare perhaps after *maculare*.

36. *Greek verbs* in *–ᾶν, -ειν*, etc., when taken into Latin, regularly end in *-are:* κυβερνᾶν > *gubernare;* βλασφημεῖν > *blasphemare*. Cf. Claussen 795.   But ψάλλειν > *psallĕre*, perhaps through the analogy of *fallere:* Claussen 796.

Germanic verbs in *-an* or *-on* regularly passed into the first conjugation in Latin: *wîtan* > It. *guidare: roubôn* > It. *rubare*. Those in *-jan* went into the fourth: *hatjan* > *hatire*, Gl. Reich.; *warnjan* > It. *guarnire*.

b. SUFFIXES FOR NOUNS.[1]

37. Some 90 endings, apparently, were used in Vulgar Latin. The Christian writers are especially rich in derivatives. Petronius, too, was very fond of diminutives: *adulescentulus*, Waters Ch. 59, Ch. 64; *porcellus*, Ch. 40; *taurellus*, Ch. 39.

The commonest endings are the following: —

-a, used to form feminines: *nepta*, Pirson 123, Bon. 366, Haag 41; *socera*, Bon. 355.

-āgo, -īgo, -ūgo were characteristic of rustic speech: Cooper 111.

-al, -āle, used to form adjectives and also nouns, especially names of parts of apparel (as *bracchiale*), was extended: *coxale*, G. 95. Cf. Olcott 238–239.

-alia, a neuter plural, as *victualia* (cf. the collective plural *-ilia*, as *mirabilia, volatilia*, G. 110–111), was used, in a collective sense, as a feminine singular with an augmentative and pejorative signification, in Italy and Gaul: *canalia < *canis*.

-anda, -enda, neuter plural of the gerundive, came to be used as a feminine singular: *facienda and *facenda.

-ans, -ens: see Adjectives.

-antia, -entia, made from present participles + *-ia* (as *benevolentia, essentia, significantia*), were used to form abstract nouns from verbs: **credentia; fragrantia; placentia;* **sperantia.* Cf. R. 49–52, G. 79–102, Olcott 73–78.

-ānus: see Adjectives.

-ar, -āre, for nouns and adjectives: *liminare*, G. 95; **pollicare.* Cf. Olcott 187–189.

-aria: see *-ia*.

-arium, used to designate a place (as *gallinarium*), was extended: *breviarium;* **calamarium.* Cf. R. 31–37, Olcott 176–182.

-arius: see Adjectives.

-aster: see *Modern Language Notes* XXIV, 240.

-ata: see *-ta*, etc.

-atīcum (as *viaticum*) was extended, to form nouns from nouns: **coraticum.*

-ātus, as *senatus* (common in Petronius, e. g., *bonatus*, Waters Ch. 74), was extended: *clericatus;* **ducatus.* Cf. *-ta*, etc.

---

[1] Cf. Cooper 1–91, Dubois 99–136, Quillacq 15–31, Bon. 453–463.

-cellus, diminutive, was used beside *-culus*: *avicula, avicella; navicula, navicella.* So *domnicellus, etc.

-ceus, -cius: see Adjectives.

-culum, -crum (as *miraculum, lavacrum*) were occasionally used: **genuculum.* Cf. G. 91-92, Olcott 131-134.

-ellus, diminutive (as *castellum*), was often used beside *-ŭlus*, which lost its diminutive force: *anulus, anellus; porculus, porcellus; vitulus, vitellus.* So *calamellus*, etc.

-enda: see *-anda*.

-ens: see Adjectives, *-ans*.

-ensis: see Adjectives.

-entia: see *-antia*.

-ĕrium, as *desiderium*, was probably somewhat extended: Old Fr., Pr. *consirier*, etc. Cf. R. 31-37. See A. Thomas, *Les substantifs en* -ier *et le suffixe* -arius, *Rom.* XXXI, 481; and *Nouveaux essais de philologie française* 110.

-eum: see *-ium*.

-eus: see Adjectives.

-ia, unaccented, used to form abstract nouns (as *victoria*), was extended: *fortia (cf. *fortia* n. pl. = 'mighty deeds of God', Koff mane 76).

-ia, unaccented, used to form feminines (as *avus, avia*): *neptia*, Pirson 123 (cf. *Zs.* XXXII, 640).

-ia, from Greek *-la* through Christian writers and speakers: *monarchía; philosophía;* etc. It was often attached to words in *-arius;* hence an ending *-aría:* **librarla.* Cf. Olcott 173-176.

-ĭca: see *Archiv für das Studium der neueren Sprachen und Literaturen* CXIV, 457.

-ĭcca (as *Bodicca, Bonica, Karica*) first appears in Africa in feminine proper names; it was then extended to Spain, Sardinia, and Dacia, and came to be used as a diminutive suffix in Spanish, Portuguese, and Rumanian: Sp. *animalico;* Rum. *manică.* It may have arisen in the first place from a childish pronunciation of *-ĭclus, -ĭcla*, being used in pet names. Cf. *Einf.* § 173. For *-accus, -iccus, -occus, -uc(c)us*, see A. Horning in *Zs.* XIX, 170, XX, 335; cf. *Gram.* II, 591. Cf. *Zs.* XXXIV, 26.

-ĭceus, -ĭcius: see Adjectives, *-ceus*.

-incus or *-inquus* (as *propinquus*), perhaps also **-ingus* and locally *-ancus*, possibly of Ligurian origin (*Rom.* XXXV, 1-21, 283ff., 333ff.), was used for many new words: Pr. *Arbonenca, ramenc;* It. *solingo, Valinca;*

Sp. *Cusanca*. It was probably confounded, in some regions, with the following.

-ing, a German patronymic ending, was used for some nouns and perhaps for adjectives (see *-incus* above): Pr. *lausenga;* It. *camerlingo*.

-īnus (as *caninus*, *Montaninus*) originally denoted appurtenance, then resemblance, then smallness; it was freely used, especially to form diminutive nouns, but sometimes to form new adjectives: *domnina* = 'young lady', Olcott 134-136; *Florentinus; serpentinus.* Cf. Olcott 200-204.

-io: see *-tio*.

-issa, from the Greek *-ισσα* (as βασίλισσα, so *pythonissa*), was used for some new formations: **dukissa;* *Germanissa*, Pirson 228; *prophetissa*, R. 251. Cf. Cooper 251.

-ĭtas: see *-tas*.

-ĭtia, *-ĭties*, used to form nouns from adjectives (as *munditia -ies*), were much extended, *-ities* especially in the south; both are rare in Rumanian (Cooper XLV): **altitia;* **granditia.* Cf. Olcott 78-80.

-ĭttus first appears during the Empire in inscriptions in Italy and Dacia, sometimes in Spain and Gaul, as a suffix for proper names: feminine *Attitta*, *Bonitta*, *Caritta*, *Julitta*, *Livitta*, *Suavitta*, etc.; masculine *Muritta*, *Nebitta*, *Sagitta*, etc. Cf. Pirson 226: *Julianeta*, *Nonnita*, *Nonnitus*. Its origin is unknown; it may have arisen from a childish pronunciation of *-ĭclus -a:* cf. *-īcca*. Meyer-Lübke, *Einf.* § 172, conjectures that it may have come from the Germanic ending that now appears as *z* in such names as *Heinz*. A. Zimmermann, *Zs.* XXVIII, 343, regards *-ăttus*, *-ĭttus*, *-ŏttus* as alternative forms of *-ātus*, *-ītus*, *-ōtus*, like *līttera* beside *lītera*, etc. It came to be very widely used as a diminutive suffix for nouns, and also for adjectives, the *i* being short in Gaul, Rætia, and central and northern Italy, generally long in the Spanish peninsula and in Sardinia: nouns, Fr. *amourette*, It. *fioretto*, Sp. *bacito;* adjectives, Fr. *doucet*, It. *grassetto*, Sp. *bonito*.

-itūdo: see *-tūdo*.

-ium, *-eum* (as *capitium*, *calcaneum*): see G. 56-59.

-īvum, *-īva:* see Olcott 224-226.

-men, *-mentum*, used to form nouns from verbs (as *certāmen*, *vestimentum*), were extended, especially *-mentum:* *gubernamentum. Cf. Olcott 123-131, R. 22-25.

-mōnium, *-mōnia:* see Olcott 81-82.

-o (*-ōnem*), originally used to indicate a characteristic (as *bĭbo*), was

commonly employed as an augmentative or pejorative, in Gaul often as a diminutive: *gŭlo;* It. *boccone;* Fr. *aiglon.* See *Archiv* V, 56, 223, XIII, 222, 415, 475. Cf. Olcott 83-87, G. 44-45.

-or (-ōrem), used to form abstract nouns (as *candor, sapor),* was employed for many new formations of the same kind, especially in Gaul: *dulcor;* **flator;* **flavor;* **lūcor;* **sentor; viror.* In Gaul these nouns came to be feminine: Bon. 503-504 *(dolor, timor,* etc.).

-or (-ōrem), used to designate the agent: see *-tor.*

-ōrium; see *-tōrium.*

-ŏttus, of unknown origin (cf. *-ĭttus),* was apparently used first of young animals, then as a general moderate diminutive: It. *aquilotto, casotta.*

-sa: see *-ta,* etc.

-sio: see *-tio.*

-sor: see *-tor.*

-sōrium: see *-tōrium.*

-sūra: see *-ūra.*

-sus: see *-ta,* etc.

-ta, -tus, -sa, -sus, later *-āta, -ātus, -uta,* perfect participles used as nouns, started perhaps with such forms as *defensa, remissa,* i. e., feminine perfect participles with a feminine noun understood, and were reinforced by neuter plural forms which became feminine and also by fourth declension nouns in *-tus,* as *collectus, narratus:* cf. C. Collin in *Archiv* XIII, 453; L. H. Alexander, *Participial Substantives of the -ata type in the Romance Languages,* 1912. They were considerably used to make abstract nouns from verbs (and *-ata* was sometimes attached to nouns, as **annata); -tus* and *-sus* were preferred in Dacia (Cooper XLV): *collecta,* G. 111; **debĭta; extensa,* R. 83; **movĭta,* Substrate IV, 122; **perdĭta; recubĭtus;* **reddĭta;* **vendĭta;* It. *andata, fossato, venuta.* Cf. Olcott 33-51, R. 82-83, G. 85-88, Bayard 24-25.

-tas (-tātem), used to make abstract nouns from adjectives, was freely employed: *falsĭtas; natīvĭtas; purĭtas; trinĭtas.* So *deĭtas* from *deus.* Cf. Olcott 58-69, G. 102-106, Bayard 19-22 (very common in St. Cyprian).

-tio, -sic (-tiōnem, -siōnem), used to form abstract nouns from verbs (as *lectio, mansio, potio),* are very common in St. Jerome, St. Cyprian, and other late writers: *abbreviatio; aggravatio,* G. 63; **nutritio; ostensio; prensio; revolutio.* Cf. Olcott 2-23, R. 69-82, Bayard 19-22.

-tor, -trix, -sor (-tōrem, -trīcem, -sōrem), used to denote the agent (as *amātor, mensor),* were very freely employed (but show few traces in Rumanian: Cooper XLV): *necātor; ostensor;* Pr. *beveire, trobaire.* Cf. Olcott 88-122, R. 55-63, G. 45-56.

-tōrium, -sōrium, used to form from verbs nouns denoting place, some-

times instrument (as *dormitorium, natatorium, cursorium*), were much extended, often taking the place of *-culum* (*cubiculum* > *accubitorium*): **cæsorium; mensorium; missorium; oratorium;* **pressorium; repositorium.* Cf. Olcott 194-196, R. 31-37, G. 96-97.

-tūdo (*-tūdĭnem*), used to make abstract nouns from adjectives (as *fortitudo*), was extended. **certitudo; servitudo.* Cf. Olcott 69-73.

-tūra: see *-ūra*.

-tus: see *-ta*, etc.

-ŭlus, -ŭla, diminutive (as *vitulus*), was used for a few new formations: **alaudula; ossulum*, Bon. 197.

-ūra and *-t-ūra, -s-ūra*, used to form abstract nouns from perfect participles (as *censura, strictura*), later from adjectives also, were extended, in late Latin often replacing *-or* (*fervor* > *fervura): **frig'dura; messura; nutritura; ornatura;* **planura; pressura; tensura;* **vir'dura*. See *Einf.* § 171. Cf. Olcott 51-58, R. 40-45, G. 88-90.

-ūta: see *-ta*, etc.

38. When Greek nouns were borrowed by Latin, the endings were adapted as follows: —

-os, -η, -ον regularly became respectively *-us, -a, -um:* Claussen 796. There are a few exceptions for special reasons (Claussen 795): ἔλαιον, influenced by *olere*, gave *oleum;* μηλόφυλλον, by popular etymology, gave *millefolium*.

-as in popular words generally became *-a* (Claussen 798-799): λαμπάς > *lampa*.

-ης, -της became *-a, -ta* or *-ης, -tus* (Claussen 798): τρώκτης > *tructa;* βωλίτης > *boletus*.

-ι in popular words either fell or became *-a, -e, -is,* or *-i* (Claussen 799): πέπερι > *piper;* σίναπι > *sinapis, sinape;* κόμμι > *gumma, gummi-s*.

-ις often became *-a*, instead of *-is* (Claussen 798): *pausis* > *pausa*.

-μα in popular words gave a feminine *-ma* (Claussen 796-797): κῦμα > *cima*.

-ρος preceded by a consonant became *-er* (Claussen 797).: Ἀλέξανδρος > *Alexander*.

-ων in popular words became *-o* (Claussen 797): λέων > *leo*.

Sometimes the genitive or the accusative was taken as a basis, instead of the nominative (Claussen 800-802): ἐλέφαντος > *elephantus;* μαγίδα > *magĭda*.

§ 39]   AN INTRODUCTION TO VULGAR LATIN.   23

The unaccented vowel of the penult was often changed in conformity with Latin habits (Claussen 802-806): διάβολος > *diabolus diabulus;* κέρασος > *cerăsus *cerĕsus;* κιθάρα > *cithăra cithĕra;* σκόπελος > *scopulus;* σπατάλη > *spatula.*

c. SUFFIXES FOR ADJECTIVES.[1]

39. The commonest endings are the following: —

–abĭlis: see *–bĭlis.*

–āceus –ācius, –īceus –īcius, used to make from nouns adjectives denoting material (as *arenaceus, pelliceus*), were extended (especially in rustic speech: Cooper 111), *-aceus* being employed later as an augmentative and pejorative suffix for adjectives and finally for nouns: *chartaceus; formaceus; mixticius,* G. 143; **setaceus;* It. *tempaccio,* etc. Cf. Olcott 215–220. See E. Wölfflin, *Die Adjectiva auf -icius* in *Archiv* V, 415.

–ālis, –īlis, used to make from nouns adjectives of appurtenance (as *regalis, gentilis*), were extended: **cortilis; *ducalis; episcopalis.* Cf. Olcott 226–238, G. 144.

–āneus –ānius, –ōneus –ōnius (as *extraneus, erroneus*) were slightly extended: **caroneus; spontaneus.*

–ans, –ens (*-antem, –entem*), present participles (as *amans, potens*), were used freely to make adjectives and nouns from verbs: *credens; *currens; *passans.*

–ānus, denoting appurtenance (as *paganus, Romanus*), was used to form adjectives of place (occasionally time) and nouns of office: *biduanus,* Bechtel 83; *medianus,* Bechtel 83; **Sicilianus; Tuscanus;—*capitanus; decanus.*

–arĭcius, a combination of *-arius* and *-ĭcius* (as *sigillaricius*), became popular in Gaul: see A. Thomas, *Nouveaux essais de philologie française* 62 (*Hacherece,* etc.).

–āris (as *singularis*) was extended: *particularis.* Cf. Olcott 182–187.

–arius, attached to nouns and adjectives, to denote connection, and used also in the masculine to form nouns of occupation (as *aquarius, argentarius, pomarius*), was much extended, especially in the latter function: *imaginarius; *leviarius;— apothecarius; *marinarius; *werrarius.* Cf. Olcott 137–173. The phonetic development of this suffix was apparently peculiar in Gaul and some other regions: the earliest examples are *glan-*

---

[1] Cf. Cooper 92–163 (diminutives, 164–195), Quillacq 32–40, Dubois 136–151 Bon. 464–467.

deria < *glandarius* + *-ia* (6th century) and *sorcerus* < *sortiarius (8th century); the earliest forms in French and Provençal are *-ers, -er,* then *-iers, -ier.* On the other hand, Spanish *-ero* and Italian *-aio* are perfectly regular, Italian *-aro* is easily explained by the analogy of the plural *-ari,* and Italian *-iere, -iero* are probably borrowed. E. R. Zimmermann, *Die Geschichte des lateinischen Suffixes* -arius *in den romanischen Sprachen,* and E. Staaff, *Le suffixe* -arius *dans les langues romanes,* try to derive all the forms from *-arius.* P. Marchot, *Zs.* XXI, 296 (cf. *Phon.* I, 34-36), postulates *-ar(i)us* and *-er(i)us,* showing that while the French forms may perhaps be derived from *-arius* and *-iarius,* the Provençal cannot. Cf. *Gram.* I, 222, § 227. Zimmermann, *Zs.* XXVI, 591, points out that many words have *e, e,* or *i* before the *a,* that *-iarius* was a real suffix (cf. *anatiarius,* Olcott 142), that *-iarius* and *-carius* may have established *-iers* in French. A. Thomas, *Rom.* XXXI, 481 (cf. *Nouveaux essais de philologie française* 119, and *Bausteine* 641), suggests that the Germans in Gaul associated *-arius* with their proper names in *-areis* or *-ari,* and when *umlaut* affected the *a* of these, pronounced *-arius,* too, as *-erius* or *-erus,* and that this pronunciation spread to the neo-Latin speakers. Cf. *Chairibertus* repeatedly used for *Charibertus* by Fredegarius: Haag 7.

-ātus, a perfect participle ending (as *sceleratus*), was much used to make adjectives in the popular language: *exauguratus;* **fatatus; timoratus.* Cf. Olcott 244-250, G. 159-160.

-bĭlis, or *-ābĭlis, -ĭbĭlis,* an objective suffix used to make adjectives from verbs (as *amabilis, terribilis*), is very common in Christian writers and was much employed in late Latin, especially in learned words; it is rare, however, in Rumanian (Cooper XLV): *acceptabilis; capabilis;* **caritabilis; diligibilis; indicibilis,* G. 137. Cf. Olcott 209-213, R. 109-116, G. 135-140.

-ceus -cius: see *-āceus*

-ens: see *-ans.*

-ensis, used to make from nouns adjectives of appurtenance (as *forensis*), was greatly extended, especially in popular speech, the derivatives being sometimes employed as nouns: **cortensis;* **Frankensis; turrensis.* G. 155; *vallensis,* G. 155; —**markensis;* **pagensis.*

-eus -ius, denoting material (as *aureus*), was slightly extended (but is rare in Rumanian: Cooper XLV); the derivative was sometimes used as a noun: *panneus; papyrius;* —*fageus; querceus.* Cf. Olcott 339-344.

-ĭbĭlis: see *-bĭlis.*

-īceus -icius: see *āceus.*

§ 40]   AN INTRODUCTION TO VULGAR LATIN.   25

–ĭcus (as *medicus*) was used especially in words from the Greek: *clericus*. Cf. Olcott 220–223.

–ĭdus (as *rapidus*) was slightly extended: *exsūcidus*, G. 155 (Tertullian); **rīpidus; sapidus*.

–īlis: see *–ālis*.

–īnus: see Nouns.

–ĭnus (as *fraxinus*) was used for a few adjectives: *quercinus*.

–ĭscus, probably a fusion of Greek *–ισκος* (*Syriscus*) and Germanic *-isk* (*Thiudiscus*), was used for *-ĭcus* in some late words: **Angliscus; *Frankiscus.*

–ĭttus: see Nouns.

–ius: see *–eus*.

–īvus (as *nativus*) occurs in a few new formations: **restīvus*. Cf. Olcott 224–226.

–ōneus: see *–āneus*.

–ōrius: see *–tōrius*.

–ōsus, also *–iōsus: Rom.* XXXIX, 217.

–sōrius: see *–tōrius*.

–tōrius, –sōrius, made up of *-t-or, -s-or* + *-ius* (as *noscere notor notorius, censēre censor censorius*), were used for some new formations: *defensorius; mansorius*. In Provençal and Rumanian *–tōrius* was extended, with the sense of *–bĭlis* or of the gerundive: Pr. *punidor;* Rum. *jurătórĭŭ*, Tiktin 597.

–ŭlus, diminutive (as *albulus*), was a favorite with Christian writers; *promptulus*, G. 158. Cf. G. 157–158.

–ŭndus (as *jocundus*) was used in Spanish and Provençal for a few words: Pr. *volon*.

–ūtus (as *canutus*) was somewhat extended: **carnutus*.

d. SUFFIXES FOR ADVERBS.[1]

40. The usual endings are as follows: —

–ce –c (as *ne nec, num nunc, tum tunc*) was apparently used to form *dunc* (*C. I. L.* IX, 4810, etc.) = *dum + ce* (cf. *Franz.* ? I, 10); Pirson 252 cites eight examples of *dunc*, one of them from Gaul. Cf. *dōnique* in *Substrate* II, 103–106. Possibly **anc* is derived from *an* in the same way: cf. *Archiv* I, 241; *Gram.* III, 552.

–e is very common in St. Jerome: G. 193–197 (*angelice*, etc.). It was

---

[1] Cf. Cooper 196–204, Dubois 163–171, Bcn. 467–470.

preserved in popular speech in *bene, longe, male, pure, tarde*, and occurs also in *Romanice*, whence such formations as *Brittanice, Normannice*, etc.

-ĭter: see *-ter*.

-o and *-um* generally coincided in pronunciation (*multum = multo*, etc.). They are rare in St. Jerome, but common in other late writers: *clanculo, multum, rato*, etc. Many such adverbs were preserved in common speech, as It. *alto, basso, caldo, chiaro, piano, poco;* hence other adjectives came to be used as adverbs (as It. *forte, soave*), and in Rumanian nearly all adjectives may be so used (as *greŭ, noŭ*).

-ter (as *brevĭter*) was not preserved in common speech, though much used in ecclesiastical Latin (G. 197–201: *infantiliter*, etc.), being especially common in St. Cyprian (Bayard 32–34).

-tim was favored by St. Cyprian (Bayard 34–35) and some other writers, but was not kept alive in popular Latin.

Some adverbial phrases on the model *ad . . . -ōnes* (in Italy also without the preposition) came into use: It. *a ginocchioni, bocconi;* Fr. *à reculons*. Cf. *Gram*. II, 689; *Rom*. XXXIII, 230; *Zs*. XXIX, 245, XXX, 337, 339.

Repetition was used, as sometimes in Classic Latin, for emphatic effect. Many examples are to be found in Petronius: *modo modo =* 'only yesterday,' Waters Ch. 37, Ch. 42, Ch. 46.

41. Adverbs of manner came to be made with the ablative *mente*. This noun was first used with an adjective to denote a state of mind, as *forti mente, obstinata mente, jocunda mente, firma mente, sana mente;* Apuleius, *dubia mente*, I, 6, and *saucia mente*, V, 23. Then it was employed in a more general sense: *pari mente*, G. 428; **bona mente;* **ipsa mente;* *mala mente. Later, perhaps after the Vulgar Latin period, *mente* was used with any adjective that could make an adverb of manner; **longa mente; sola mente*, *Gl. Reich*. This formation is not common, however, in Rumanian: *Lat. Spr*. 487. In the Romance languages *mente* was sometimes added to adverbs: Fr. *comment;* It. *insiememente*.

e. CHANGE OF SUFFIX.

42. The popular language sometimes substitutes one suffix for another, as *manuplus* for *manipulus*. The principal types are: —

(1) Subsitution of a new or common suffix for an old or rare one: —

-*cĭllus* > -*cĕllus*: see -*ĭllus*.

-*cŭlus* > *cĕllus*: see -*ŭlus*.

-*ēlus* > -*ĕllus* (common in late Latin): *camēlus* > *camĕllus*, Cohn 213–216, R. 460; *loquēla* > *loquĕlla*, Corssen I, 227, R. 460; *querēla* > *querĕlla*, S. 131, R. 321, 460; *suadēla* > *suadĕlla*, R. 460. Cf. Caper (Keil VII, 96): "*querela, loquela per unum l.*"

-*ēnus* > -*īnus*: "*Byzacenus* non *Byzacinus*," *App. Pr.*; *venēnum* > *venīnum. Cf. Cohn 219–226.

-*ex(-ĕcem)* > -*ix(-īcem)*: *vervēcem* > *berbīcem*. Cf. Cohn 41–42.

-*ĭllus* > -*ĕllus*: *axĭlla* > *ascĕlla*, etc. Cf. Cohn 42–52.

-*or(-ōrem)* > -*ūra*: *calor* > *calūra; *pavor* > *pavura; *rancor* > *rancūra, etc. Cf. Cohn 172–180.

-*ŭlus* > -*ĕllus*: *anŭlus* > *anĕllus*; *avicŭla* > *avicĕlla*, etc. Cf. Cohn 17–28.

-*ŭus* > -*ĭtus*: *vacuus* > *vŏcĭtus (cf. § 195).

(2) Indiscriminate use of two suffixes: —

-*ānus* = -*āneus*: *extraneus* *extranus; *subterraneus* *subterranus. Cf. Cohn 160–172.

-*ātus* = -*ītus* = -*ūtus*: *barbatus* *barbutus; *carnatus* *carnutus; *caudatus cauditus*, Cohn 184; *lanatus lanutus*, Cohn 184. Cf. Cohn 180–205.

-*īceus* -*īcius* = -*īceus* -*īcius*: *erīcius* *erīcius. Cohn 30–31.

-*icŭlus* = -*icŭlus*: *capītŭlus* *capĭtŭlus; *cornīcŭla* *cornĭcŭla; *lentīcŭla* *lentĭcŭla. Cf. Cohn 151–154.

-*icŭlus* = -*ucŭlus*: *ossĭculum ossŭculum*, Waters Ch. 65; *pedīculus pedŭculus*.

-*īlius* = -*ĭlius*: *consīlium* *consĭlium; *fămīlia* *famīlia. Cf. Cohn 154–160.

-*īx(-īcem)* = -*ĭx(-ĭcem)*: *sōrĭcem* *sorīcem. Cf. Cohn 147–151.

(3) Alteration of a suffix: —

-*ărius*: see Suffixes for Adjectives, -*ārius*. Cf. Cohn 274–291.

-ēnus > -īnus through late pronunciation of Greek η as ī: σαγήνη > saginæ (Vok. III, 121: 7th century) > Old Fr. saïne, etc.
-ĭcŭlus? > -ŭcŭlus: *genŭcŭlum; *ranŭcŭla, etc. Cf. Cohn 226-264.
-ūdo (-ūdĭnem) > -ūmen (-ūmĭnem): consuetudo *costumen, Substrate I, 553-554; incus incūdo *incūmĭnem, etc. Cf. Cohn 264-274.

4. COMPOUNDS.

a. NOUNS.

43. Acer arbor (> Fr. érable); alba spīna; avis strūthius; bene placĭtum, G. 131; bis cŏctum; in ŏdio; mĕdio die; mĕdio lŏco.

b. ADJECTIVES.

44. These compounds generally belonged to the literary style. G. 130-134, 160-170: magnisonans; omnimodus; unicornis; unigenitus; etc. But male habĭtus, etc., were popular.

c. PRONOUNS.

45. See §§ 24, 65.

d. VERBS.

46. Calce pistare; crucifĭgĕre, G. 191; fŏris mĭttĕre; genuflectĕre, G. 191; ĭnde fŭgĕre (> Fr. enfuir); intra vidēre; manu tenēre; mente habēre (> Pr. mentaver); mĭnus pretiare. So antemĭttĕre, etc., in Gl. Reich. In church writers there are many verbs in -ficare, as mortificare: G. 190.

e. ADVERBS.

47. There were many compounds made up of a preposition and an adverb: ab ante, R. 234; ab intus, R. 231, Bon. 483; ab olim, Bechtel 101; a contra, Bechtel 101; a foras, Bechtel 101; a foris, R. 231, Bon. 483; a longe, G. 203, Bon. 483; a modo, R. 232, Bon. 483; a semel, Bechtel 101; — ad horam = 'presently', 'just now', G. 426; ad mane, Bechtel 101; ad semel, Bon. 194, 484; ad sero, Bechtel 101; ad subito, Bechtel 101;

ad tunc, Bechtel 101; — *de contra*, Bechtel 101; *de deorsum*, R. 232; *de foris*, R. 232, G. 203; *de intro*, Bechtel 102; *de intus*, R. 232, G. 203; *de magis*, *Lat. Spr.* 487; *de retro*, R. 232; *de semel*, Bechtel 101; *de sursum*, R. 233, G. 203, Bon. 484; — *e contra*, G. 203; *ex tunc*, R. 433; — *in ante*, Bon. 484, *Lat. Spr.* 487; *in contra*, R. 235; *in hodie*, Bechtel 102; *in mane*, Bechtel 102; **in semel*, Substrate III, 268.

Petronius (Waters Ch. 38) says: *Ubi semel res inclinata amici de medio.*

The following compounds are of a still different nature: *ac sic*, *Per.* 40, 8, etc.; *et sic*, *Per.* 39, 17, etc.; *usque hodie*, G. 426, *Per.* 68, 13.

f. PREPOSITIONS.

48. Some of these adverbial compounds, and some others similar to them, were used as prepositions: *ab ante*, *Lexique* 40; — *de ante*, Bechtel 102; *de inter*, Bechtel 102, Haag 75; *de intus; de retro; in ante; in contra.* Cf. E. Wölfflin, *Abante*, in *Archiv* I, 437. Slightly different is *intus in*, Bechtel 102.

A compound made up of preposition + noun is found in: *in giro* (followed by the ablative or the accusative), Bechtel 102; *in medio*, Bechtel 102; *per girum* and *per giro = circa*, Bechtel 102.

Some compounds consist of two prepositions: **de ad* (> It. *da*)[1]; *de post*, R. 235; *de sub*, R. 235; *de super*, Bon. 484.

g. CONJUNCTIONS.

49. *At ubi* and *ad ubi*, Bon. 484–486 (cf. *Per.* 74, 28, 85, 15, etc.); *et at ubi*, *Per.* 72, 19, 75, 3.

---

[1] Romance *da*, *dad* may be the result of a fusion rather than a combination of *de* and *ad*. In any case it is probably a late product. Some have thought it came from *de+ab*. Mohl, *Lexique* 38–47, says *da* is found from the 7th century on; he would derive It. and Old Sp. *da*, Sardinian *dare*, *das*, Rætian *dad* from the Oscan *da*, *dat* and from a southern Latin **dabi*, **dabs*.

II. SYNTAX.[1]

A. ORDER OF WORDS.[2]

50. The Romance order is simpler and more rational than that of Classic Latin. It does not permit the arbitrary separation of members that belong together, such as the preposition and the word it governs, or the adjective and the noun it modifies, as in Ovid's "In nova fert animus mutatas dicere formas corpora." Neither does it allow the collocation of words of the same part of speech that belong logically in different places, as in the "In multis hoc rebus dicere habemus" of Lucretius. The most irrational features of the Classic Latin construction were surely artifical, and were not characteristic of daily speech. Nevertheless there is really a fundamental difference between the old order and the new: Romance has, so to speak, a *crescendo*, Latin to a certain extent a *diminuendo* movement (*Lat. Spr.* 491); Romance puts the emphasis at the end, Latin very frequently in the middle. The principle, however, is not primarily rhythmic, but psychic, the difference being due to a diverse conception of the structure of language: Romance inclines more to put the modifier after the word modified. The modern order is the more logical, proceeding from the known to the unknown. The old arrangement is exemplified by this sentence: "Fabius

---

[1] See Meyer-Lübke, *Gram.* III, for a comprehensive account of Romance syntax.
[2] See Elise Richter, *Zur Entwicklung der romanischen Wortstellung aus der lateinischen*, 1903, from which work most of the matter of this chapter was taken.

æquatus imperio Hannibalem et virtute et fortuna superiorem vidit." The following examples illustrate the later structure: "Mors perfecit tua ut essent omnia brevia," "Hæc loca sunt montuosa et natura impedita ad rem militarem." The change constitutes a progress in language; all cultivated peoples have made it. It is indigenous in Latin, not imitated from the Greek, which independently effected the same transformation.

51. The modern order was not abruptly substituted for the old. On the contrary, it is to be found in Latin, with generally increasing frequency, in inscriptions and popular writers, from the earliest texts down; it occurs sporadically also in literary authors, especially in Cicero. Petronius has notably short periods and an approach to the new structure. But until the fourth century the majority of Latin sentences have the old arrangement. Classic Latin may be said to represent an intermediate stage, while the revolution was in progress; there was a long struggle, and for centuries the ancient and the modern type were used side by side. By the fourth century the new order prevailed. Here is a characteristic passage from the *Peregrinatio:* "Hæc est autem vallis ingens et planissima, in qua filii Israhel commorati sunt his diebus, quod sanctus Moyses ascendit in montem Domini, et fuit ibi quadraginta diebus et quadraginta noctibus" (*Per.* 37,21-24). The following is a good sample of the style of the Vulgate: "Cui respondit Dominus: Qui peccaverit mihi, delebo eum de libro meo; tu autem vade, et duc populum istum quo locutus sum tibi; angelus meus præcedet te. Ego autem in die ultionis visitabo et hoc peccatum eorum" (*Exodus* XXXII, 33, 34).

52. There was always a tendency to put a stressed word first, followed by an unaccented one, such as a connective or an atonic pronoun (*Lat. Spr.* 490). According to Meyer-

Lübke, *Zs.* XXI, 313, personal pronouns, when unstressed, were always enclitic in Latin, and were attached preferably to the first word in the sentence; and so it was in the early stages of the Romance languages: cf. It. *vedolo* but *non lo vedo, aiutatemi* but *or m'aiutate;* Fr. *voit le* but *qui le voit.* The definite article, however, precedes its noun in all the Romance languages except Rumanian and Albanian (Zauner 40).

53. In dependent clauses, which were naturally of less importance, the old order survived longer than in independent. In a few other respects the old arrangement lingered and under certain conditions is still preserved: negative and intensive adverbs precede their verb; under some circumstances the object may come before the verb, and sometimes the whole predicate precedes; in certain constructions the dependent infinitive may stand before the finite verb (as Pr. *morir volgra*).

B. USE OF WORDS.

54. There were great changes in the functions of pronouns, prepositions, conjunctions, and adverbs. Many uses of prepositions are connected with the loss of inflections: these will be discussed under the Use of Inflections. A definite and an indefinite article developed out of *ille* and *unus*.

1. NOUNS AND ADJECTIVES.

55. For the simplification of inflections, see the Use of Inflections.

Repetition for intensive effect is not uncommon in late writers: Commodian, *malum malum*, Wölfflin 4; *bene bene, bonis bonis, fortis fortis, malus malus*, etc., R. 280. Cf. § 40.

a. COMPARISON.

56. Little by little the old comparative and superlative lost their precise sense from being employed frequently with merely an intensive force (Wölfflin 83). The comparative came to be used for a superlative, as *omnium levior* (Wölfflin 68–71), and also for a positive, as Ovid's *inertior ætas* (Wölfflin 63–68); and the superlative was often really a positive in meaning, as in St. Augustine's *sancta atque dulcissima* (Wölfflin 57–63), and in *hic est filius meus carissimus*, etc. (R. 415–417). From early times certain periphrases were used to emphasize the comparative idea, as Plautus, *melius sanus* (Wölfflin 16); Anthimus, *plus congruus* and *maxime congruus* (Wölfflin 16; cf. *maxime pessima*, etc., R. 280); Vitruvius, *magis melior*, etc. (Wölfflin 46); Commodian, *plus levior*, etc. (Wölfflin 47). To avoid ambiguity, the *plus* and *magis* constructions were employed more and more to express a distinct comparison: *plus miser* in Tertullian, *plus formosus* in Nemesianus, *plus dulce*, *plus felix*, etc., in Sidonius Apollinaris (Wölfflin 29). Finally, toward the end of the Vulgar Latin period, this formation came to be popularly regarded as the regular one: *magis mirabilem*, Sepulcri 232; *plus popularis, magis . . . præclarum*, Bon. 451. Many old comparative forms remained, however, in common use. Cf. Adverbs. In the Romance languages a substitute for the superlative was made by prefixing the definite article to the comparative; it is likely that this device existed in late Vulgar Latin, but no example of it has been found. See *Archiv* VIII, 166–170.

b. NUMERALS.[1]

57. *Unus* was used as an indefinite article, occasionally in Classic Latin, frequently in late and popular writers: *lepida*

---
[1] For the forms of numerals, see Morphology.

... *una* ... *mulier*, Plautus, *Pseud.* 948 ; *unus servus*, Petronius, Waters Ch. 26 ; *accessit ad eum una sorella*, R. 425 ; cf. *Per.* 48, 25, etc.

58. Ordinal numerals, except a few of the smallest, were apparently not much used in popular speech after the fifth century.

2. PRONOUNS.

59. Pronouns were much more used than in Classic Latin: G. 408–409.

a. PERSONAL AND POSSESSIVE PRONOUNS.

60. The personal pronouns came into more and more frequent use. *Ego* and *tu* are very common in Petronius. The demonstratives, especially *ille*, were employed as personal pronouns of the third person. The adverb *inde* came to be used occasionally as a genitive neuter pronoun: *nemo inde dubitat*, Regnier 10; *exinde* = Fr. *en*, Bon. 580.

Many pronouns developed double forms, according as they were accented or unaccented (as *suus* and *sus*): see Morphology. Cf. § 158.

There was great irregularity in the use of reflexives, especially the possessives, *suus* being generally substituted for *ejus*. See *Lat. Spr.* 489, G. 403–404, Hoppe 102–103, Dubois 333–336.

b. DEMONSTRATIVES.

61. *Idem* went out of popular use, being replaced by *ille* and *ipse*. For the encroachment of *ipse* on *idem*, see Hoppe 104, Bayard 133.

62. *Is*, too, was often replaced by *ille* and *ipse* (Bechtel 145), and eventually was preserved in vulgar speech only in the combination *eccum* (= *ecce hum*), where it was not recognized,[1] and in the extremely common phrase *id ipsum* (> It. *desso*), where likewise the *id* lost its significance. This last compound was used as a neuter pronoun, meaning 'it' or 'that,' as *id ipsum sapite*, R. 424 (cf. R. 424-425, G. 407, Quillacq 126), and also as a demonstrative adjective, generally invariable, as *id ipsum velam*, R. 424, *in id ipsum monastyriu*, *Franz. ∂* II, 2, *in id ipsam rem*, *Franz. ∂* II, 2.

63. *Hic, ille,* and *iste* came to be used indiscriminately (G. 405-406, Hoppe 104, Bayard 130-132); there are examples of *iste* for *hic* in Cæsar's time (Densusianu 178). *Hic* and *is*, too, were confused by late writers (Bayard 132). Toward the end of the Vulgar Latin period *hic* was apparently going out of common use, with the exception of the neuter *hoc*.

64. A combination of two demonstratives was common in Christian writers: *is ipse, iste ipse, ipse ille, ille ipse, iste ille, iste hic, hic ipse*. The last three have left no trace.

65. *Ecce* and *eccum* (pronounced *eccu*) were used as demonstrative prefixes (cf. § 24): we find early *ecce ego, ecce tu, ecce hic, ecce nunc;* also *ecce iste, ecce ille*, such combinations being common in Plautus. The final stage, probably not reached until the end of the Vulgar Latin period, is the fusion of the two parts into one word.

Atque, too, was perhaps used as a prefix (*Gram.* II, 646): Plautus, *atque ipse illic est* (*Epidicus* 91), *atque is est* (*Stichus* 582). G. Ascoli, however, *Intorno ai continuatori neolatini del lat. "ipsu–"* in *Archivio glottologico italiano* XV, 303 (discussing Sp. *aquese*, Pg. *aquesse*, Catalan *aqueix*, etc.), maintains that *eccu'* was the basis in all the Empire. At any rate, *eccu'* was influenced in some regions, especially in Spain and southern Gaul, by *atque* or *ac* (as in *ac sic*).

---

[1] Cf. Plautus, *Mil. Glor.* I, 25: "Ubi tu's? — Eccum."

When *iste* and *ille* lost their distinctive force, people said for 'this' *ecc'iste* or *eccu'iste*, for 'that' *ecc'ille* or *eccu'ille*. These compounds developed into *ecceste, *acceste, *ceste, *eccueste, *accueste, *cueste and *eccelle, *accelle, *celle, *eccuelle, *accuelle, *cuelle.

66. The suffix –*met* was used also as an intensive prefix, *ipsemet* becoming *metipse* through such combinations as *temet ipsum* (*Ecclus.* XXX, 22), *semet ipsum* (*Philip.* II, 8). Cf. §24. *Ego met ipse* is blamed by Donatus (*Lat. Spr.* 484).

Beside *ipse*, there was an emphatic form *ipsĭmus* (used by Petronius: Waters Ch. 69, etc.). This, with the prefix *met-*, became *metipsĭmus.

67. *Ille, hic, ipse, is*, especially *ille*, were used as personal pronouns of the third person. Cf. §60.

68. *Ille, hic, ipse, is* were used also as definite articles. *Ille* in this function is very common: R. 419–420 (*cito proferte mihi stolam illam primam*). Examples of the others are by no means infrequent: *hic*, R. 427 (*virum hunc cujus est zona hæc*); *ipse*, R. 423 (*in ipsa multitudine*); *is*, R. 423–425. This use of *is* was probably more literary than popular.

c. INTERROGATIVES AND RELATIVES.

69. The forms were greatly confused by late writers. In Bon. 391–396 we find *qui* used as n. sg. and pl.; *quæ* as m., as n., as acc. f. sg., as acc. m. pl.; *quod* as m., as f. pl., as n. pl.; *quem* as n.; *qua* very often as n. pl. (395–396).

In popular speech *qui* was apparently used regularly for *quis:* Audollent 549, Quillacq 126–127, Bon. 391–392; it is common in inscriptions. Furthermore, the masculine *qui* took the place of the feminine *quæ;* it occurs in Christian inscriptions from the fifth century on: cf. R. 276 (*qui, quem* for *quæ, quam*), Haag 51, Bon. 390-391, 394 (*qui* f. sg. and f. pl., *quem* f.), *Archiv* I, 53 (*qui* for *quæ* in 528 A. D.). *Quid*, moreover, gradually encroached on *quod:* Bon. 393.

70. *Qualis* was kept, and was used as an interrogative and as a relative. The adverb *unde* came to have occasionally the meaning of French *dont* (Bon. 580; *Zs.* Beiheft 7, 178), and eventually *de unde, **d'unde*, was employed as a relative pronoun. Cf. § 84.

d. INDEFINITE PRONOUNS.

71. Some Classic Latin pronouns fell into disuse, and some new compounds were made. The principal indefinite pronouns and adjectives used in late popular speech are as follows: —

aliquanti took the place of *aliqui* and *aliquot: aliquanta oppida cepit*, G. 415.

alĭquis flourished especially in the west: Sp. *alguien*, Pg. *alguem*. The neuter *aliquid* was more extended: Pr. *alques*.

alĭqui ūnus > **aliqu'ūnus* *alicūnus.

alius and *alter* were confused in common speech: G. 415-417; Plautus, *alius filius*, G. 417. This confusion is more frequent in late Latin: St. Jerome, *nemo judicat alterum*, G. 416. There is evidence of the retention of the old neuter *alid* (Lucretius I, 263): *Archiv* I, 237.

cata was probably introduced, along the Mediterranean, by Greek merchants, in such phrases as *cata unum* = καθ' ἕνα, *cata tres* = κατὰ τρεῖς. Hence *cata ūnus, **cat' ūnus*, etc. Cf. § 19.

hŏmo was used sometimes like French *on: Per.* 55, 25.

ĭnde came to mean, in certain constructions, 'some' or 'any.'

magis: see *plus*.

mŭltus.

*nec ente or *ne ente was apparently used as an equivalent for *nihil* Meyer-Lübke, *Gram.* II, 650, conjectures *ne inde.

*ne ipse ūnus, **ne'ps'ūnus*.

nec unus.

nēmo was kept in Italy, Sardinia, and Dacia: *Lat. Spr.* 485.

nūllus.

omnis: see *tōtus*. *Omnis* and *omnia* were kept in Italy.

paucus.
persona.
plus and *magis* were confused: G. 427, Regnier 108–109 (*quanto plus tenetur tanto plus timetur,* 109).
qualis.
quantus, tantus replaced *quot, tot.* There are examples as early as Propertius: Densusianu 179. Cf. Dräger 104, § 53, R. 336–337, G. 413–415 (St. Jerome, *quanti justi esuriunt,* 414; Claudian, *tantis lacrimis,* 415).
quī.
quīque.
quĭs.
quĭsque, quĭsquis. *Quisque* was much extended (G. 409–411), being used for *quisquis* and *quicumque* (Bayard 135).
res and *res nata* = 'anyone', 'anything': R. 345.
talis.
tantus : see *quantus.*
tōtus, pronounced also *tottus* (S. 121) and perhaps *tūttus,* was sometimes used for *omnis :* Plautus, *totis horis, Mil. Glor.* 212. This use was common in late Latin: Densusianu 178, Bechtel 143, R. 338, G. 402–403 (*tota tormenta diaboli in me veniant,* 403). Cf. §§ 163, 204, (2).
ūnus.

3. VERBS.

72. Frequent in late Latin is a pleonastic use of *debeo,* Bon. 691–693: *commonens ut . . . custodire debeant,* 692. Cf. § 117. Compare the old Italian use of *dovere.*

There is also a common pleonastic use of *cœpi* with the infinitive, instead of the perfect: see § 124.

Videri, too, is often used pleonastically: Bayard 99–100.

4. ADVERBS.

73. The words referring to the "place in which" and the "place into which" were confused, *ubi* being used for *quo, ibi* for *eo. Lat. Spr.* 488. *Unde* was employed in the sense of 'where' (*Zs.* Beiheft 7, 157); also 'therefore' and 'wherefore': *Dic amice unde tristis es*, Regnier 110; cf. § 84.

74. *Plus* was often substituted for *magis*, and *magis* for *potius:* Bayard 110. *Plus* and *magis* were used more and more for comparison, and the old comparative and superlative forms became rarer: see § 56. Repetition was used for intensive effect: Seneca, *semper semper*, Wölfflin 5. *Bene, multum, satis* were employed as intensives more than in Classic Latin. *Totum* occurs often as an adverb: *Per.* 37, 14, and many other places; Dubois 332.

75. Double negation is frequent: R. 446–447 (*nec facio nihil*, etc.). *Non* for *ne* with the subjunctive is common: G. 435, Regnier 110. The absolute use of *non*, meaning 'no', occurs occasionally: *Dicit unus ex uno angulo: Ecce hic est. Alius ex alio angulo: Non, sed ecce hic est*, Regnier 111.

5. PREPOSITIONS.

76. The functions of prepositions were very much extended (Bayard 137–158): see Use of Inflections, Cases.

77. *Ab*, according to Mohl, *Lexique* 43, is not found in any of the Italic dialects except Latin. It apparently has no successors in the Romance languages, having been replaced by *de*, which also, from the third century on, usurped the place of *ex* (*Lat. Spr.* 487, R. 395–396, Hoppe 38): *de palatio exit*, Bechtel 105; *egredere de ecclesia*, Bechtel 105; *de utero matris nati sunt sic*, R. 395; *egressus de arca*, G. 339; *muri de lapide jaspide*, G. 342; *vivo de decimis*, G. 341; *de adversario . . . aliquid postulare*, Hoppe 38; *nec de cubiculo . . . procedit*, Hoppe 38.

78. *Ad* for *apud* occurs in Plautus, Terence, and others

(Oliver 5–6), and is common in late writers (R. 390–392, Urbat 10): *ad ipsum fontem facta est oratio*, Bechtel 103; *ad nos*, Bechtel 104; cf. *Per.* 42,27. For the most part *apud* was replaced by *ad*, except in Gaul, where it was kept with the sense of *cum:* Haag 74, Urbat 27 (*tractans apud me metipsum;* also *ab una manu pallas altaris tenerem*, etc., where *ab* seems to be used for *apud*). *Apud* is used for *cum* by Sulpicius Severus, and more frequently by later authors: *Lat. Spr.* 489. According to F. G. Mohl, *La préposition* cum *et ses successeurs en gallo-roman* in *Bausteine* 61, *apud* is repeatedly found for *cum* in the Latin writers of Gaul, and *cum* for *apud* in Gregory of Tours; *cum* probably disappeared from actual use in Gaul by the fourth century; *apud*, being, as he says, a new word, had a great vogue in authors of the second and third centuries, a critical period for Gaul, and so came to supplant *cum* in that country.[1]

79. *Pro* often had the sense of 'for,' and replaced *ob* and *propter: fides pro una muliere perfida*, G. 343; *volo pro legentis facilitate abuti sermone vulgato*, G. 343; *attendimus locum illum pro memoria illius*, Bechtel 106. *Pro* itself was partially replaced by *per* (cf. §14), but was substituted for *per* in other regions (Urbat 34–35).

80. *Circa*, in the Empire, frequently meant 'concerning': *frustrati circa veritatem*, Hoppe 37. *Juxta* often signified 'according to': *juxta consuetudinem*, Bechtel 105; *juxta drachmæ exemplum*, Hoppe 37. *Super* sometimes replaced *de: fallere vos super hanc rem*, Bechtel 106; *super anima commendatus*, Hoppe 41.

---

[1] Mohl would derive the Old It. *appo*, not from *apud*, but from *ad post (p. 71); Fr. *avec*, not from *apud* + *hoc*, but from *ad hoc* (pp. 75–76). Pr. *ab* he takes from *apud*, but Pr. *am* from Italic *amb*, *am*.

81. *Retro, subtus, de foris, foris, foras* were freely used as prepositions (R. 398-400, G. 334): *vade retro me*, R. 399; *subtus terram*, R. 399.

6. CONJUNCTIONS.

82. *Quod, quia, quoniam* (and after *jubere, ut:* R. 427-428) are used very often by late writers instead of the accusative and infinitive construction: R. 402, Regnier 112-113. *Ut* with the infinitive is not infrequent: R. 445-446. *Quod* for *ut* is very common: Audollent 549. *Eo quod* came to be much used in the sense of 'that': *Per.* 48, 27, etc. Eventually *ut* was generally discarded.

Cur, quare sometimes replaced *quod* and *quia:* G. 431-432. *Quia,* which in late Latin was often reduced to *qui* or *qua* (see § 168) frequently took the place of *quod:* Regnier 111-112. *Quomodo* became a great favorite, often supplanting *quando, quod,* and *quoniam:* R. 403. *Quando* displaced *cum* in the temporal sense. *Qua,* 'when', encroaches on *quando* in the *Peregrinatio:* 46, 22, etc.; cf. Bechtel 119-120.

83. *Si* took the place of *an* and *utrum* (R. 403-405, Regnier 111), and was often used for *ne* and *num* (G. 430): *videte si potest dici,* Regnier 111. *Ac si* frequently did service for *quasi: Per.* 39, 13, and many other places; Bon. 323.

84. *Aut . . . aut* is sometimes equivalent to *et . . . et: Per.* 49, 24; cf. Bayard 161. *Ac sic* recurs continually in the *Peregrinatio,* meaning 'and so' or 'so': 40, 8, etc. *Tamen* in the same text (37, 2, etc.) seems to be used, in most cases, merely to indicate a subordinate clause. *Magis* is much employed for 'but' by late writers. *Unde* sometimes means 'therefore' and 'wherefore': G. 424 (*unde inquit Dominus*); cf. §§ 70, 73.

C. USE OF INFLECTIONS.

1. CASES.[1]

85. In popular speech prepositions were more used, from the beginning, than in the literary language; prepositional constructions, as time went on, increasingly took the place of pure case distinctions, and the use of cases became more and more restricted. Hence arises in late writers a great irregularity in the employment of cases[2]: G. 302–326, Quillacq 96–103; for African Latin, *Archiv* VIII, 174–176; for confusion after verbs and adjectives, R. 412–415.

a. LOCATIVE.

86. The locative, rare in Classic Latin, remained eventually only in names of places. There are, however, several examples in the *Peregrinatio:* Bechtel 110, *et sic fit missa Anastasi, ut fit missa ecclesiæ*, etc. We find remnants of the locative genitive in *Agrigentī > Girgenti, Arimĭnī > Rimini, Clusĭī > Chiusi, Florentiæ > Firenze, Palestinæ* (G. 322), etc.; of the locative ablative singular in *Tĭbŭrī > Tivoli;* of the locative ablative plural in *Andecāvīs > Angers, Aquīs > Acqui Aix, Astīs > Asti, Fīnĭbus > Fimes, Parīsiīs > Parigi Paris*, etc. Cf. B. Bianchi in *Archivio glottologico italiano* IX, 378. With other words, and very often with place names also, the locative was replaced by *in* with the ablative (Hoppe 32: *in Alexandria*) or by *ad* with the accusative (Urbat 10); the *domi* or *domo* of Cicero becomes *in domo* in Seneca. When the locative of names of localities was kept, it generally came to be regarded as an in-

---

[1] Cf. Pirson 169–202.

[2] There is confusion even in Petronius, who occasionally uses the accusative for the dative and the ablative.

variable form; we find such locatives used as nominatives from the third century on: *Lat. Spr.* 481.

b. VOCATIVE.

87. The vocative is like the nominative in most words in Classic Latin, and such words as had a separate vocative form tended to discard it: vocatives in *-us*, instead of *-e*, occur in Plautus, Horace, and Livy; *meus* for *mi* is very common (Regnier 34). In Vulgar Latin the vocative form probably disappeared entirely, except perhaps in a few set phrases, such as *mī dŏmĭne*.

c. GENITIVE.

88. The genitive, little by little, was supplanted by other constructions, generally by the ablative with *de* (which occurs as early as Plautus), sometimes by the dative. Examples abound: *expers partis ... de nostris bonis*, Terence *Heaut.* IV, 1, 39; *partem de istius impudentia*, Cicero, *Verr.* II, 1, 12; *clerici de ipsa ecclesia*, Bechtel 104; *de aceto plenum*, R. 396; *de Deo munus*, R. 396; *curator de sacra via*, R. 426; *de colentibus gentilibusque multitudo magna* (also *quidam ex eis*), Acts XVII, 4; *possessor de propria terra*, Urbat 20; *de sorore nepus*, Pirson 194; *terminus de nostra donatione*, 528 A. D., *Archiv* I, 53; cf. Bon. 610 ff. For the partitive genitive we find: *nil gustabit de meo*, Plautus, cited by Draeger I, 628; *aliquid de lumine*, Hoppe 38; *neminem de præsentibus*, Hoppe 38; *de pomis* = 'some apples,' *Per.* 40, 10; *de spiritu Moysi*, Bechtel 104; *de animalibus, de oleo*, etc., R. 396; *aliquid habet de verecundia discipuli*, R. 342; *numquid Zacchæus de bono habebat*, Regnier 54; *quid de scientia*, Sepulcri 217; *de studentibus*, Pirson 197. Cf. Oliver 14.

89. According to Meyer-Lübke, *Lat. Spr.* 487, the genitive probably ceased to be really popular, save in set combinations, by the beginning of the third century. In late Latin a wrong form was often used: *a deo honorem* in an inscription in Gaul, *Zs. fr. Spr.* XXV, ii, 135; *matre meæ, alta nocte silentia*, etc., Bon. 341–342; *in fundo illa villa*, etc., D'Arbois 13; *in honore alme Maria*, etc., D'Arbois 91–93.

The genitive was retained, however, in some pronouns, in a good many set phrases, in certain words that belonged especially to clerical Latin, and probably in some proper names: *cūjus, illūjus, illōrum*, etc.; *lūnæ dīes, est ministĕrīī, de noctis tempore* > It. *di notte tempore* (later *di notte tempo*), etc.; *angelōrum, paganōrum*, etc.; It. *Paoli, Pieri*, etc.

d. DATIVE.

90. The dative was more stable than the genitive: *Lat. Spr.* 487. We find, however, as early as Plautus, a tendency to replace it by the accusative with *ad: ad carnuficem dabo*, Plautus, *Capt.* 1019; *ad me magna nuntiavit*, Plautus, *Truc.* IV, 1, 4; *si pecunia ad id templum data erit*, inscription of 57 B.C., *C. I. L.* IX, 3513; *apparet ad agricolas*, Varro, *De Re Rustica* I, 40; *ad propinquos restituit*, Livy II, 13 — constructions freely used by Classic authors. Inasmuch as the dative, in the singular of most nouns and in the plural of all, was identical in form either with the ablative or with the genitive (e. g., *causæ causis, muro muris, mari maribus*), the fear of ambiguity naturally fostered this practice and the substitution became very general in most of the Empire: *ait ad me, Per.* 64, 8; *dicens ad eum*, etc., Bechtel 102–103; *cum hæc ad vestram affectionem darem*, Bechtel 103; *fui ad episcopum* = ' I went to the bishop', Bechtel 104; *loquitur ad Jeremiam*, G. 329; *ad quem promissio facta*, G. 329; *ad quem dixit*, Sepulcri 218; *Dominus ad Moysen dicit*, Urbat 12; *ad me restituit omne regnum*, Urbat 12; *ad Dei officio paratus*, Pirson 194. Cf. *Lat. Spr.* 488, Oliver

§ 92] AN INTRODUCTION TO VULGAR LATIN. 45

3-4. Sometimes *super*, not *ad*, was used: *imposuerat manus super eum*, Bechtel 105; *super me misericordiam præstare*, Bechtel 105.

91. The dative remained in Dacia, and lingered rather late in Gaul (*Lat. Spr.* 481); elsewhere it probably disappeared from really popular speech by the end of the Empire, except in pronouns (*cūi, illūi illī*, etc., *mī, tĭbi*, etc.).

Rumanian has kept the dative, in its original function and also as a genitive, in the first declension (as *case*), and so in feminine adjectives (as *romîne*).

e. ABLATIVE.

92. The analytical tendency of speech, reinforced by the analogy of prepositional substitutes for the genitive and dative, favored the use of prepositions with the ablative, to distinguish its various functions. For *de* = 'than,' see *Zs.* XXX, 641.

Ab is common: *ab omni specie idololatriæ intactum*, Hoppe, 36; *ab sceleribus parce*, G. 335; *a carne superatur*, G. 337; *ab scriptura sancta commemoratos*, Regnier 51; *a præmio minorem esse*, St. Cyprian, cited by Wölfflin 52; *ab Ariulfi astutia deceptus*, Sepulcri 218.

De is the most frequent: *erubescens de infamia sua*, Hoppe 14; *de singularitate famosum*, Hoppe 33; *nobilior de obsoletiore matrice*, Hoppe 33; *digni de cælo Castores*, Hoppe 34; *gaudet de contumelia sua*, Hoppe 34; *de victus necessitate causatur*, Hoppe 35; *de vestra rideat æmulatione*, Hoppe 36; *de manibus suis*, Bechtel 104; *de oculis*, Bechtel 104 (cf. *de se*, Bechtel 105); *occidam de lancea*, R. 393; *patrem de regno privavit*, R. 426; *de virgine natus est*, Regnier 54; *de te beati sunt*, Regnier 56. Cf. R. 392-395, G. 339-342, Regnier 54-56.

Ex occurs also: *ex causa humanæ salutis*, Hoppe 33; *ex infirmitate fatigata*, Sepulcri 218.

In is often found: *in illo die*, Hoppe 31; *quo in tempore*, Hoppe 31; *in maxilla asinæ delevi mille viros*, R. 397; *in camo et freno maxillas eorum constringe*, Ps. XXXI, 9; *in amore Dei ferventes*, G. 347; *in bonis operibus abundetis*, Regnier 60. Cf. R. 396–397, G. 344–347, Regnier 58 ff.

93. Sometimes *ad* or *per* with the accusative is substituted for the ablative: *per hoc*, Hoppe 33; *ad diem*, Bechtel 103; *ad horam sextam aguntur*, etc., Bechtel 103–104; *per nomen vocavit*, Sepulcri 218; *pugnare ad ursos, ad unum gladii ictum caput desecare*, Lat. Spr. 488.

94. The use of prepositions became really neccessary in the late spoken language, because, after the fall of final *m* and the loss of quantitative distinctions in unaccented syllables, the ablative differed little or not at all from the accusative in the singular of most words: *causăm causā, donŭm donō, patrĕm patrĕ, fructŭm fructū, diĕm diē*. It is likely that before the end of the Empire the ablative plural form was generally discarded, the accusative being used in its stead, and that the ablative and accusative singular were pronounced alike, in all words, in most of the Latin territory. The fusion of the two cases was doubtless helped by the fact that certain prepositions might be combined with either accusative or ablative.

95. There is evidence of the confusion of accusative and ablative as early as the first century, but it was probably not very common before the third. *Cum* with the accusative is very frequent: *cum suos discentes, cum sodales*, in inscriptions, Lat. Spr. 488; *cum epistolam*, Bechtel 95; *cum res nostras*, D'Arbois 27. Cf. E. K. Rand in *Modern Philology* II, 263, footnote 5.

The accusative form is substituted for the ablative after

other prepositions: *a monazontes*, Bechtel 94;—*de eo torrentem*, Bechtel 96 ; *de actus*, Bechtel 96 ; *de hoc ipsud*, Bechtel 96 ; *de martyrium*, Bechtel 96; *de carnem*, etc., R. 406–412; *de ipsas villas*, D'Arbois 27 ; *de rigna nostra*, D'Arbois 70–71 ;— *ex fines tuos*, etc., R. 406–412;— *videbo te in publicum*, Waters Ch. 58; *in finem Deus fecit cœlum et terram*, etc., Hoppe 40–41 ; 12 examples of *in* + acc. for abl. in *Per.*, Bechtel 97–98; *erat in medium maris*, R. 410;—*pro hoc ipsud*, Bechtel 101; *pro nos*, D'Arbois 152;—*sine fructum*, etc., R. 406–412.

96. Conversely, the ablative form is very often written for the accusative: *ad ecclesia majore*, Bechtel 94; —*ante sole*, *ante cruce*, Bechtel 95; *ante sole*, etc., R. 406–412;—*circa puteo*, Bechtel 95; —*contra ipso loco*, Bechtel 95;—*foras ecclesia*, Bechtel 96; —*in carne conversa*, etc., Hoppe 40–41; in the *Per.*, *in* + abl. for acc. is three times as common as the correct use of *in* + acc., Bechtel 94–101; *venit in civitate sua*, etc., R. 406–412;—*intra civitate sua*, Bechtel 99; *intro spelunca*, Bechtel 99;—*juxta aqua ipsa*, Bechtel 99;—*per valle illa*, and 21 other cases of *per* + abl., Bechtel 100;—*post lectione*, Bechtel 100; *post morte*, etc., R. 406–412;—*prope luce*, Bechtel 101; — *propter populo*, Bechtel 101; — *super civitate hac*, Bechtel 101.

97. The ablative was kept only in some fixed expressions, such as *hōrā, ist' annō, quōmŏdo, parī mente*, etc.; perhaps in such phrases as It. *vendere cento soldi*, etc.; probably in some proper names with *de*, as *Della Casa*. It is likely, too, that the ablative absolute survived in a few common expressions, like It. *ciò fatto;* generally, however, in popular speech, the nominative absolute took its place: Bechtel 109–110, *et benedicens nos episcopus profecti sumus, visa loca sancta omnia* (*Per.* 45, 8), etc.

f. ACCUSATIVE.

98. After verbs of motion *ad* was often used, sometimes *in*, instead of the simple accusative: *eamus in forum*, Waters Ch. 58; *fui ad ecclesiam*, Bechtel 103; *ad Babyloniam duxit*, G. 327; *consules ad Africam profecti sunt*, G. 328; *ad istam regionem venit*, Regnier 52. Cf. Regnier 51–52.

99. Duration of time was expressed by *per* with the accusative, also by the ablative: Bechtel 108–9, *per totos octo dies is ornatus est, tota autem nocte vicibus dicuntur psalmi*, etc.

g. FALL OF DECLENSION.

100. By the end of the Vulgar Latin period there probably remained in really popular use (aside from pronouns and a number of set formulas) in Dacia only three cases, in the rest of the Empire only two — a nominative and an accusative-ablative. Clerics, however, naturally tried to write in accordance with their idea of correct Latin.

2. VERB-FORMS.

101. Many parts of the verb went out of popular use, and were replaced by other locutions; these obsolete parts were employed by writers with more or less inaccuracy. In the parts that remained many new tendencies manifested themselves.

a. IMPERSONAL PARTS.

102. Only the present active infinitive and the present and perfect participles were left intact.

(1) SUPINE.

103. The supine disappeared from general use, being replaced, from the first century on, by the infinitive: as *cum* *veneris ad bibere*, St. Augustine, *Sermones* 225, Cap. 4. Cf. *Lat. Spr.* 490, Dubois 275. In Rumanian, however, the supine was preserved: Tiktin 596.

(2) GERUND.

104. With the exception of the ablative form, the gerund came to be replaced by the infinitive, sometimes with a preposition: *dat manducare, Lat. Spr.* 490; *quomodo potest hic nobis carnem dare ad manducare*, R. 430; *potestatem curare, necessitas tacere*, etc., G. 363.

The ablative form of the gerund became more and more a substitute for the present participle: *ita miserrimus fui fugitando*, Terence, *Eun.* V, 2, 8; Draeger II, 847-849, cites Livy, *conciendo ad se multitudinem*, and Tacitus, *assurgens et populando; hanc Marcion captavit sic legendo*, Hoppe 57; *multa vidi errando*, Densusianu 179; *qui pertransivit benefaciendo et sanando*, R. 432. Cf. R. 432-433. The ablative gerund was sometimes used for a conditional clause: *cavendo salvi erimus*, Hoppe 57.

(3) GERUNDIVE.

105. The gerundive was used as a future passive participle, with *esse*, from the third century on, in place of the future: *filius hominis tradendus est*, R. 433. Cf. R. 433-434, G. 386-388. Eventually, however, the gerundive was discarded, except in some standing phrases.

(4) FUTURE ACTIVE PARTICIPLE.

106. The future active participle was probably rare in late Vulgar Latin, except when it was used with *esse* as a substitute for the future (as *facturus sum*). Sometimes, in a literary style, it took the place of a relative clause: *faveant mihi pro ejus nomine pugnaturo*, G. 389. Cf. G. 388-389.

(5) Present Participle.

107. The present participle was kept, and was used as an adjective and as a noun: see Derivation, Suffixes for Adjectives, *–ans*. Sometimes it was employed periphrastically with *esse: si ipse est ascendens in cælos*, G. 389. Writers occasionally substituted it for a relative clause: *nemo mentiens plorat*, G. 388. Often, however, it was replaced by the ablative gerund: see Gerund above.

(6) Perfect Participle.

108. The perfect participle was kept, and, as will presently be seen, its use was greatly extended through new methods of forming the passive and the perfect tenses. Verbs that had no perfect participle were obliged to make one.

(7) Infinitive.

109. The perfect and passive infinitive forms eventually disappeared: see Voice and Tense below. In late writers, however, the perfect instead of the present infinitive is very common: R. 431–432 (*malunt credidisse*, etc.).

110. The infinitive + accusative construction was more and more avoided from the third century on: G. 371–375. It was replaced sometimes by the passive, but often by a clause introduced by *quia, quod, quoniam, ut*, etc.: *Eva vidisse describitur*, G. 371; *legitur dixisse Deus*, Regnier 63;—Bechtel 112–115, *dicent eo quod filii Israhel eas posuerint, sciens quod libenter haberetis hæc cognoscere, credidit ei quia esset vere filius Dei*, etc.; *perspicue exposuit quod ager mundus sit*, G. 377; *nesciebat quia Jesus erat*, G. 383; *de corpore loquor, ut spiritu valeat non ignoramus*, G. 385. Cf. G. 375–385, Bon. 659–671.

Late writers, wishing to avoid vulgarisms, often misused the infinitive + accusative: G. 371–373.

111. On the other hand, the infinitive assumed many new functions: see Supine and Gerund above. Cf. Hoppe 42–52: *Ninus regnare primus, amant ignorare, aliter exprimere non est, bonus et dicere et facere,* etc.

It was often used as a noun: *totum vivere animæ carnis est,* Hoppe 42; *ipsum vivere accedere est,* Regnier 106; *per malum velle perdidit bonum posse,* Regnier 106.

It replaced the subjunctive with *ut* and similar constructions: *vadent orare,* Bechtel 117; *revertitur omnis populus resumere se,* Bechtel 117: *valeamus assumi,* G. 363; *quæ legi digna sunt,* G. 366; *timuisti...facere,* G. 368; *non venit justos vocare,* G. 370; *venit aliquis audire,* Regnier 73; *male fecisti dare Spiritum sanctum,* Regnier 74; *mihi præcepit hæc loqui,* Bon. 673. Cf. G. 363–370, Regnier 73, Bon. 647, 671–675; P. Thielmann, *Facere mit dem Infinitiv* in *Archiv* III, 177.

It took the place of a relative or indirectly interrogative clause after certain verbs: *nesciendo quæ petere,* Venantius Fortunatus, cited in *Lat. Spr.* 490; *non habent unde reddere tibi,* R. 430.

b. VOICE.

112. Under the influence of *carus est,* etc., *amatus est* came to mean 'he *is* loved', etc. Hence *amatus fuit* signified 'he *was* loved': see Draeger I, 276 ff. Then a whole passive inflection was made up of the perfect participle + *esse* (in northern Italy *fieri*). The old passive forms—except the perfect participle and, to some extent, the gerundive—gradually disappeared from ordinary speech. Although authors kept up the classic practice as far as they were able, some examples of the popular formation may be culled from late writings: *denuo-factus filius fui,* Hoppe 60; *mors salva erit cum fuerit devorata,* Hoppe 60; *conjectus in carcerem fuerat,* Hoppe 61; *permissa est accedere,* Regnier 63.

113. As the passive inflection disappeared, deponent verbs became active. Even in Classic Latin there is often hesitation, as in the case of *frustrare frustrari*, *irascere irasci*, etc. Many deponent verbs are used as active verbs by Petronius. In late vulgar speech *mori*, *sequi*, etc., followed the same course. Cf. Bonnet 402–413.

114. In the intermediate period the passive was frequently replaced by reflexive and active constructions. When *littera scribitur* seemed archaic, and *littera scripta est* vulgar, people said *littera se scribit* and *litteram scribunt* or *litteram scribit homo*: cf. *facit se hora quinta*, Bechtel 126; *se sanare = sanari* in the 4th century, *Rom.* XXXII, 455 (cf. *Zs.* XXXIII, 135); for the use of *homo* with the force of French *on*, see *Per.* 55, 25.

c. MOOD.

(1) IMPERATIVE.

115. The imperative came to be restricted to the second person singular and plural of the present, the subjunctive being used for the third person, and also for the first. Dubois 275 notes that the forms in *–o* are very rare in Ennodius, who lived in southern Gaul in the fifth century.

116. In negative commands the imperative was often replaced by the subjunctive, by the indicative (found in Pirminius), and in Italy, Gaul, and Dacia by the infinitive: *Lat. Spr.* 490.

(2) SUBJUNCTIVE.

117. The subjunctive was limited to fewer functions, being replaced by the indicative in many constructions: *cum hi omnes tam excelsi sunt*, Bechtel 115; *si scire vultis quid facitis*, Regnier 69; etc. At the end of the Vulgar Latin period it was probably used, in popular speech, very much as it is used in the Romance languages. Late writers, while trying to follow the traditional practice, were less logical and evidently less spontaneous than Classic authors in their employment of the subjunctive.

Sometimes the subjunctive was replaced by *debeo* with the infinitive: *debeant accipi = accipiantur*, G. 418. Cf. § 72.

Sometimes, after *facio*, its place was taken by the infinitive: Regnier 27-28, *ecce Pater fecit Filium nasci de vergine*, etc. Cf. § 111.

In conditions not contrary to fact, in indirect discourse and indirect questions, in dependent clauses that are not adversative nor dubitative, the indicative was often substituted for the subjunctive: R. 428-430, G. 355-357, Regnier 68-71.

On the other hand, late writers often put the subjunctive where Classic authors would have put the indicative: G. 357-362.

118. The imperfect subjunctive gradually gave way to the pluperfect: this use is common in the *Bellum Africanum* (*Lat. Spr.* 489); cf. Sittl 133-134. It apparently began with *debuisset, potuisset, voluisset*, used freely for the imperfect by Gregory the Great (Sepulcri 226) and others, and with perfect infinitives like *tacuisse* for *tacere* (*Lat. Spr.* 489: examples from the 4th century).

The imperfect subjunctive ultimately went out of use, except in Sardinia. Writers of the third and fourth centuries show uncertainty in the use of it; R. 431 cites many examples, as *timui ne inter nos bella fuissent orta*.

In Rumanian the pluperfect subjunctive has assumed the function of a pluperfect indicative: *căntáse*, etc.

119. The perfect subjunctive was apparently confused with the future perfect indicative. It was thus preserved in Spain

and in Italian and Rumanian dialects: cf. C. De Lollis in *Bausteine* 1, and V. Crescini in *Zs.* XXIX, 619; Tiktin 596. Cf. § 124.

d. TENSE.

120. The present and imperfect indicative and the present subjunctive remained, in general, with their old functions; see, however, § 117. For the imperfect and pluperfect subjunctive, see § 118; for the perfect subjunctive, § 119. In the perfect, pluperfect, future, and future perfect indicative great changes took place, which led also to the formation of a new perfect and pluperfect subjunctive.

(1) THE PERFECT TENSES.

121. In Classic Latin *habeo* with the perfect participle was used to express a lasting condition: *Hannibal quia fessum militem præliis operibusque habebat*, Part. perf. 376. It was used in the same way with adjectives: *miserum habere*, etc., *Part. perf.* 372 ff. Even in Classic Latin, however, the meaning of this locution began to shift to the perfect, or something akin to it: Cato the elder, *quid Athenis exquisitum habeam*, Part. perf. 516; Plautus, *illa omnia missa habeo, omnis res relictas habeo*, *Part. perf.* 535; in legal phraseology, *factum habeo*, *Part. perf.* 537–538; Sallust, *compertum ego habeo*, Draeger I, 295. The construction is very common in Cicero in a sense that closely approaches the perfect: *satis habeo deliberatum. Part. perf.* 415; *scriptum habeo*, Part. perf. 422; *rationes cognitas habeo*, Densusianu 181; *pecunias magnas collocatas habent*, Draeger I, 294; cf. *Part. perf.* 405, 414–415, 423, 518–521, Draeger I, 294–295.

122. In late Latin this compound often had simply a perfect meaning: *metuo enim ne ibi vos habeam fatigatos*, Regnier 28; *episcopum invitatum habes*, Bon. 690. Cf. Bon. 689–691.

In popular speech it supplanted more and more the original perfect form, which was increasingly confined to its aorist function: *Lat. Spr.* 489. In the Spanish peninsula, however, and to some extent in Italy, the old perfect meaning was not entirely lost.

123. On the model of this new perfect, a compound pluperfect was constructed: Cicero, *quas in ærario conditas habebant*, Draeger I, 294; *si Dominum iratum haberes*, Regnier 28; *quam semper cognitam habui*, Sepulcri 227. In the same way a future perfect was made: *de Cæsare satis dictum habebo*, *Part. perf.* 537. Eventually an entire perfect inflection was built up with *habere* or, in the case of neuter verbs, with *esse;* its vogue began in Gaul in the fifth century, elsewhere in the sixth: *Part. perf.* 543, 541.

124. The old perfect form remained in popular use, generally with the aorist sense. Some late writers were fond of substituting for it *cœpi* with an infinitive: Waters Ch. 70, etc. Cf. § 72.

The old pluperfect indicative became rarer, but still lingered, sometimes with its original sense, sometimes as a preterit, sometimes as a conditional. The preterit use occurs in *dixerat, ortaret, transalaret* in the *Gl. Reich.; auret, furet, pouret*, etc., in the Old French *Sainte Eulalie; boltier'* in the Old Italian *Ritmo Cassinese* (*Zs.* XXIX, 620); etc. The conditional function, which came down from the Classic Latin use in conditional sentences, was preserved in Spanish, in Provençal, in some southern Italian dialects (notably in the *Rosa fresca aulentissima*), and in the Italian *fora* < *fueram*.

The old future perfect was apparently confused with the perfect subjunctive, and continued to be used, with the force of a future indicative or subjunctive, in the Spanish peninsula.

in some dialects of Italy, and in Dacia: Sp. *cantáre*, Old Sp. *cantáro*. Cf. § 119.

The old pluperfect subjunctive was used as an imperfect: see § 118.

(2) FUTURE AND CONDITIONAL.

125. The Latin future was not uniform in the four conjugations; the formation in *-bo*, which was used in three of them and prevailed in two, was native, according to Mohl, *Pr. Pers. Pl.* 141-142, only in Rome and the immediate vicinity. Furthermore, the future in the first two conjugations was suggestive of the imperfect, and in the other two, in late pronunciation, was liable to confusion with the present subjunctive and indicative. These causes or others made the future unpopular. As the tense became rare in speech, mistakes were made in writing: *Vok.* I, 98; Regnier viii. The old *audibo*, *dormibo* forms were kept late (*Futurum* 161), and we find such errors as *respondeam* for *respondebo* (*Futurum* 158).

126. Classic Latin had some circumlocutions, such as *facturus sum*, *delenda est*, *habeo dicere*, which approached the meaning of the future. During the Empire there was a strong tendency to substitute these or other constructions for the future forms (such periphrases are particularly frequent in African church Latin):—

(1) The present indicative for the future is common in Cicero in conditional sentences: Lebreton 188-190. The substitution became frequent in all sorts of constructions: *nam si vis ecce modo pedibus duco vos ibi*, Bechtel 112; *cum volueris ire imus tecum et ostendimus tibi*, Bechtel 112; *pervidet*, Bechtel 90-91; *quando corrigis, quando mutaris? cras, inquis*, Regnier 64; *jam crastina non eximus*, Sepulcri 225. Cf. Draeger I, 286 ff.; Sepulcri 225-226.

(2) The future participle + *esse* was a favorite with late writers: *sic et nos futuri sumus resurgere*, Regnier 29. Cf. Bayard 256. See §§ 105, 106.

(3) *Velle* and *posse* + infinitive were frequent: G. 423. *Velle* in this sense was preserved in Dacia; the oldest Rumanian future is *voĭŭ jurá* or *jurá voĭŭ:* Tiktin 599.

(4) *Debere* + infinitive was another substitute. It was kept in Sardinian.

(5) *Vadere, ire, venire* + infinitive were used also.

127. The form that prevailed, however, was *habeo* with the infinitive: In Classic Latin *habeo dicere = habeo quod dicam*, being so used by Cicero and many others; later, as in Suetonius, it means *debeo dicere: Futurum* 48 ff. Cf. Varro, *De Re Rustica* I, 1, *ut id mihi habeam curare;* Cicero, *Ad Famil.* I, 5, *tantum habeo tibi polliceri;* Lucretius VI, 711, *in multis hoc rebus dicere habemus;* Ovid, *Trist.* I, 1, 123, *mandare ... habebam*. In these senses it was very cómmon in late writers: *habes spectare*, Hoppe 43; *filius Dei mori habuit*, Hoppe 44; *probare non habent*, Hoppe 44; *non habent retribuere*, R. 447; *multa habeo dicere*, R. 447; *unde mihi dare habes aquam vivam*, R. 448; *exire habebat*, R. 449; *nec verba nobis ista dici habent*, Regnier 28. Cf. R. 447–449.

128. This *habeo* construction finally took the sense of a simple future: Tertullian, *aliter prædicantur quam evenire habent, cui dare habet Deus corpus*, etc., Hoppe 44–45;—Servius, *velle habet, Futurum* 180;—St. Jerome, *qui nasci habent*, G. 370;—St. Augustine, *tollere habet*, Densusianu 181; *et sic nihil habes invenire in manibus tuis, videre habetis, venire habet*, etc., Regnier 28. It had become common in Italy by the sixth century.

129. In the early stages of the Romance languages, or

possibly in the latest stage of Vulgar Latin, the infinitive came to stand regularly, though not immutably, just before the *habeo*. Finally the two words were fused into one, but this union was not completed until after the beginnings of the Romance literatures, and in Portuguese it is not completed yet: Old Sp. *cantaré* or *he cantar;* separation is common in Old Provençal, and occurs in Old Italian; Pg. *fazel-o-he*. The earliest examples of the Romance future are found in Fredegarius: *Justinianus dicebat 'daras'*, Haag 54; *addarabo*, Haag 55. See Morphology.

130. On the model of this new form, an imperfect of the future, or *conditional*, was constructed. The phrase existed, ready for use, in Classic Latin, where it was employed with an implication of obligation or necessity. So it seems to be used by Tertullian, although sometimes with him the meaning borders on a real conditional: *non traditus autem traduci habebas, ista civitas esterminari haberet, quod esset venturus et pati haberet*, etc., Hoppe 43–45.

In Classic Latin, in place of *amassem* in the conclusion of a conditional sentence, *amaturus eram* or *fui* was often used; and when *amaturus sum* was replaced by *amare habeo*, it was natural that *amaturus eram* should give way to *amare habebam*. Furthermore, to match such a sentence as *dicit quod venire habet*, there was needed a past construction like *dixit quod venire habebat* or *habuit;* and corresponding to *si possum venire habeo*, something like *si potuissem venire habebam* or *habui* was called for.

St. Cyprian and St. Hilary seem to show a simple conditional use of the compound: *quod lex nova dari haberet*, Bayard 256; *manifestari habebat*, Bayard 257;—*Herodes principes sacerdotum ubi nasci habebat Christus interrogat*, Quillacq 116. There are sure examples from the fifth century on: *Lat. Spr.* 489.

The development of this form in the Romance languages was, in general, parallel to that of the future: see Morphology.

The origin of the Rumanian conditional, *cîntareaşĭ*, is not obvious; for a full discussion of the question, see H. Tiktin, *Die Bildung des rumänischen Konditionalis* in *Zs.* XXVIII, 691.

III. PHONOLOGY.

A. SYLLABICATION.

131. The principles of syllabic division are rather difficult to establish. The Latin grammarians seem to have given no heed to actual speech, but to have followed the usage of Greek spelling, supporting it with purely theoretical considerations. Cf. S. 132–151. According to these writers, the syllable always ended in a vowel, or in a liquid or nasal followed by another consonant in the next syllable, or in half of a double consonant: *a-ni-ma, no-ctem, pro-pter, a-mnis; al-ter, in-fans; sic-cus, mit-to.* The division of *s* + consonant they regard as uncertain (*a-s-trum*); doubtless in reality the *s* was nearly syllabic, as in Italian. They add that etymological considerations often disturb the operation of the rule, as in *ob-liviscor*, etc.

132. In point of fact, however, all consonant groups, except a mute + a liquid, made position and attracted the accent: *perféc-tus*, and not *pérfe-ctus*. It is altogether likely, then, that a consonant group, in the spoken language, was usually divided after the first consonant: *noc-tem, prop-ter*. A single consonant between vowels certainly went with the second: *po-si-tus.*

The group mute + liquid makes position in the older dramatists: Nævius accents *intégram*, *Lat. Spr.* 466. In the Classic poets it may or may not make position. Quintilian I, 5 recommends *ténebræ, vólucres, pháretra*, etc. In Vulgar Latin this combination almost invariably attracts the accent: *cathédra.* It is likely that in Old Latin the division came before the liquid, but subsequently, after the accent had become fixed on the preceding vowel, both consonants were carried over: *có-lub-ra*, *co-lúb-ra*, *co-lú-bra*.

133. We have reason to believe that in closely connected speech a final consonant was carried over to the next word, if that word began with a vowel: *cor exsultat = co r-exsultat*.

B. ACCENT.

134. The Latin accent was probably from the beginning a stress accent. In the earliest stage of the language it apparently fell regularly on the first syllable: Corssen II, 892–906; S. 30–34; *Franz.* ǝ I, 13. The Classic Latin system — according to which the accent falls on the penult if that syllable is long, otherwise on the antepenult — developed as early as literature began, and remained, both in the literary and in the spoken language, through the Classic period; even after the distinctions of quantity were lost, the place of the accent was unchanged: *bonitátem*, *cómputo*, *delĕcto*.

The penult vowel before mute + liquid (cf. § 132) normally has the stress in Vulgar Latin: *cathédra*, *colúbra*, *intégram*. There seem to be a few exceptions to the rule: Old Fr. *palpres < pálpebras*, Old Fr. *poltre < *púllitra*, and perhaps some others.

1. PRIMARY STRESS.

135. We have seen that Vulgar Latin regularly accents according to the Classic quantitative accentuation. There are, however, some cases in which the Classic principle fails to operate or the Classic stress has been shifted: —

a. VOWELS IN HIATUS.

136. Accented *e* and *i*, when immediately followed by the vowel of the penult, became *y*, the accent falling on the

following vowel: *mulĭĕris* > *muljéris*, S. 51, *Lat. Spr.* 468; *putĕŏlis* > *putjólis*, C. I. L. X, 1889 (PVTEÓLIS); so *parĭĕtes* > *parjétes* > *parētes*,[1] C. I. L. VI, 3714 (PARETES). This change seems to be due to a tendency to shift the stress to the more sonorous of two contiguous vowels: cf. O. Jespersen, *Lehrbuch der Phonetik*, p. 192. It was favored also by the analogy of *múlier, púteus, páries*, etc., in which the vowel in hiatus is atonic.

137. Accented *u*, when immediately followed by the vowel of the penult, became *w*, the accent falling on the *preceding* syllable: *bat(t)uĕre* > *báttuere > *báttere; consuĕre* > *cónsuere > *cónsere; habuĕrunt* > **hábuerunt; tenuĕram* > *ténueram. Here the shift was apparently due in each case to analogy, *battuere* being influenced by *báttuo, consuere* by *cónsuo, habuerunt* by *hábuit, tenueram* by *ténui*, etc.

138. Aside from these cases, hiatus seems to have had no effect on the accent in Latin. It is possible, however, that *dúos, súos, túos* were sometimes pronounced *duós, suós, tuós*.

b. COMPOUND VERBS.

139. Verbs compounded with prefixes were generally reconstructed with the accent and the vowel of the simple verb, provided the composite nature of the formation was understood and the parts were recognized (cf. § 31): *déficit* > **disfácit, displĭcet* > **displácet, ímplĭcat* > **implícat, réddĭdi* > *reddédi, réquĭrit* > **requǽrit, rétĭnet* > *reténet, etc. Cf. *Gram.* II, 668-670. So *calefacis*, S. 56; *condedit, perdedit, reddedit, tradedit*, S. 54; *addedi, adsteti, conteneo, credédi, inclausus, presteti*, etc., Sepulcri 213-215. On the same plan new verbs were formed: **de-mínat, re-négat*, etc.

---

[1] *Ĭĕ* regularly became *ē;* but if the preceding consonant was *l*, it was palatalized; hence *parétes*, but **mul'éres*. Cf. § 225.

Recípit became *recipít, the composite character of the word being felt, although the compound was no longer associated with *capere*.

In *cólligo* and some others not even the composite nature was perceived, the simple verbs having become rare or having taken a different sense: *legere*, for instance, came to be used only in the sense of 'read.'

c. ILLAC, ILLIC.

140. The adverbs *illāc*, *illīc* accented their last syllable through the analogy of *hāc*, *hīc*. Priscian says "*illíc* pro *illíce*": S. 42.

d. FICATUM.

141. There existed in Greek a word συκωτόν (Pirson 40), 'figlike', which was applied by cooks to a liver. It is found in late Latin in the form *sycotum*, which should properly have been pronounced *sȳcōtum*; for some unknown reason, perhaps under the influence of a vulgar *hēpāte for *hēpar*, 'liver', it probably became *sęcotum.

Through this word there came into use the culinary terms *fīcátum*, *fícatum, *fęcatum, *fęcotum, *fęcitum, all meaning 'liver.' *Fīcátum*, a simple translation of συκωτόν, prevailed in Dacia, Rætia, and northern Italy. *Fęcatum* or *fęcotum*, a fusion of *fīcátum* and *sęcotum, was preferred in central and southern Italy. *Fícatum*, a cross between *fęcatum* and *fīcátum*, was kept in Sicily and in the Spanish peninsula. Sardinia preserved both *fīcátum* and *fícatum*. Gaul had *fícatum* and *fęcatum*; later, by a change of suffix, *fęcitum*. See G. Paris in *Miscellanea linguistica in onore di Graziadio Ascoli* 41; H. Schuchardt in *Zs.* XXV, 515 and XXVIII, 435; L. Clédat in *Revue de philologie française et de littérature* XV, 235.

e. NUMERALS.

142. The numbers *vīgĭntī, trīgĭnta, quadrāgĭnta, quīnquāgĭnta,* etc., were sometimes accented on the antepenult: Consentius mentions a faulty pronunciation *trĭginta,* Keil V, 392, lines 4–5; *quarranta* occurs in a late inscription, *Vok.* II, 461, Pirson 97. See M. Ihm in *Archiv* VII, 69–70; G. Rydberg in *Mélanges Wahlund,* 337. The shift was probably due to a natural tendency to differentiate the numerals from one another: compare the floating accent in English *thirteen, fourteen,* etc.

d. GREEK WORDS.

143. The accentuation of Greek words was varied. Sometimes the Greek stress was preserved, sometimes the word was made to conform to the Latin principle.

(1) GREEK OXYTONES.

144. Greek oxytones, when borrowed by Latin, were stressed according to the Latin system: δραχμή > *drách(ŭ)ma,* ἐπιστολή > *epístŭla –ŏla,* λαμπάς > *lámpa(s),* μηχανή > *mác(h)ĭna,* παραβολή > *parábŭla,* πειρατής > *pirăta,* σπασμός > *spásmus,* ταπεινός > **tapínus.* Cf. S. 42 ff., Claussen 809.

Συκωτόν, however, apparently stressed the first syllable: see § 141.

(2) GREEK PAROXYTONES.

145. Greek paroxytones were mostly accented according to the quantity of the penult: γραφίον > *gráphĭum,* κιμάρα > *cámĕra,* μαγίδα > *mágĭda,* παλάμη > *pálma,* πολύπους > *pólÿpus,*[1] πορφύρα > *púrpŭra,* φαρέτρα > *phárĕtra* or *pharĕtra* (cf. § 134).

Πτισάνη (> *ptĭsăna*) > It. *tisána,* φιάλη (> *phiăla*) > It. *fiăla,* χολέρα (> *chŏlĕra*) > It. *colĕra,* etc., may represent popular terms borrowed by ear from the Greek, with the Greek stress,

---

[1] Occasionally the accent was kept by doubling the consonant, as *polippus.*

but it is more likely that the Italian forms are book-words with a shifted accent.

Cf. S. 42 ff., Claussen 810–811.

146. The ending *-ĭa* was at first generally assimilated to the Latin *-ĭa*: βιβλία > *bíblia*, βλασφημία > *blasphémia*, ἐκκλησία > *ec(ec)lésia*, ἱστορία > *história*, σηπία > *sépia*, συμφωνία > *symphónia*. Later a fashionable pronunciation *-ía*, doubtless favored by Christian influence, penetrated popular speech (σοφία > *sophía*, etc.) and produced a new Latin ending *-ía*, which was used to form new words: see Derivation, Suffixes for Nouns. Cf. Claussen 812. The pronunciations *melodĭa*, etc., and *sophīa*, etc., are attested: S. 55–56.

The endings *-εῖα*, *-εῖον* sometimes became *-ĕa -ĭa*, *-ĕum -ĭum*, sometimes *-ēa, -ēum*: βαλανεῖον > *bálnĕum*, κωνωπεῖον > *conopēum -ĕum -ĭum*, πλατεῖα > *platēa platĕa*. Cf. Claussen 813–814.

(3) Greek Proparoxytones.

147. The treatment of proparoxytones is complicated. Cf. S. 42–49, Claussen 814–821, *Gram.* I, 35, § 17, A. Thomas in *Rom.* XXXI, 2–3. Late Latin grammarians mention a pronunciation of Greek words with the Greek accent (S. 42), but their statements are too vague to be of use.

A few early borrowed words perhaps show the Old Latin accentuation: κυπάρισσος > *cúparissos* > *cupressus*. Cf. Claussen 809.

148. When the penult was short, the accent remained unchanged: γένεσις > *génĕsis*, κάλαμος > *cálămus*, κόλαφος > *cólăphus*, πρεσβύτερον > *presbýtĕrum* (with a new nominative *présbyter*).

149. When the penult vowel was in position, it took the accent: ἄβυσσος > *abýssus*, βάπτισμα > *baptísma*, τάλαντον > *taléntum*.

Ἔγκαυστον, however, became both *encáustum* and *encaústum*. Occasionally the consonant group was simplified and the accent remained: καρυόφυλλον > *garófŭlum*.

150. When the penult vowel was long and not in position, it apparently took the accent in book-words but not in words learned by ear (S. 48–49): κάμηλος > *camēlus -ĕllus*, κάμινος > *camīnus*, κροκόδειλος > *crocodīlus*, φάλλαινα > *ballēna;* ἄγκῡρα > *áncŏra*, βλάσφημος > *blásphēmus* (Prudentius), βούτυρον > *bútȳrum* (Æmilius Macer), Ἰάκωβος > *Jácobus*, σέλινον > *sélinum*.

Some words have both pronunciations: εἴδωλον > *īdŏlum* (both in Prudentius: *Lat. Spr.* 466), ἔρημος > *erēmus erĕmus* (Prudentius), σίναπι > *sínapi sināpi*.

e. OTHER FOREIGN WORDS.

151. Some words borrowed from other languages kept their original accent, contrary to Latin rules (S. 49): Umbrian *Pisaúrum* > It. *Pésaro*, etc.; Celtic *Baiócasses* > Fr. *Bayeux*, *Duróasses* > Fr. *Dreux*, *Trícasses* > Fr. *Troyes*, etc., Dottin 103.

152. Germanic words were apparently made to conform to Latin types: *Hûgo Hûgun* > *Húgo Hugónem* > Fr. *Húes Huón;* Kluge 500.

2. SECONDARY STRESS.

153. As far as we can determine the rhythm of Vulgar Latin, judging from phonetic changes and from semi-popular late Latin verse, it consisted in a tolerably regular alternation of accented and unaccented syllables. Thus Sedulius, at the beginning of the fifth century, writes:

> Beátus áuctor sǽculí
> Servíle córpus índuít,
> Ut cárne cárnem líberáns
> Ne pérderét quos cóndidít.

§ 156]   AN INTRODUCTION TO VULGAR LATIN.   67

The secondary stress, then, fell on the second syllable from the tonic: *cupǐdītósus, felīcītátem; dōlōrósa, lăcrĭmósa; Cæsărĕm, Gálliās*. In some derivatives, however, the root syllable may have received an irregular stress through the analogy of the primitive: *árborǐcéllus.

In late formations *e* or *i* in hiatus did not count as a syllable: *comǐnitiáre.

154. When the secondary stress *preceded* the tonic, it was strong, and the vowel bearing it was apparently treated as an accented vowel: *amīcītátem > Pr. *amistát;* so, in Italian, *Buólognino* beside *Bológna*, *Fióréntino* beside *Fírénze*, *véttováglia* beside *vittória*.

When it *followed* the tonic, it was weak, but probably the vowel bearing it had more force than a wholly unaccented final vowel: *sócĕrí* > Pr. *sózer*, *plácĭtúm* > Pr. *plach;* but *clérĭcúm* > Pr. *clérgue* while *clér'cum* > Pr. *clerc*, *cólăphúm* > Pr. *cólbe* while *cól'pum* > Pr. *colp*.

155. In many cases the intervening vowel fell out or lost its syllabic value. Then the primary and the secondary accent were brought together, and the secondary was shifted or lost: *parábuláre > *paráuláre > **párauláre, cálidús* > *cáldus, fílius* > *fílius*.

UNSTRESSED WORDS.

156. Short, unemphatic words, in Latin as in other languages, had no accent, and were attached as additional syllables to the beginning or end of other words (S. 38–39): *non-ámat, áma-me, te-vídet, dó-tibi, cave-fácias, circum-lítora* (Quintilian I, 5). Many words, especially prepositions and conjunctions, as well as some adverbs and pronouns, were used only as enclitics or proclitics.

157. If such particles had more than one syllable, they tended to become monosyllabic: unstressed *magis*, perhaps influenced by *plus*, became *mais and *mas. A dissyllabic proclitic beginning with a vowel seems to have regularly lost that vowel: *illum vídet* > *'lu' vídet; ecce híc* > *'c'ic* (but *écce híc* > *ecc'íc*); *eccum istúm* > *'cu' istu'* (but *éccum ístum* > *eccu'ístu'*). For elision, see *Franz.* ⱝ II, 73–79, 379–390.

158. Words sometimes stressed and sometimes unstressed tended to develop double forms: *illās* > *illas* and **las, sŭa* > *súa* and *sa*. Cf. S. 56–57.

C. QUANTITY.

159. We must distinguish between the quantity of vowels and the quantity of syllables. Every Latin *vowel* was by nature either long or short; how great the difference was we do not know, but we may surmise that in common speech it was more marked in stressed than in unstressed vowels. A *syllable* was long if it contained (1) a long vowel or a diphthong or (2) any vowel + a following consonant. If, however, the consonant was final and the next word began with a vowel, the consonant, in connected speech, was doubtless carried over to the next syllable and did not make position: see § 133. For the syllabication of mute + liquid, see §§ 132, 134.

1. POSITION.

160. In some of the Romance languages position checked the development of the preceding vowel, and it is probable that the beginnings of this differentiation go back to Vulgar Latin times: *pa-rem* > Old Fr. *per, par-tem* > Fr. *part*. Mute + liquid did not prevent the development: *pa-trem* > Fr. *pere*. Neither, apparently, did a final consonant (cf. § 133): *sa-l* > Fr. *sel*.

Compare Italian *fiero* < *fĕ-rus*, *ferro* < *fĕr-rum ; petto* < *pĕc-tus, pietra* < *pĕ-tra, fiel(e)* < *fĕ-l; — fuore* < *fō-ris, collo* < *cŏl-lum; corpo* < *cŏr-pus, cuopre* < ** cŏ-p'rit, cuor(e)* < *cŏ-r*.

161. Early in the Empire *ss* after diphthongs and long vowels was apparently reduced to *s* (S. 112–120): *cāssus* > *cāsus, caussa* > *causa, formōssus* > *formōsus, glōssa* > *glōsa, mīssit* (S. 118: mIssIt) > *mīsit*. This did not occur, however, in the contracted endings *–āsse –āssem* etc., *–ēsse –ēssem* etc., *–īsse –īssem* etc.

Similarly one *l* was lost in *māllo, mīllia* (but not in *mīlle :* Pompeius, S. 127), *nōllo, paullum*.

162. In Latin texts there is much confusion of single and double consonants, especially before the accent: *bal(l)æna, buc(c)īna, cot(t)idie,*[1] *ec(c)lesia,*[2] *glut(t)īre, mut(t)īre, tap(p)ēte, ves(s)īca*, etc. Cf. S. 111–132, Stolz 223–224. In some words this may result merely from bad spelling; but often it must represent an actual difference in pronunciation, as seems to be the case with the doublet *cĭto* > Sp. *cedo, cĭtto (C. I. L.* VIII, 11594) > It. *cetto*. Cf. § 163.

163. Many words certainly had two forms, doubtless belonging to different Latin dialects, — one with a long vowel + a single consonant, the other with a short vowel + a double consonant : *brāchium brăcchium; būca bŭcca; camēlus camĕllus*, where we have perhaps only a change of suffix, cf. § 42 ; *cīpus cĭppus; cūpa, cŭppa,* giving Sp. *cuba,* Fr. *cuve*, It. *cupola* and Sp. *copa,* Fr. *coupe*, It. *coppa ; glūto glŭtto ; hōc erat hŏcc erat*, S. 125–126 (Velius Longus and Pompeius) ; *Jūpiter Jŭppiter;* perhaps *lītera lĭttera; mūcus mŭccus; pūpa pŭppa; stūpa stŭppa; sūcus sŭccus*. Cf. Stolz 222–225.

---

[1] The antiquity of double *t* is attested by an old inscription : *Lexique* 101.
[2] The single *c*, which prevailed in Romance, is common in Greek and Latin manuscripts : S. 129.

To these may perhaps be added: *bāca bacca; bāsium *băssium (> It. bascio); brāca bracca; *būtis (< βοῦτις) *bŭttis (> It. botte); cāseus *căsseus (> It. cascio); chāne(< χάνη) channe; conservāmus conservammus, Vok. I, 261; jubēmus jubemmus, Vok. I, 261 (iubimmus iobemmus); lītus littus; mīsi * mĭssi (> It. messi).

Beside the two forms indicated, there was occasionally a third, seemingly a cross between the other two, having both the long vowel and the double consonant: anguīla (> Sp. anguila) + anguĭlla = *anguīlla (> It. anguilla); *stēla (> Old Fr. esteile: cf. Lexique 95–98) + stĕlla (> It. dialect stẹlla) = *stēlla (> It. stẹlla; cf. Vok. I, 339, stilla); strēna (> Old Fr. estreine) + strĕnna = *strēnna (> It. strenna, Sic. strinna); tōta (> Sp. toda) + tŏtta (Keil V, 392¹) = *tōtta (> Pr. tota, Fr. toute).[2] So perhaps Diomedes' littera: Archiv XIV, 403.

1**64.** In late Latin inscriptions and manuscripts a consonant was sometimes doubled before r or u: acqua, bellua, frattre, lattrones, mattrona, strennuor, suppra, suppremis, tennuis. Cf. S. 122, Stolz 223. This doubling indicates in most cases a local pronunciation, prevalent in Africa or in Italy. According to F. G. Mohl, Zs. XXVI, 612, a consonant was doubled before i and u in the old Italic dialects: compare the Italian doubling in fabbro, tenne, volle, etc. In aqua the double consonant, attested by inscriptions and by Christian poets, was very widespread and prevailed in Italy, Rætia, and a large part of Gaul. See Clara Hürlimann, *Die Entwicklung des lateinischen* aqua *in den romanischen Sprachen*, reviewed by Meyer-Lübke in *Ltblt.* XXIV, 334.

---

[1] Consentius: "per adjectionem litteræ *tottum* pro *toto*." Cf. *Gram.* I, 488, § 547; *Lexique* 98–104. According to *Lat. Spr.* 485, *tottus* was used by Pirminius.

[2] For *tūttus see § 204(2).

2. VOWEL QUANTITY.

165. Originally, perhaps, long and short vowels were distinguished only by duration, the vowels having, for instance, the same sound in *lātus* and *lătus*, in *dēbet* and *rĕdit*, in *vīnum* and *mĭnus*, in *nōmen* and *nŏvus*, in *ūllus* and *mŭltus*. However this may have been, long and short *e*, *i*, *o*, and *u* were eventually differentiated, the short vowels being open while the long were close: *vẹndo sẹntio, pinus pịper, sọlus sọlet, mụlus gụla*. That is, for the vowels of brief duration the tongue was not lifted quite so high as for those held longer. Later, in most of the Empire, *ị* and *ụ* were allowed to drop still lower, and became *ẹ* and *ọ*: see §§ 201, 208. In the case of *a*, which is made with the tongue lying flat in the bottom of the mouth, there was no such differentiation.

According to Meyer-Lübke, *Lat. Spr.* 467, the distinction was clear by the first century of our era. In *Vok.* I, 461, II, 146, III, 151, 212, is given the testimony of grammarians, all of later date; in *Vok.* II, 1 ff., the evidence of inscriptions. Marius Victorinus, about 350 A. D., distinguishes two *e*-sounds (S. 174, 182); Pompeius, about 480, cites Tertullian for an *ẹ* similar to *i*, and several fifth century grammarians plainly distinguish *ẹ* from *ę* (S. 176, 182); from the second century on *æ* was often used for *ę* in inscriptions (S. 183-184). Terentianus Maurus, by 250, distinguishes *ọ* from *ǫ* (S. 175, 211), and so do other grammarians (S. 211). Writers do not clearly distinguish *i̯* and *ị̆*, until Consentius, in the fifth century (S. 193); *e*, however, is often used for *ị* in inscriptions, as *menus*, etc., and *i* for *ẹ*, as *minses*, etc. (S. 195, 200-201). None of the grammarians apparently distinguished *u* and *ụ*, but *o* is used for *ụ* in inscriptions, as *ocsor, secondus*, etc. (S. 216-217).

166. In open syllables, if the word is used in verse, the quantity of the vowel is in general easily ascertained. In closed syllables and in words not used by poets the quantity is in many cases doubtful; but it is sometimes given by grammarians, sometimes marked in inscriptions, sometimes conjectured from the etymology, and often shown by subsequent developments in the Romance languages. Occasionally the testimony conflicts: some inscriptions have CARĪSSIMO, etc., others KARESSIMO, etc. (S. 98, 99); Aulus Gellius prescribes *dĭctum*, but an inscription has DICTATORI (S. 105); Classic Latin offers *frīgĭdus* (cf. FRÍGIDA, S. 105), but the Romance languages, except Spanish, require a short *i;* some Romance forms support Classic *nūtrīre*, others demand *ŭ; ūndĕcim*, *lūrĭdus, ūltra* were apparently pronounced also with short *u* (S. 81–82); Fr. *loir* calls for *glĭrem beside *glīrem*.

a. VOWELS IN HIATUS.

167. Vowels in hiatus with the last syllable offer difficulties. The Classic rule that a vowel before another vowel is short is not absolute even for verse, and the practice of poets was not always in accordance with spoken usage. *Dīes, pīus* kept their originally long vowel, attested by inscriptions (DIES PIVS PIIVS, S. 93; cf. *Substrate* II, 101–102); so *cūi*, proved by old inscriptions; and, at least in part, *fūi*, found in inscriptions, in Plautus, and in Ennius (S. 93): these preserved their close vowel in the Romance languages.

Naturally long vowels, then, probably kept their original quantity in hiatus. Naturally short vowels doubtless had their regular development also: *dĕus = dẹus*, although we do find the spellings *dius* and *mius* (S. 187); *dŭo > dŭi = dụi; vĭa = vịa*. At a later stage, after *u* had become *ọ* (see §§ 165, 208), any *ọ* before *u* was apparently differentiated into *ọ: ōvum > ọum* (cf. § 324) *> ǫum* (and also *ọvum*, with a restoration of the *v* through the plural *ova*); *sŭus > sọus > sǫus* (S.

216, Pirson 16). There may have been other special variations in different countries. Cf. § 217.

For a different theory, see *Gram.* I, 246-248. For another still, see A. Horning in *Zs.* XXV, 341.

168. *Quĭa*, used for *quod* in late Latin, had a peculiar development from the sixth century on: before a vowel it was pronounced *quĭ'* and was confused with *quĭd*, which had begun to assume the functions of *quod* (see §§ 69, 82; cf. *Franz.* ⸗ II, 352-355); before a consonant, under the influence of *qua* and *qua(m)*, it became *qua*. Cf. *Franz.* ⸗ II, 357-390; J. Jeanjaquet, *Recherches sur l'origine de la conjonction 'que' et des formes romanes équivalentes*, 1894.

169. *Plŭere* was supplanted in popular usage by *plŏvere* (*Lat. Spr.* 468). *Plŭvia*, on the other hand, gave way to *plŏja. Cf. § 208,(4).

b. LENGTHENING BEFORE CONSONANTS.

170. According to some grammarians, vowels were lengthened before *j*, as in *ējus*, *mājor*. The Romance languages, however, point to open vowels in *pejor*, *Troja*. The apparent contradiction disappears if we accept the statement of Terentianus Maurus, 250 A. D., who says (S. 104) that the vowels in these words were short, but the *j* was doubled — that is, there was a glide from the vowel to the *j*, which prolonged the first syllable: not *pējor*, *Trōja*, but *pĕijor*, *Trŏija*. We find in inscriptions such spellings as *Aiiax, coiiux, cuiius, eiius, maiiorem*, etc.: S. 236, Pirson 74. Quintilian states that Cicero preferred *aiio, Maiiam*, with double *i* (S. 236). Velius Longus adds that as Cicero approved of *Aiiacem, Maiiam*, we should write *Troiia* also (S. 236). Priscian analyzes *pejus*, etc., into *pei-ius, ei-ius, mai-ius* (Édon 207).

171. When *n* was followed by a fricative (*f*, *j*, *s*, or *v*), it regularly fell early in Latin, and the preceding vowel was lengthened by compensation: *cēsor, cōjugi, cōventio, īferi.* But inasmuch as *n* occurs before *f*, *j*, and *v* only at the end of prefixes, it was usually restored by the analogy of the full forms *con–, in–:* so *infantem* through *indignus*, etc.; *conjungere* through *conducere*, etc.; *convenire* through *continere*, etc. Before *s*, however, *n* occurred in the middle of many words, and the fall was permanent, the *n* being restored only in compounds before initial *s: cōsul, īsula, mēsis, spōsus;* but *insignare.* Cf. § 311.

It is altogether likely that the *n* fell through nasalization of the vowel: *consul cõnsul cō̃sul cōsul.* If so, all trace of the nasality disappeared, but the length and the close quality of the vowel remained. Cf. *Archiv* XIV, 400.

Romance and late Vulgar Latin words with *ns* (except in compounds as above) are either learned terms or new formations: so *pensare*, beside the old popular *pēsare.

See S. 77–78; for the usage of Cicero and others, S. 86; for inscriptions, S. 89.

172. (1) Vowels were apparently lengthened before *ŋk: quīnque, sānctus*, etc. Cf. S. 78; for inscriptions, S. 90.

(2) Before *gn* vowels were lengthened according to Priscian (S. 91), and inscriptions mark length in *dīgnus, rēgnum, sīgnum* (cf. *sigillum*), S. 91. The Romance languages, however, call for *dignus, lignum, pignus, pugnus, signum.* Priscian, who wrote in the sixth century, is a very late authority, and some philologists regard the passage in question as an interpolation of still later date; still the evidence of the inscriptions remains. According to Meyer-Lübke (*Gram.* I, 54, *Lat. Spr.* 467), the vowel was lengthened, but only after *ĭ, ŭ* had become *i̯, u̯*, so that the result was *ī̯, ū̯*, not *ī, ū;* cf. BENEGNVS

in *C. I. L.* XII, 2153, which is doubtless equivalent to the BENĪGNUS of *C. I. L.* XII, 722. This seems a very plausible explanation. C. D. Buck, however, in the *Classical Review* XV, 311, prefers to regard such forms as *dĭgnus*, in so far as they existed at all, as due to a vulgar or local pronunciation.

c. DISAPPEARANCE OF THE OLD QUANTITY.

173. The difference in quantity was probably greater and more constant in accented than in unaccented vowels. The distinctions in quality, resulting from the original quantity, remained, in stressed syllables, through the Latin period and developed further in the Romance languages; in unaccented syllables the distinctions were doubtless weaker, and were often obliterated.

174. The old quantity itself was lost, for the most part during the Empire. It seems to have disappeared from *unstressed syllables* by the third or fourth century; but confusion set in as early as the second. The nominative singular *-ĭs* and the plural *-ēs* were confounded by 150 A. D. (S. 75), and *æ* was often used for *ĕ* in inscriptions (S. 183–184: *benæ*, etc.). Terentianus Maurus, about 250, tells us that *au* is short in unaccented syllables, as in *aut* (S. 66). Other grammarians warn against quantitative mistakes. Servius says, in the fourth century, "*miseræ* dativus est non adverbium," etc. (S. 226). The poetry of Commodian, in the third or fourth century, seems to observe quantity in stressed and to neglect it in unstressed syllables, and we find numerous metrical errors in other late poets: cf. J. Cornu, *Versbau des Commodian* in *Bausteine* 576.

On the other hand, Latin words borrowed by the Britons, mostly in the third and fourth centuries, show, through a shift of accent, the preservation of quantity in post-tonic syllables: Loth 72, 65. Moreover, Latin words borrowed by Old High German indicate a retention of long *i* and *u* before the accent: Franz.

It is possible that the quantity of unstressed vowels was better kept in the provinces than in Italy.

175. In *accented syllables* there are sporadic examples of confusion by the second century, as *æques* for *ĕques* in 197 (S. 225); but probably the disappearance of the old distinction was not general before the fourth and fifth centuries, and not complete before the end of the sixth. Servius, in the fourth century, criticizes *Rŏma* (S. 106). St. Augustine declares that "Afræ aures de correptione vocalium vel productione non judicant" (*Lat. Spr.* 467). Pompeius and other grammarians blame the confusion of *æquus* and *ĕquus* (S. 107, 178). Much late poetry disregards quantity altogether.

On the other hand, Latin words borrowed by the Britons from the second to the fifth century, but mostly in the third and fourth, show the preservation of the quantity of stressed vowels: Loth 64. Latin words in Anglo-Saxon, taken over in the fifth and sixth centuries, retain the quantity of vowels that bear the accent: Pogatscher. The Latin words in Old High German, too, distinguish by quantity *ī* and *ĭ*, *ē* and *ĕ*, *ō* and *ŏ*, *ū* and *ŭ*; *ĕ*, *ŏ* are distinguished by quality also, for *ē* > *î* while *ĕ* > *e* or *i*, *ō* > *û* or *ô* while *ŏ* > *o*: Franz.

d. DEVELOPMENT OF A NEW QUANTITY.

176. At the end of the Latin period a new system of quantity grew up, entirely diverse from the old, and based on the situation of the vowel. In most of the Empire accented vowels not in position were pronounced long, all other vowels short: *sănctŏ vālĕs, vĕndŏ vēnĭs, dĭxĭ plīcăs, fŏrmās fŏrĭ, frŭctŭs*

§ 178]   AN INTRODUCTION TO VULGAR LATIN.   77

gŭlĭ; că-thẹ-dră tĭ-nẹ-brăs; cọ-r mẹ-l nọ-s rẹ-m trẹ-s. In Spain and in some parts of Gaul, *all* stressed vowels were apparently long: tẹmpŭs, pọrta.

This new pronunciation doubtless sprang up with the disappearance of the old, which it displaced. Meyer-Lübke in *Gram.* I, 561-562, says that the development was different and independent in the several Romance languages; in *Einf.* 103-104, he describes it as common to all, but as posterior to the fifth century; in *Lat. Spr.* 467, he puts it in the fourth and fifth centuries.

177. It is likely that these new long vowels were pronounced in most regions with a circumflex intonation, which in the transition from Latin to the Romance languages resulted in diphthongization in a large part of the Empire, particularly in northern Gaul: vẹnis > It. *vieni*, gụ̂la > Old Fr. *goule*, cộr > It. *cuor*, nộs > Fr. *nous*, trệs > Old Fr. *treis*. Portugal, southern Gaul, Lombardy, and Sicily apparently did not participate in this early breaking; and the conditions of diphthongization were very diverse in different localities. The vowels most affected were ẹ and ọ.

An isolated example, perhaps only a blunder, occurs in an inscription made a little before 120 A. D.: NIÉPOS, beside NEPOTIS (A. Zimmermann in *Zs.* XXV, 735). In 419 A. D. we find VOBIT for *obiit* (S. 213).

D. VOWELS.

178. Latin had the vowels ă, ĕ, ĭ, ŏ, ŭ, and in unaccented syllables before a labial (as in *proxumus*) a short ü; furthermore, the groups æ, au, eu, œ, also ui. We have seen (§ 165) that ē, ī, ō, ū were pronounced close, and ĕ, ĭ, ŏ, ŭ open, while ă was not affected by quantity. We shall see presently

(§§ 209, 210) that œ > ę and œ > ẹ, while au, eu generally remained áu̯, éu̯ (cáutus, céu), and ui (as in cui) was úi̯.

179. The foreign vowels of borrowed words were assimilated in some fashion to the Latin system. In the few Celtic words that were taken over there are no important peculiarities. In the Germanic vocabulary there is not much to be noted: *ai* in words adopted early apparently became *a*, as *waiðanjan > **wadaniare;* *eu* (or *iu*) appears in *treuwa* (or *triuwa*), which became **trẹwa;* *iu* is found in *skiuhan* > *skivare.

The history of Greek vowels is very complicated: —

GREEK VOWELS.

180. According to Quintilian (Édon 64–65), the Greek letters were sounded as in Greek. This pronunciation was doubtless the ideal of people of fashion, but popular speech substituted for unfamiliar vowels the sounds of the vernacular. The inconsistencies in this substitution arise partly from the different dates at which words were borrowed, partly from the channel (written or oral) through which they came, and partly from the various pronunciations of the vowels in the several Greek dialects.

181. *A*, long or short, was pronounced *ă:* Φᾶσις > *Phāsis*, φάλαγξ > *phălanx*.

182. *H* was in Greek originally a long *ę*, but early in our era it became *ī*. In book-words it was assimilated to Latin *ē:* ἀποθήκη > *apothēca* > It. *bottega;* so in some late words, as βλασφημία > *blasphēmia* > It. *bestemmia*. In words of more popular origin it often had the Greek open sound: ἐκκλησία > *eclẹsia;* σηπία > *sæpia*, but also *sēpia* > It. *sẹppia;* σκηνή > *scæna scēna*. Late words often show *i:* ἀσκητής > *ascitis*, Per.

§ 186]   AN INTRODUCTION TO VULGAR LATIN.   79

40, 1, etc.; ἐκκλησίαι > ecclisiæ, Neumann 9; μοναστήριον > monastirium, μυστήριον > mistirium, etc., Claussen 854–855; ταπήτιον > Fr. *tapis*, Pr. *tapit*.

183. *E* was close in some Greek dialects, open in others. In book-words it was assimilated to Latin *ĕ*: γένεσις > *gĕnĕsis*. In popular words it was sometimes close, sometimes open: ἔρημος > *er'mus er'mus* > It. *ermo*, Sp. *yermo*; κέδρος > *cĕdrus* > It. *cedro*; πέπερι > *pĭper*; Στέφανος > *Stĕphanus Stephanus*. Cf. Claussen 853–854.

184. *I*, at least in the principal dialects, seems to have had a very open sound, even when long. In book-words it was assimilated to Latin *ĭ*: φῖμός > *phīmus*; φίλος > *phĭlus*. In popular words *ī* apparently became *ĭ*, later *e* or *ę*; *ĭ* apparently became *ĕ*, later often *ę*: ἀρθρῖτικός > *arthrīticus* > It. *artetico*; ἀρτεμῖσία > *artemīsia* > Old Fr. *armeise*; βωλίτης > *boletus*; ὀρίγανος > It. *regamo*; χρῖσμα > *chrīsma* > It. *cresima*, Old Fr. *cresme*; Χρῑστός > *Chrīstus Chrestus*, cf. *Christianus Chrestianus*; etc.;—ἀντίφονος >*antefona* > Old Fr. *antiefne*; βλίτον > *blītum* > It. *bieta*; μίνθη > *menta* > It. *menta*, Sp. *mienta*; σίναπι > *sīnapi* > It. *senape*; etc. Cf. Claussen 855–857.

185. Ω was probably *ǭ*, but perhaps dialectically *ǭ* (cf. ὥρα > *hǭra*). In book-words it was assimilated to Latin *ō*: φώκη > *phōca*. In popular words it apparently became *ǫ*, occasionally *u*: γλῶσσα > It. *chiosa*; πτωχός > It. *pitocco*; τρώκτης > *trŭcta*. Cf. Claussen 869–870.

186. *O* in most dialects was *ǫ*. In book-words it was assimilated to Latin *ŏ*: κόφινος > *cŏphĭnus*; ὀρφανός > *ŏrphănus*. In popular words it was generally close, but sometimes open, and occasionally the same word had both pronunciations: ἀμόργη > *amŭrca*; δοχή > *dǭga* > It. *doga*, etc.; κόμμι > *gŭmmi*; ὀσμή >? It. *ǫrma*; πορφύρα > *pŭrpŭra*; τόρνος > *tǫrnus* > It.

tǫrno, etc.; — κόγχη > *cǫncha;* στρόφος > *strǫppus;* χορδή > *chǫrda;* — κόλαφος > *cǫlaphus cǫlaphus.* Cf. Claussen 857–860.

187. *Y* was originally pronounced *u;* later in Attic and Ionic it became *ü*, which subsequently, in the 9th or 10th century, was unrounded into *i*.

In the older borrowed words, perhaps taken mostly from Doric (Claussen 865), υ regularly was assimilated to Latin *u* (S. 219–221): βύρσα > *bŭrsa;* κρύπτη > *crŭpta;* κύμβη > *cŭmba;* μύλλος > *mŭllus;* μύρτος > *mŭrta,* App. Pr.; πύξος > *bŭxus.* It. *busta* seems to represent a peculiar local development: cf. *buxida* (= *pyxis*) in Theodorus Priscianus and in glosses, Lat. Spr. 468. Cf. *Zefurus,* Audollent 536; "*tymum* non *tumum,*" App. Pr.; *Olumpus,* etc., Pirson 39. In τρῠτάνη > *trŭtĭna* the υ was shortened. In ἄγκυρα > *ancŏra,* στύραξ > *stŏrax,* and a few other words the υ for some reason became *ŏ;* these probably have nothing to do with καλύπτρα > It. *calǫtta,* κρύπτη > It. *grǫtta,* μῦδος > It. *mǫtto,* in which the *ǫ* is a later local development. For some words we find an occasional spelling *œ*, which may represent a Greek dialect pronunciation between *u* and *ü: γ*ῦρος > *gyrus gœrus;* Μυσία > *Mysia Mœsia;* etc.

Towards the end of the Republic, cultivated people adopted for Greek words the Ionic-Attic pronunciation, which is generally represented, in the case of υ, by the spelling *y*. Cicero says: "*Burrum* semper Ennius, nunquam *Pyrrhum*" (S. 221). According to Cassiodorus, *u* is the spelling in some words, *y* in others (S. 221). In the *App. Pr.* we find: "*Marsyas* non *Marsuas,*" "*myrta* non *murta,*" "*porphyreticum marmor* non *purpureticum marmor,*" "*tymum* non *tumum.*" Among the common people the unfamiliar *ü* was assimilated to *i*. The spelling *i* occurs sometimes before Augustus: ἀγκύλια > *ancilia;* Ὀδυσσεία > *Odissia,* Livius Andronicus; Ὀλυσσεύς > *Ulixes.* In inscriptions we find *misteriis,* etc., S. 221. The *App. Pr.*

has "*gyrus* non *girus.*" Cf. *giro, misterii*, etc., Bechtel 76–77; *giret*, Audollent 535; *Frigia*, etc., Pirson 39. This *i*, if long, was usually pronounced *į;* if short, *i̯*, which became *ẹ:* γῦρος > It. *giro;* κῦμα > It. *cima;* σύριγγα > It. *scilinga;* — κύκνος > It. *cęcino;* etc. For σῦκωτόν, see § 141; γύψος > It. *gęsso* is probably a local development. Κυ frequently became *qui:* κολοκύντη > *coloquinta*, etc.; cf. § 223.

The modern Greek pronunciation is represented by some Romance words: ἄμυλον > It. *amido;* βυζαντίς > It. *bisante;* τύμπανον > Fr. *timbre;* etc.

Cf. Claussen 860–869.

188. *AI* originally became *ai*, as in Αἴας > *Aiax*, Μαῖα > *Maia;* later *æ* (as in αἰγίς > *ægis*), which came to be pronounced *ẹ*, as in Αἰθιοπία > *Æthiopia Ethiopia*. Cf. Claussen 871–872.

189. *AY* > *au:* θησαυρός > *thesaurus*. Cf. Claussen 872–873.

190. *EI* was doubtless originally pronounced *ei* in Greek, then, from the sixth to the fourth century B. C., *ẹ̄;* finally, about the third century, *ī*, except before vowels. In Latin, ει became *ī* before consonants, *ē* or *ī* before vowels; εἴδωλον > *īdōlum;* παράδεισος > *paradīsus;* πειρατής > *pīrāta;* — Κλειώ > *Clīo;* Μήδεια > *Medēa*. In -ειος -εια -ειον, the penult was often shortened: πλατεῖα > *platĕa*. Cf. Claussen 873–875.

191. *EY* generally became *eu:* Εὖρος > *Eurus*. Such forms as "*ermēneumata* non *erminomata*" (*App. Pr.*), *toreomatum* from τόρευμα, may be merely misspellings; cf. *Clepatra* for *Cleopatra*. Some Romance forms show *u:* κέλευσμα > ? It. *ciurma*. Cf. Claussen 875–877.

192. *OI* originally became *oi*, as in ποινή > *poina;* later *æ* (as in *pœna*), which came to be pronounced *ẹ*, as in Φοῖβος > *Phœbus Phebus* (S. 277). Sometimes, however, it became *o*,

as in ποιητής > *poēta*. *Cimiterium cymiterium*, for *cœmeterium* < κοιμητήριον, perhaps indicates an ignorant confusion of *ü* and *ö*. Cf. Claussen 877–878.

Like οι, ῳ became *æ:* κωμῳδία > *comœdia*.

193. *O Y* was doubtless originally pronounced *ou* in Greek, then *ō*, then *ū*. In Latin it usually became *ū:* βροῦχος > *brūchus;* οὐρανός > *Ūrănus*. Cf. Claussen 878–879.

1. ACCENTED VOWELS.

a. SINGLE VOWELS.

N.B.— For vowels in hiatus, see § 167. For nasal vowels, see § 171.

a

194. *A* regularly remained unchanged in the greater part of the Empire: *caput, dare, factum, latus, manus, patrem, tantus.* But in Gaul, especially in the north, it probably had a forward pronunciation tending somewhat toward *ę:* cf. *crepere* (probably for *crepare*) in *Gl. Reich.;* and *agnetus* (for *agnātus?*) in Fredegarius, Haag 6.

195. Some words had a peculiar development:—

(1) Beside *alăcrem* the Romance languages seem to postulate *alęcrem* and *alęcrem*. It is possible that *álăcer* (whence *alăcrem*) > *álĕcer* (whence *alęcrem*), then *alĭcer* (whence *alĭcrem alęcrem*).

(2) For the suffix *-arius*, see § 39, *-arius*.

(3) Beside *cĕrăsus* (< κέρασος) there must have been a Latin *cĕrĕsus*. So beside *cĕrĕsĕus*, which was used in southern Italy, Rome, and Sardinia, there was a *cĕrĕsĕus*, which was used elsewhere: *Lat. Spr.* 468; cf. *Substrate* I, 544.

(4) Beside *grăvis* there was a *grĕvis*, under the influence of *lĕvis:* GREVE, *Lat. Spr.* 468; cf. *Substrate* II, 441.

(5) Beside *mălum* (< Doric μᾶλον) there was a *mĕlum* (< μῆλον), used by Petronius and others: *Lat. Spr.* 468.

(6) Beside *vacuus* there was a *vŏcuus: vocuam, C. I. L.* VI, 1527 d 33; cf. *vocatio, C. I. L.* I, 198, etc. Cf. S. 171, Olcott 33. The *o* was probably

original; old *vocáre, vocívus* regularly became *vacáre, vacívus* (> *vacuus*), whence by analogy *vácat* for *vócat: Lat. Spr.* 466. By a change of suffix *vŏcuus* became *vŏcĭtus.

ē

196. Long *e*, which was pronounced *ẹ* (§ 165), probably remained unchanged in Vulgar Latin, at least in most regions: *debēre, dēbet, habētis, mercēdem, vēndere, vērus*.

In Sicily, Calabria, and southern Apulia *ẹ* has become *i*. In old Oscan, which was spoken in nearly the same region, *ē* became *i* in late Republican times, as in *cinsum, dibeto*, etc. (*Lexique* 106). There is, however, no proof of historical connection between the phenomena: cf. *Lat. Spr.* 468.

197. *I* is very often used for *ē* in inscriptions and late writings: Gregory the Great has *crudilitas, dulcido, ficit, filix, minsam, vindo*, etc., *-ido* for *-edo*, *-isco* for *-esco*, *-isimus* for *-esimus;* and conversely *ver* for *vir*, etc.: Sepulcri 193–194. Cf. S. 189–190; Carnoy 15 ff. (*ficet* in the 3d century, etc.). Also *Vok.:* for the confusion of *-ēre* and *-īre*, I, 260 ff., II, 69 ff.; for *-ēsco* and *-īsco*, I, 359–364; for *-ēlis* and *-īlis*, *-ēlius* and *-īlius*, I, 287–289; for *vindimia* instead of *vindēmia*, I, 328, III, 127 (*Lexique* 115). These spellings are due in the main to the identity of *ē* and *ĭ* in late pronunciation: see § 165.

A. Sepulcri, in *Studi Medievali* I, 614–615, conjectures that *s* + consonant may have tended to raise *ẹ* to *i*, *ọ* to *u*. This would account for *bistia* (= *bēstia*) found in late Latin, *Studi Medievali* I, 613; for *crisco* and other verbs in *-isco* for *-ēsco;* for *adimplisti*, etc.; for *fistus*, etc.;—also for *colustru;* for *cognusco* and other verbs in *-usco* for *-ōsco*. Some of the *-ēsco* > *-īsco* cases are surely due to a shift of conjugation: see §§ 414–415.

198. In Gaul this substitution of *i* for *ē* was so very common that it must signify something. It probably indicates an extremely close pronunciation of the *e* (cf. *ǫ*); later, in northern Gaul, this very high *ẹ* > *ei* (*vērum* > Old Fr. *veir*): *Lat. Spr.* 468. It is interesting to note that Celtic *ē* also became *i:* Dottin 99.

Lexique 104–105: *criscit, riges, tris, vexit,* etc. Pirson 2–5: *ficerent, ficit, requiiscit, rictu, rigna,* etc. Neumann 10–11: *adoliscens, minses, quiiscit, rigna.* Bon. 106–113: *minse, quinquaginsima,* etc. Haag 8–9: *adoliscens, criscens, ingraviscente, seniscit, tepiscit; delitus, fedilis, habitur, minsis, sidibus, stilla,* etc. Cf. *Vok.* I, 311 ff.

ĕ

199. Short *e*, which was pronounced *ę* (see § 165), remained unchanged: *bĕne, ĕxit, fĕrrum, fĕrus, fĕsta, tĕneo, vĕnit.*

For the development of diphthongs, see § 177.

(1) According to *Lat. Spr.* 466, *voster*, which supplanted *vester*, is to be regarded as a new formation on the model of *noster* rather than as the old form.

ī

200. Long *i*, pronounced *i* (§ 165), remained unchanged: *audīre, dīco, mīlle, quīnque* (*Substrate* I, 546), *vīlla, vīnum.*

(1) *Frīgĭdus*, except in Spain, must have become **frīgĭdus* (> *frĭgĭdus*), perhaps through association with *rĭgĭdus*. Cf. § 166.

(2) Beside *īlex* there was an *ēlex*, found in Gregory of Tours: *Archiv für das Studium der neueren Sprachen* CXV, 397. Cf. *Lexique* 114.

(3) Beside *sīcula* there was a *sęcula* (*Lexique* 119) > It. *segolo.* Varro (*Lexique* 119) mentions a rustic *speca* for *spīca.* It. *stęgola*, Sp. and Port. *esteva* postulate **stēva* for *stīva;* cf. *C. G. L.* IV, 177, l. 1.

(4) For *sī*, see § 229, (4).

ĭ

201. Short *i*, pronounced *ị* (§ 165), became, doubtless by the third century and sporadically earlier, *ẹ* in nearly all the Empire: *bĭbo, cĭrculus, ĭlle, mĭnus, pĭscem, sĭtis, vĭtium.* The spelling *e* for *ĭ* is common from the third century on: *frecare,* *legare, menus,* etc., S. 200–201; *elud* (= *illud*), Audollent 535; *minester,* etc., Pirson 8–10; *karessemo,* etc., Carnoy 15 ff.; *minester, sebe, semul, sene, vea,* Neumann 23–25; *corregia,* etc., R. 463; *accepere, trea,* etc., Bon. 117–123; *æteneris, trebus,* etc., Haag 11. Conversely *i* is often used for *ē* (cf. §§ 197, 198): *minses,* etc., S. 195; *benivolus,* etc., R. 463. Quintilian and Varro mention (S. 166) a rustic *e* for *ĭ*, attested also by inscriptions (S. 202).

In Sardinia and a part of Corsica this change did not take place, and both *ī* and *ĭ* > *i*. These two islands were taken from Rome by the Vandals in 458 and added to the African kingdom; after that they were perhaps isolated: *Einf.* 106.

In southern Italy *ẹ* from *ĭ*, like *ẹ* from *ē*, became *i:* cf. § 196.

(1) Beside *camīsia* there was a *camĭsia: Substrate* I, 541.

(2) Beside *sĭmul* there was a **sĕmul,* perhaps through the analogy of *sĕmel: Lat. Spr.* 468.

(3) *Sinĭster* was replaced by *sinĕxter*, under the influence of *dĕxter: Lat. Spr.* 469.

ō

202. Long *o*, pronounced *ọ* (§ 165), remained unchanged in Vulgar Latin, at least in most regions: *colōrem, fōrma, hōra, nōmen, sōlus, spōnsus.* In Sicily, Calabria, and southern Apulia *ọ* has become *u*, as it did in old Oscan: cf. the change of *ẹ* to *i*, § 196.

For *agnusco, cognusco,* etc., used by Gregory the Great and others, see the end of § 197. The popular *ūstium* for *ōstium* (*Lat. Spr.* 468; *Studi Medievali* I, 613) is perhaps to be explained in this way.

For *ou* > *ọu*, see § 167.

203. The spelling *u* for *ō* is very common in Gaul (*Lat. Spr.* 468): *furma,* etc., S. 214; *amure,* etc., Pirson 13; *victurias,* etc., Bon. 126–130; *cognusco, gluria, nun, puni*, etc., Haag 13. It probably represents a very close sound, which later, in northern Gaul, became *ou* or *ų: cŏrtem* > Old Fr. *court.* Cf. § 198.

204. There are a few peculiar cases: —

(1) Fr. and Sp. *meuble, mueble* postulate *ǫ* in *mōbilis*, presumably through the analogy of *mŏveo.* Cf. § 217.

(2) Beside *tōtus* and *tottus* (§ 163), some of the Romance forms point to **tūttus* or **tūctus*, or at least to a nom. pl. **tūtti* or **tūcti:* It. sg. *tutto*, pl. *tutti;* Neapolitan sg. *totto*, pl. *tutte;* old Fr., Pr. sg. *tot*, pl. *tuit.* The Italian *tutto* may have come through the plural. Such a form seems to be attested by the *Gl. Cassel:* "aiatutti. uuela alle," where *tutti* is defined as *alle.* No satisfactory explanation has been proposed; the most plausible, perhaps, is that of Mohl, *Lexique* 102–104, namely, the influence of *cūncti* on *tōti.* Cf. *Zs.* XXXIII, 143.

ŏ

205. Short *o*, pronounced *ǫ* (§ 165), remained unchanged: *bŏnus, fŏlia, fŏris, fŏrum, lŏcus, mŏrtem, sŏlet, sŏrtem.* The rustic Latin *funtes, frundes* (for *fŏntes, frŏndes*) are perhaps connected with Italian *fǫnte* and other words containing *ǫ* for *ǫ* before *n* + dental.

U is occasionally used for *ŏ* in inscriptions: *lucus*, etc., S. 211–212. Cf. *App. Pr.*, "*formica* non *furmica.*"

For the development of diphthongs, see § 177.

ū

206. Long *u*, pronounced *ų* (§ 165), remained unchanged in most of the Empire: *cūra, dūrus, nūllus, ūna.* Grammarians mention the protrusion of the lips: S. 216.

But in Gaul, a large part of northern Italy, and western Rætia it was probably formed a little forward of its normal position. It was certainly not *ü*, cf. K. Nyrop, *Grammaire historique de langue française* I, § 187; but it doubtless slightly approached it. This pronunciation may have been due to the linguistic habits of the Celts: cf. Windisch 396–397. Celtic $\bar{u} > \bar{\imath}$ in Great Britain by the second century; in Latin words borrowed by the Celts $\bar{u}$ is generally treated like Celtic $\bar{\rho}$ (*mūrus* > *mur*), but in a few, presumably taken very early, $\bar{u} > \bar{\imath}$ (*cūpa* > *cib*, *crūdus* > *criz*): Loth 67–68.

207. The following special cases are to be noted:—

(1) Beside *lūrĭdus* there probably was a *lŭrdus: *Substrate* III, 517.

(2) *Nūptiæ*, through the analogy of *nŏvius ("bridegroom," from *nŏvus*) and *nŏra*, became *nŏptiæ*: *Lat. Spr.* 469. Cf. *Substrate* IV, 134.

(3) Beside *pūmex* there was a *pōmex*: Bon. 136, *pomice*. Cf. F. G. Mohl in *Zs.* XXVI, 617–618.

ŭ

208. Short *u*, pronounced *u* (§ 165), became, probably by the fourth century or earlier, ρ in most of the Empire: *bŭcca*, *cŭlpa*, *gŭla*, *rŭptus*, *ŭnda*. The spelling *o* is common in late documents: "*columna* non *colomna*," "*turma* non *torma*" (cf. "*coluber* non *colober*," "*formosus* non *formunsus*," "*puella* non *poella*"), *App. Pr.; tomolus*, etc., Pirson 15–17; *tonica*, etc., Bon. 132–135; *corso*, *covetum* (= *cŭbĭtum*), *toneca*, Haag 14. The old spelling *o* for *u* after *v* (*voltus*, *servos*, etc.), which lasted down into the Empire, is perhaps only orthographic: *Lat. Spr.* 464.

In Sardinia, a part of Corsica, Albania, and Dacia this change did not take place, and both $\bar{u}$ and $\bar{u} > u$: *Lat. Spr.* 467.

For $\rho u > \rho u$, see § 167.

(1) Beside *angŭstia* there must have been *angŏstia.

(2) Fr. *couleuvre*, *fleuve*, *jeune* call for local ρ in *colŭbra*, *flŭvium*, *jŭvĕnis*. There are other local irregularities. Cf. § 217.

(3) In place of *nŭrus* we find *nŏrus* (R. 465) and *nŏra* (S. 216), due to the analogy of *sŏror* and *nŏvia ("bride," from *nŏvus*).

(4) Instead of *plŭere* and *plŭvia* people said *plŏvere* (used by Petronius and others) and *plŏja: *Lat. Spr.* 468. Cf. §§ 169, 217.

b. DIPHTHONGS.

æ

209. *Æ* was originally written and pronounced *ai*, but through the mutual attraction of its two parts it became *æ*, later *ẹ: cæcus, cælum, quæro*.

In certain words a vulgar and dialect pronunciation *ē*, common to Volscian and Faliscan (Hammer 7, 8), came into general use: *fēnum, prēda, sēpes, sēptum, sēta*. Cf. S. 166–168, 188; Carnoy 79–80. For *fēnum fænum, prēda præda, sēpes sæpes* both forms were preserved. Hence, by analogy, such spellings as *fæcit*, etc., S. 190. Cf. Neumann 13 (and *Fortsetzung* 21–23): *fæmina, quiæti*, etc.

210. The regular change of *æ* to *ẹ* took place largely in Republican times in unaccented syllables; in stressed syllables in the first century of our era and later. *E* for *æ* in dative endings occurs early: Corssen I, 687 ff. About the middle of the first century B. C., when Varro cited *edus* for *hædus* as a rural form, stressed *æ* was probably still a diphthong in the city but had become *ẹ* in rustic Latium; some hundred years later *ẹ* came into the city and pervaded the provinces: *Lat. Spr.* 465. Terentius Scaurus, in the first century, says that *æ* represents the sound better than *ai:* S. 224. *E* is found early in Campania, especially in Pompeii (*presta*, etc.): S. 225. In Spanish inscriptions *e* occurs from the first century on (Carnoy 78): *questus* (2d century), etc., Carnoy 69–84. It was probably general everywhere by the second century: *Einf.* § 78. Pompeius blames the confusion of *æquus* and *ĕquus:* S. 178. The spelling *e* for *æ* was usual in unaccented syllables (as *sancte*) before the third century, in stressed syllables (as *questor*) from the fourth century on; it may be called regular by the fifth century: S. 178, 225. Cf. Bechtel

75-76: *cedat, grece*, etc. Conversely *æ* was often erroneously used for *ĕ* (S. 183-184) and for Greek η (as *scænam*, *Lexique* 104).

au

211. *Au*, pronounced *áṳ*, generally remained in Vulgar Latin: *aura, gaudium, taurus*. In Rumanian and Provençal it was preserved as *au*, in Portuguese as *ou*; its existence in the earliest stage of French is proved by the treatment of *c* in *causa > chose*; in Italian and Spanish it did not become *ọ* until original *ọ* had broken into *uo* or *ue*.

(1) The spellings *Cladius, Glacus, Scarus*, etc., with *a* for *au* when there is an *u* in the next syllable, are pretty common in various countries: S. 223; Carnoy 86-95. Perhaps they represent a provincial pronunciation, or possibly they are only orthographic.

(2) *Clūdo* for *claudo* is common, coming through derivatives, such as *occlūdo*: *Vok*. II, 304; Carnoy 100 (*cludo* in two Sp. inscriptions of the 1st and 2d centuries); Bayard 6. Cf. Carnoy 85-86 (*clusa*, etc.).

212. Umbrian and Faliscan had *o* in place of Latin *au*: Hammer 4-5, 8. So, in general, the dialects of northern and central Italy: *Chronologie* 158-164. There are some examples in Pompeii, in Oscan territory, where *au* was normally preserved; this pronunciation was used also in the country around Rome, and in the first and second centuries B.C. crept into the city, where it was used by the lower classes: *Lat. Spr.* 465-466. In Umbrian inscriptions we find *toru*, etc.: Hammer 4. In Latin, *Clodius* and *Plotus* are common in first century inscriptions: Carnoy 85, Pirson 27. *Closa*, etc., occur in the second century: Carnoy 85.

The grammarians — Probus, Diomedes, Festus, and others — speak of a rustic or archaic *o* for *au*: Corssen I, 655-663; *Vok*. II, 301 ff.; S. 162-164; Hammer 15-19. Festus cites *orum*; Priscian, *cotes, ostrum, plostrum*: Carnoy 95. Cf. *App. Pr.*, "*auris* non *oricla*"; R. 464, *coda, orata, orum*.

Conversely, *au* was occasionally used for *ō* (*Chronologie* 160): Festus, *ausculum;* Marius Victorinus, "*sorex* vel *saurex*." Cf. *aucīdere for *occīdere*, postulated by some Romance forms.

213. This rustic and vulgar *ō*, — which was pronounced *ǫ*, while the Romance *o* from *au* was *ǫ*, — was generally adopted in Vulgar Latin in a few words: *cōda; fōces;* *ōt (cf. Umbrian *ote*, Hammer 4) = *aut; plōdere*. Cf. Classic *fauces, suffōco; plaudo, explōdo; si audes, sōdes*. Cicero used *loreola, oricla, plodo, pollulum:* Carnoy 95. *Ōla, cōdex, cōles* = *caulis, lōtus, plōtus* occur also.

eu

214. *Eu*, pronounced *éu̯* (as in *ceu, eu, Europa, eurus, eheu, heu, neu, neuter, seu*), was not preserved in any popular words. Cf. S. 228.

œ

215. *Œ* was originally written and pronounced *oi*, but through the mutual attraction of its two parts it became presumably *ö*, later *ẹ: cœpi, pœna, pœnitet*. It may be that the intermediate stage is reflected by the spelling PHYEBÆ for *Phœbe*, S. 227.

E is attested by inscriptions in the first century of our era: *ceperint*, Carnoy 84; *Phebus*, *C. I. L.* IV, 1890; etc. Cf. S. 227, *Lat. Spr.* 464. In the *Per*. we find *amenus, cepi*, etc., Bechtel 76. The confusion of *œ* and *e* is mentioned by late grammarians: S. 227. In late Latin a bad spelling, *œ* for *æ* and *e*, became popular: *cœcus, cœlum, cœmenta, fœmina, fœnum, mœrore, mœstus, pœnates*. Cf. S. 228; *Vok.* II, 293 ff.

ui

216. *Ui*, pronounced *úi̯*, was preserved: *cūi, hūic, illūi*. For the development of *fui*, see § 431.

c. INFLUENCE OF LABIALS.

217. According to some philologists, a following labial tends to open a vowel: *colŭbra* > *colobra*, *flŭvium* > *flovium*, *jŭvĕnis* > *jovenis*, *mōbĭlis* > *mobĭlis*, *ōvum* > *ovum*, *plŭĕre* > *plovĕre*, etc. A general influence of this kind can hardly be regarded as proved for any combination except *ou*, which became *ou*: see § 167.

S. Pieri, *La vocal tonica alterata dal contatto d'una consonante labiale* in *Archivio glottologico italiano* XV, 457, maintains that *i̧, ȩ, o̧, u* were lowered one stage — to *ȩ, ȩ, o̧, o̧* — by a preceding or following labial, even if it was separated from the vowel by a liquid. Although many examples are cited, the evidence is not convincing. For a criticism of the theory, see G. Ascoli, *Osservazioni al precedente lavoro*, ibid., p. 476. The discussion is continued by Pieri, *La vocal tonica alterata da una consonante labiale* in *Zs*. XXVII, 579.

d. CLERICAL LATIN.

218. In clerical Latin the vowels were probably pronounced for the most part as in vulgar speech, until the reforms of Charlemagne. After that, in general, *ă = a*, *ĕ = ȩ*, *ĭ = i̧*, *ŏ = o̧*, *ŭ = u* (or *ü*), *œ* and *æ = ȩ*, *au = o̧* or *au*.

2. UNACCENTED VOWELS.

N. B. — For secondary stress, see §§ 153–155.

219. Among unstressed vowels, those of the first syllable had most resistance, possibly through a lingering influence of the Old Latin accent: cf. § 134.

The vowels of the final syllable lost much of their distinctness, but did not fall, except sporadically, until long after the Vulgar Latin period, and then only in a part of the Empire

Grammarians testify to the confusion of *o* and *u:* S. 212. *Quase, sibe* are found in place of *quasi, sibi:* S. 199–200. According to Quintilian I, iv, 7, "in *here* neque *e* plane nequi *i* auditur."

Weakest were medial vowels immediately following the secondary or the primary stress. In early Latin there was an inclination to syncope: *ar(i)dōrem, av(i)dēre, bál(i)nĕum, cal(e)fácĕre, júr(i)go*, etc. This tendency continued, in moderation, in Classic and Vulgar Latin: *cal(i)dus, ŏc(u)lus, frĭg(i)daria, vĭr(i)dis*, etc. In inscriptions we find such forms as *infri, vetranus:* S. 251.

For the confusion of unaccented *e* and *i*, see Pirson, 30–36, 47–48; for *o* and *u*, see Pirson 41–47. Fredegarius is very uncertain in his use of unstressed vowels: Haag 15–24.

220. *Ŭ* was employed only before labials, in unaccented syllables: cf. S. 196–198, 203–208; Lindsay 25–26, 35; *Franz.* ? I, 21–24. During the Classic period it generally became *ĭ: decumus > decimus, maxumus > maximus, pontufex > pontifex, quodlubet > quodlibet*, etc.; cf. *Lat. Spr.* 466. In Spanish inscriptions we find *maximus*, etc., spelled both with *u* and with *i:* Carnoy 65–69.

Sümus, being sometimes accented, developed two forms, *sŭmus* and *sĭmus*. The former was the one generally adopted in Classic Latin, but *sĭmus* was favored by Augustus and by some purists of his time (Lindsay 29). According to Marius Victorinus (Keil VI, 9), "Messala, Brutus, Agrippa pro *sumus simus* scripserunt." In the vulgar speech *sĭmus* seems to have prevailed in Italy and southern Gaul. Cf. § 419, (1).

221. In general Latin quantity did not sensibly affect the quality of unstressed vowels, except in initial syllables, and even there the difference must have been small. In final syllables, however, *ĭ* was certainly distinct from *ī: sentīs,*

§ 224]   AN INTRODUCTION TO VULGAR LATIN.   93

sentĭt > It. *senti, sente; fēcī, fēcĭt* > Pr. *fis, fes*.   In *sĭbi, tĭbi* the final vowel was sometimes long, sometimes short.

a. UNACCENTED VOWELS IN HIATUS.

222. *I* and *u* followed by a vowel and beginning a syllable were apparently pronounced as consonants from the earliest times. Quintilian says that *u* and *i* in *uos* and *iam* are not vowels: S. 232. Quintilian and Velius Longus cite the spellings *Aiiax, aiio, Maiiam* as approved by Cicero: S. 236. Bonnet notes that *a*, not *ab*, is used before *Joseph, Judæis*, etc. These, then, will be treated as consonants, and will be left out of consideration in the present chapter.

223. After gutturals, *u* followed by a vowel was originally a vowel itself, but lost its syllabic value in early Classic times: *acua* > *aqua, distinguere* > *distinguere*.   So it was in *qualis, quæro, quem, qui*.   In Greek transliterations κυ for *qui* (as in ἀκύλας) is very common: Eckinger 123-125; cf. § 187.

In perfects, however, such as *nocuit, placuit*, the *u* was apparently not reduced to a semivowel until the end of the Classic period.

In some other words the syllabic value of *u* was kept, at least in theory, rather late: Velius Longus distinguishes *aquam* from *acuam*, S. 234; *App. Pr.*, "*vacua* non *vaqua*," "*vacui* non *vaqui*."

224. Otherwise, *e, i*, and *u* in hiatus with following vowels lost their syllabic value probably by the first century of our era, and sporadically earlier. Occasional examples (such as *dormio, facias, fluviorum*) are found in Ennius, Plautus, Lucilius, Lucretius, Horace, Virgil, Ovid, Juvenal, and Seneca: e.g., *deorsum* in Lucretius; *vindemiator* in Horace; *abiete, abietibus* in Virgil. *Italia* counts as three syllables in poets of the early Empire. Cf. S. 232. Valerius Probus has *pariĕtibus:* Édon 208. Consentius declares that trisyllabic *soluit* and four-syllable *induruit* are barbarisms; Cæsellius is undecided whether *tenuis* has three syllables or two: S. 234. *Suavis,* however, was used as a trisyllable by Sedulius in the fifth century; it was probably a semi-learned word, as it became *soef* in French, *soave* in Italian.

The pronunciation *ẹ, į, ų* was probably regular in popular speech by the first century or before; by the third century, with a narrowing of the mouth-passage, the semivowels presumably developed into the fricative consonants *y* and *w:* S. 231–232. So *alea > alẹa > alja, fīlius > fĭlįus > filjus, sapui > sapųi > sapwi*. In the same way *filíolus > filjólus* (§ 136), *tenúeram > ténweram* (§ 137); likewise *eccu'hīc > *eccwic, eccu'ista > *ecwįsta* (§ 65), etc. We have, then, in late Latin, a new *y* and a new *w*.

Hence arises, in late Latin spelling, a great confusion of *e* and *i* in hiatus: CAPRIOLVS (cf. § 136), S. 187; Caper, "non *iamus* sed *eamus*," "*sobrius* per *i* non per *e* scribendum," Keil VII, 106, 103; *aleum, calcius, cavia, coclia, fasiolus, lancia, lintium, noxeus, solia, vinia, App. Pr.; abias, abiat, exiat, Lauriatus, valiat,* Audollent 535; *palleum,* etc., R. 463; *calciare, liniamenta,* Bayard 4; *eacit* (=*jacet*), *eam* (=*jam*), *Vok.* II, 43; cf. Carnoy 33–35.

225. But the combinations *eé, ié, oó, uó* developed differently, *eé* and *ié* apparently being contracted into *ē, oó* and *uó* into *ō,* at an early date: *ariĕtem* (§ 136) > *arētem* (Varro, "*ares* veteres pro *aries* dixisse": Carnoy 43); *dē-ĕxcĭto > *dēxcĭto > It. *desto; faciēbam* > **facēbam; muliĕrem* (§ 136) > *mul'ērem,* the *i* remaining long enough to palatalize the *l* (the Romance *ẹ* was doubtless a later analogical development); *pariĕtes* (§ 136) > *parētes, C. I. L.* VI, 3714 (Rome); *prĕhĕndĕre* >

prēndĕre, then *prĕndĕre through the analogy of rĕddĕre and perhaps also of ascĕndĕre, defĕndĕre, pĕndĕre, tĕndĕre; quiētus > quĕtus, common in late inscriptions, Pirson 57 (cf. requebit, Carnoy 43); — cŏhŏrtem > cŏrtem; cŏŏpĕrīre > cŏpĕrīre, then *cŏpĕrīre *cŏp'rīre through the analogy of cŏ- and perhaps also of ŏpĕra, ŏpus; dŭŏdĕcim > dōdĕcim (Pirson 58: dodece).

226. Furthermore, *u* after all consonants fell before unaccented *u* probably by the middle of the first century, before unaccented *o* by the second century: antīquus > antīcus; carduus > cardus; cŏquus > cŏcus (App. Pr., "coqui non coci," "coqus non cocus"; cf. S. 351); distīnguunt > distīngunt (according to Velius Longus, some writers use no *u* in distinguere, Édon 130); ĕquus > ĕcus (App. Pr., "equs non ecus"; cf. Velius Longus, S. 217); innŏcuus > innŏcus, Koffmane 111; mŏrtuus > mŏrtus; suus > sus, tuum > tum, Carnoy 117; — battuo > batto (cf. abattas, Gl. Reich.); cŏquo > cŏco (App. Pr., "coquens non cocens"; hence *cocīna); quat(t)uor > quattor (S. 218) quator (Pirson 58) quatro (7th century, Carnoy 221); quot(t)īdie > cottīdie, S. 352; stīnguo > stīngo; tīnguo > tīngo (Caper, "tinguere . . . non tingere," Keil VII, 106); tŏrqueo > *torquo > *tŏrco; ŭnguo > ŭngo (ungo, unguntur, ungi, Bayard 7; Caper, "ungue non unge," Keil VII, 105; uncis = unguis, Audollent 536). So apparently aruum > *arum, ĕruum > ĕrum (Lat. Spr. 472: ero). Vĭduus, however, doubtless under the influence of the commoner vĭdua, kept its *u*: Old Fr. vef.

After gutturals, *u* fell before stressed *u* and *o*: quum > cum; quōmŏdo > cōmŏdo, Audollent 536. See § 354.

U often fell irregularly in contin(u)ari, Febr(u)arius, Jan(u)arius: Vok. II, 468–469; S. 217–218.

227. Similarly, *i* after a consonant fell before unaccented *i*: audīi > audi, consĭlīi > consĭli, ministĕrīi > ministĕri. Velius

Longus found it necessary to say that *Claudii, Cornelii, Julii*, etc., should be spelled with double *i:* Keil VII, 57.

Some late words, however, kept *-iī* and *-iīs: Dionysii* > It. *Dionigi, Parisiis* > It. *Parigi*.

b. INITIAL SYLLABLE.

228. As far as one can judge from spellings and subsequent developments, *ă* was pronounced *a; æ, ĕ, ĭ, œ* all came to be sounded *ẹ; ī* remained *i; ō* and *ŭ* were finally all pronounced *ọ* or *u; ŏ* remained *ọ; au* became *a* if there was an accented *u* in the next syllable, but otherwise remained unchanged (cf. *Lat. Spr.* 470): *rādīcem, vălēre; ætātem, dēbēre, tĕnēre, vĭdēre, fœdāre; rīdēmus, cīvĭtātem, hībernus; plōrāre, frūmentum, sŭbĭnde; cōlōrem, dŏlēre, mŏvētis; A(u)gŭstus, A(u)runci, a(u)scŭlto, audēre, gaudēre, naufragium*. For the confusion of *e* and *i*, see Audollent 535, Carnoy 17–33, Bon. 135–138. Cf. *ecclesia*, Bechtel 76 ; "*senatus non sinatus,*" *App. Pr.; golosus gylosus* (for *gulōsus*), Koffmane 110; *moniti* (for *mūnīti*), Bon. 136. *Agustus* is frequent from the second century on, S. 223 (cf. *agustas*, Pirson 26); *Arunci* occurs in manuscripts of Virgil; Caper says "*ausculta non asculta,*" S. 223; *agŭrium must have existed also.

229. In a few words the vowel of the initial syllable was lost before an *r:* *corrŏtŭlare > **c'rŏt'lare; dīrēctus* generally > *d'rēctus* (*Vok*. II, 422: *drictus*); *quĭrĭtare* > **c'rītare*. *Jejūnus* after prefixes lost its first syllable: *dis-junare.

Some minor peculiarities are to be noted: —

(1) *A* after *j* apparently tended to become *e:* Old Latin *jajŭnus* > Classic *jejŭnus* (the original *a* seems to be preserved in some Italian dialect forms); Classic *Januarius* > *Jenuarius* (common in inscriptions, S. 171–172, *Lat. Spr.* 470); Classic *janua* > *jenua > Sardinian *genna*.

(2) *E*, long or short, is very often replaced by *i* in Gallic inscriptions (*Lat. Spr.* 470): *divota, mimoriæ*, etc.; *dilevit*, Bon. 109; cf. *Vok*. I,

422-424. This perhaps indicates a close pronunciation: cf. § 198. *Di-* for *de-*, possibly through confusion with *dis-*, is common in Gregory the Great: *dirivare*, etc. According to Mohl, *Lexique* 105-108, *e* became *i* in southern Italy from the fourth to the sixth century: RIVOCAVERIT, etc. A form *ni* for *ne* is found from early times: Pirson 3.

(3) *Ĭ* was occasionally assimilated to a following accented *a*: *gĭgántem* > *jagante > Old Fr. *jaiant*, Pr. *jaian*, Old Genoese *zagante*; *sĭlváticus* > *salvaticus* (*Gl. Reich.*, cf. *Lat. Spr.* 470) > Old Fr. *salvage*, It. *salvatico*, Rum. *sălbatec*. Cf. *Einf.* § 111.

(4) *Ī* tended to become *e*, by dissimilation, if there was an accented *ī* in the next syllable:[1] *dīvīděre* > **devīděre; dīvīnus* > *devīnus*, in fourth century inscriptions, *Lexique* 122; *fīnīre* > *fenīre*, in manuscripts and inscriptions, *Lexique* 123; *vīcīnus* > *vecīnus*, attested by Servius, *Lexique* 104 ff. *Sī*, in late Latin, sometimes became *se*, attested from the sixth century on (*Vok.* II, 87; *Lexique* 120; *Franz. ∂* II, 224 ff.; Bon. 126; Haag 11; cf. *nise, C. I. L.* I, 205); in very late texts there is frequent confusion of *si* and *sed* (*Franz. ∂* II, 225, 234-235); the *e* is perhaps due to the analogy of *que < *quĭd* = *quod* (cf. §§ 69, 82), cf. Italian *sed* on the model of *ched: si* is preserved in French, Provençal, and Spanish, *se* in Portuguese, Old French, Italian, and Old Rumanian. In *mīrabīlia* the *ī* apparently became *e* and *a*.

(5) *Ū* was kept by analogy in many words: *dūrare, mūrare, mūtare, nūtrire* (beside *notrire). *Jūnĭpĕrus* > *jeniperus* (*Lat. Spr.* 470) and *jiniperus* (*App. Pr.*).

(6) *O* appears as *u* in *furmica* (*App. Pr.*, cf. *Rom.* XXXV, 164), *putator* (*Bon.* 127), *turrente* (Bon. 131). *O* is changed to *e* in *retundus* (*Vok.* II, 213; cf. Vitruvius, *retundatio, Lat. Spr.* 470), through the influence of the prefix *re-;* also sometimes in *serore* (*Lat. Spr.* 470; cf. *serori, seroribus*, Carnoy 107).

(7) *Au* in vulgar speech was often replaced by *o* (cf. §§ 212, 213): *oricla, App. Pr.*, Pirson 27; so *ot (for *aut:* cf. Umbrian *ote*, Lindsay 40), which prevailed in Vulgar Latin.

230. *S* before a consonant was doubtless long and sharp, as in modern Italian, so that at the beginning of a word it had a syllabic effect — *s-chola*. This led to the prefixing of a front vowel (until the seventh century nearly always an *i*, later

---

[1] Mohl's view, *Lexique* 122-126, is that original Latin *ei*, if *i* followed, became *e* instead of *ī*.

often *e*) to the *s* when no vowel preceded — *in i-schola.* This *i* or *e* came to be regarded as a regular part of the word. The prosthetic vowel occurs first in Greek inscriptions. The earliest Latin example is probably *iscolasticus*, written in Barcelona in the second century; it is found repeatedly, though not frequently, in the third century (Carnoy 114-116); in the fourth and fifth it is very common: *espiritum, ischola, iscripta, isperabi, ispose, istatuam, istudio*, S. 317; *ismaragdus*, Pirson 60; *estatio, Estephanus, iscola, istare*, R. 467. Grammarians took no note of it until St. Isidore, in the seventh century. But in late Latin texts *ab* rather than *a* was used before words beginning with *sc, sp, st: ab scandalo*, Dubois 171; *ab sceleribus*, Bon. 445; cf. Dubois 171-172, Bon. 445-446.

The *es-, is-* thus produced was confounded with *ex-, exs-* (pronounced *es-*) and *ins-, his-* (pronounced *is-*): *explendido, splorator, instruo* for *struo, Spania*, etc., S. 317; *hispatii* for *spatii*, Bechtel 78; *spiratio* for *inspiratio*, Koffmane 109; *scalciare* for *excalceare, scoriare* for *excoriare, spandere* for *expandere, Spania, Spanus, stantia* for *instantia, strumentum*, etc., R. 469-470; *spectante* for *expectante*, etc., Bon. 148. Cf. *Vok.* II, 365 ff.; S. 316-319; Pirson 59-60.

c. INTERTONIC SYLLABLE.

N. B. — By this term is meant the syllable following the secondary and preceding the primary stress.

231. Vowels so situated probably became more and more indistinct towards the end of the Empire, and occasionally disappeared. In some regions they began to fall regularly before the close of the Vulgar Latin period, but *a* was generally kept: *bón(i)tátem, cáp(i)tális, cárr(i)cáre, cérebéllum, cív(i)tátem, cóll(o)cáre, cómparáre cómperáre, dél(i)cátus, dúb(i)táre, eleméntum eliméntum, frígidária frigdária, mirabília,*

§ 233]   AN INTRODUCTION TO VULGAR LATIN.   99

sácraméntum, sépuráre séperáre, vérecúndia. Frigdaria occurs in the second century B. C.: Franz. ↄ I, 12. Cf. dedcavit, Pirson 52; vetranus, Pirson 51; cornare for coronare, Koffmane 111; stablarius, R. 467. The fall of the vowel of course disturbed the Vulgar Latin rhythm: see § 153. Cf. F. Neumann in Zs. XIV, 559.

Mĭnĭstērium apparently became mĭnstērium early enough for the n to fall before the s: see § 171. Cf. Substrate IV, 116.

d. PENULT.

232. The Vulgar Latin rhythmic principle tended to obliterate one of the two post-tonic syllables of proparoxytones. The penult, being next to the accent, was weaker and more exposed to syncope. We find in late Latin much confusion of e and i: anemis, meretis, etc., Neumann 22; dixemus, etc., Bon. 118. Likewise o and u: ambolare, etc., R. 464; insola, etc., Bon. 131–135; cf. Sepulcri 201–202.

The treatment of this vowel, however, was apparently very inconsistent in Vulgar Latin, and the conditions differed widely in different regions. There was probably a conflict between cultivated and popular pronunciation, both types often being preserved in the Romance languages: thus while the literary and official world said (h)ŏmĭnes (> It. uomini), the uneducated pronounced 'ŏm'nes (> Pr. omne); similarly beside sŏcĕrum there was sŏcrum.

As far as the general phenomena can be classified, we may say that in popular words in common speech the vowel ot the penult tended to fall under the following conditions: —

(1) BETWEEN ANY CONSONANT AND A LIQUID.

233. A vowel preceded by a consonant and followed by a liquid weakened and fell in the earlier part of the Vulgar

Latin period: *altra; anglus; aspra; dedro* for *déderunt, Lexique* 63; *fecrunt fecru, Lexique* 64; *íns(u)la; juglus; maníplus; socro,* Pirson 51. In some words we find *a* weakened to *e: cítera, App. Pr.; hilerus,* Carnoy 12; *Cæseris, compera, seperat* (about 500 A. D.), *Vok.* I, 195–196; *Eseram* for *Isaram,* Bon. 96. For a vowel between a *labial* and a liquid, see (2) below.

But if the first consonant was a palatal, the vowel seems to have been kept, at any rate in some regions: *bájulus, frágilis, grácilis, vírginem.* In *vígilat > *víglat* the vowel fell before the *g* began to be palatalized (so apparently in *dígitum > dictum, Franz. ⒐* I, 15–16; *frígidus > frigdus, App. Pr.*). Cf. § 259.

234. Latin originally had the two diminutive endings *-clus* (*< -tlo*), as in *sæclum,* and *-cŭlus* (*< -co-lo*), as in *aurĭcŭla.* These were kept distinct by Plautus. Later they were confused, both becoming *-cŭlus* in Classic Latin, both *-clus* in vulgar speech: *artíc(u)lus, bác(u)lus, másc(u)lus, óc(u)lus, spéc(u)lum, vernác(u)lus, víc(u)lus. Oclus* and some others occur in Petronius: see W. Heræus, *Die Sprache des Petronius und die Glossen,* 1899; cf. *peduclum,* Waters Ch. 57. Many examples are found in inscriptions: *oclos, scaplas,* Audollent 538; *aunclus, felicla, masclus,* Pirson 49–50. Cf. *Franz. ⒐* I, 16–18.

To *-clus* was assimilated in popular Latin the ending *-tŭlus: capítulus > *capiclus; fístula > *fiscla; vétulus > veclus, App. Pr.* (cf. *vitlus,* Pirson 51). But a few words, which must have been slow in entering the common vocabulary, escaped this absorption: *crústulum > crustlum* (found in 18 A. D.); *spatula > *spatla.* Cf. § 284.

(2) BETWEEN A LABIAL AND ANY CONSONANT.

235. A vowel preceded by a labial and followed by a consonant was inclined to fall early: *bublus; cóm(i)tem; comp'tus;*

§ 238]   AN INTRODUCTION TO VULGAR LATIN.   101

déb(i)tum; dóm(i)nus; fíb(u)la; póp(u)lus; sablum; tríb(u)la; vápulo baplo. In *dóm(i)nus* the *mn* form may be the older: *domni*, Pirson 50; *domnus* in St. Augustine, Koffmane 109; *domnicus*, R. 467; *domnulus*, Koffmane 111. *Lamna* occurs in Horace and Vitruvius, *Franz.* ⸮ I, 13. Petronius has *bublum*, Waters Ch. 44, *offla*, Waters Ch. 56. Cf. *fibla, poplus, sablum*, etc., in R. 467.

In some words, however, the vowel was kept, either everywhere or in a large region: *árb(o)rem; hámula; hóm(i)nes; júv(e)nis; nébula; trémulat*.

236. When *ab* or *av* was brought next to a consonant by the fall of a following vowel, it generally became *au*, but often there were double forms; the process began very early: *ávica > *auca*, found in glosses; *ávidus* > *audus*, Plautus (cf. *avunculus* > *aunculus*, Plautus); *clávido > *claudo* (cf. *navifragus > *naufragus*); *fábula* > *faula **fabla; gábata* > *gauta **gabta;* *návitat > **nautat; parábula* > *paraula **parabla; tábula* > *taula *tabla. Cf. *Franz.* ⸮ I, 12.

(3) BETWEEN A LIQUID AND ANY CONSONANT.

237. A vowel preceded by a liquid and followed by a consonant was subject to syncope at all periods: *ardus*, Plautus; *caldus*, Plautus, Cato, Varro, Petronius; *cól(a)phus* (cf. *percolopabat*, Waters Ch. 44; *colpus, Gl. Reich.*); *fúlica fulca*, *Franz.* ⸮ I, 13; *lardum*, Ovid, Martial, Juvenal, Pliny; *merto*, Pirson 51, *Franz.* ⸮ I, 15; *soldus*, Cæsar, Horace, Varro; *valde; virdis, App. Pr.* (cf. *virdiaria*, Vegetius, 4th century). Cf. *Franz.* ⸮ I, 12 ff.

(4) MISCELLANEOUS.

238. In some words the vowel fell under different conditions: *dígitum* > *dictum*, *Franz.* ⸮ I, 15–16 (cf. § 233); *frígidus*

>*frigdus* (cf. § 233), *App. Pr.* (*fricda*), Pompeii (FRIDAM); *máxima* > *masma*, 2d century, Suchier 732; *nítidus* > **nittus*, *pútidus* > **puttus*, probably late; *postus*, Lucretius, Pirson 50, *Franz. ∂* I, 13-14 (cf. *posturus*, Cato).

239. In the transition from Vulgar Latin to the Romance languages the vowels in classes (1), (2), (3), — in so far as they had not fallen already, — were syncopated with some regularity; and a number of vowels otherwise placed fell under different conditions in various regions: *pónere* > **ponre*, *tóllere* > **tolre*; *fémina* > **femna*, *hábitus* > **abtus*, *rápidus* > **rapdus*; *cárrico* > **carco*, *cléricus* > **clercus*, *cóllocat* > **colcat*; *déc(i)mus*, *fráx(i)nus*, *pérs(i)ca*, *séd(e)cim*. Cf. *Gl. Reich.*: *carcatus*, *culicet culcet* = *collŏcat*.

In a part of Gaul *ámita* > **anta*, *débita* > **depta*, *domínica* > **dominca*, *mánica* > **manca*, *sémita* > **senta*. Some of these shortened forms were used in other regions.

A vowel preceded by *d* or *t* and followed by *c* seems to have remained longer than most other vowels that fell at all: *júdico*, *médicus*, *viáticum*, *víndico*, etc.

e. FINAL SYLLABLE.

240. The vowels regularly remained through the Vulgar Latin period. Later, about the eighth century, they generally fell, except *a* and *ī*, in Celtic, Aquitanian, and Ligurian territory.

241. In the *App. Pr.* we find "*avus* non *aus*," "*flavus* non *flaus*," "*rivus* non *rius*." *Aus* and *flaus* have left no representatives, but *rius* is evidently the ancestor of Italian and Spanish *rio*. All three forms are probably examples of a phonetic reduction that affected certain regions.

Through a large part of the Empire *-āvit* > *-aut*: *triumphaut* is found in Pompeii. See Morphology.

242. Final vowels, as in modern Italian, must have been often elided or syncopated in the interior of a phrase, especially *e* after liquids: Caper, "*bibere* non *biber*"; *haber* in an inscription; *conder, præber, prædiscer, tanger* in manuscripts. See *Franz. ə* I, 41. So, perhaps, *autumnal(e), tribunal(e)*, etc.

The *App. Pr.* has "*barbarus* non *barbar*," "*figulus* non *figel*," "*masculus* non *mascel*." These curious forms are probably not the result of a phonetic development, but are rather due to a local change of inflection, which left no trace in the Romance languages. Cf. Old Latin *facul = facilis, famul = famulus*.

243. *A*, long or short, was naturally pronounced *a*; *æ, ĕ, ĭ*, according to the testimony of numerous inscriptions (*Lat. Spr.* 469), were all probably sounded *e*, which in Sicily became eventually *i; ī* remained *i; ŏ* was *o*, which became *u* in Sicily; *ŭ* was *u*. In some localities this *o* and this *u* were kept distinct, but generally they were confounded (*Lat. Spr.* 469). Examples: *ămās, ămăt; sanctæ, trīstēs, trīstĕm, trīstĭs; fēcī, bŏnī, sĕntīs; bŏnōs, mŏriŏr; cŏrpŭs, frūctū*. About the eighth century *a* probably became *ə* in northern Gaul.

244. The changes in pronunciation led to great confusion in spelling. It is likely that final vowels were especially obscure in Gaul in the sixth and seventh centuries.

Neumann 7–8 cites ten cases of *e* for *a: Italice*, etc.

E and *æ*, in late Latin, were not usually distinguished (cf. § 210): *apte = aptæ, cotidiæ*, etc., Bechtel 75–76.

E and *i* came to be used almost indiscriminately. Quintilian I, vii, says that Livy wrote *sibe* and *quase;* in I, iv and I, vii, he describes the final vowel of *here* as neither quite *e* nor quite *i*. Cf. *mihe, tibe*, etc., *Lexique* 118. *E* for *i* is frequent in the dative and ablative, Carnoy 45: *luce*, dative; *uxore*, ablative.

Es and *is* are continually interchanged: *Vok.* I, 244 ff., III, 116; *mares = maris*, etc., Audollent 535; *Joannis*, etc., Neumann 11–13; *jacis, omnes = omnis* (3d century), etc., Carnoy 13–15; *regis = reges*, etc. Bon. 111; *omnes =omnis*, etc., Bon. 121. So *et* and *it:* Bechtel 88–89, very common in *Per.; tenit*, etc., Neumann 11–13; *posuet*, etc., Carnoy 13; *movit*, etc., Bon. 115; Sepulcri 229–230.

With *o* and *u* it was the same. In *Vok.* II, 91 ff., there are 61 examples of *u* for ablative *o* between 126 and 563 A. D., as well as frequent instances of ablative in *um*, of *om* for *um, os* for *us*, and *us* for *os*. The confusion of *o* and *um* is very common in *Per.;* also in Gregory the Great, Sepulcri 203–204; cf. Carnoy 48, *monumento = monumentum.* Bon. 131 has *spoliatur* for *spoliator. Os* and *us* were interchanged from the third century on: *anus = annos*, Carnoy 48; *bonus = bonos*, etc., Sepulcri 201. The accusative plural in *us* was particularly common in Gaul: *filius =filios*, etc., Bon. 128; cf. Haag 42.

245. In words often used as proclitics final *–er, –or* became *–re, –ro: ĭnter > *intre; quat(u)or > quatro*, Carnoy 221; *sĕmper > * sempre; sŭper > *supre.* Cf. *Lat. Spr.* 474.

Mĭnus, used as a prefix (cf. § 29) as in *minus-pretiare*, became in Gaul *mis–*, perhaps at the end of the Vulgar Latin period, under the influence of *dis–*. Cf. *Phon.* 43–44.

E. CONSONANTS.

246. The Latin consonant letters were B, C, D, F, G, H, I, K, L, M, N, P, Q, R, S, T, V, X, Z. *I* and *V* were used both for the vowels *i* and *u* and for the consonants *j* and *v*. *K*, an old letter equivalent to *C*, was kept in some formulas; it need not be separately considered. *Q* was generally used only in the combination *QV = kw* (cf. § 223). *X* stands for *ks*. *Z* in Old Latin apparently meant *s* or *ss* (S. 319-320); later it represented a different Latin version of Greek ζ, which will be treated below (§§ 338-339).

In addition to the above, Vulgar Latin had a new *w* and *y* coming from originally syllabic *u*, *e*, or *i* in hiatus: see § 224. In words borrowed from Greek and German there were several foreign consonants, which will be discussed after the native ones.

247. Double consonants regularly kept their long pronunciation: *annus, nullus, passus, terra, vacca*. For *ss > s* and *ll > l* after long vowels, see § 161. For double forms like *cīpus cippus*, see §§ 162, 163.

In late spelling there is some confusion of single and double consonants: *anos*, Pirson 88; *fillio*, Pirson 85; *serra*, Bon. 158; cf. Pirson 83-91. For Fredegarius see Haag 39-40. Double consonants are often written single in early inscriptions.

248. The principal developments that affected Latin consonants may be summed up as follows: *b* between vowels was opened into the bilabial fricative β, and thus became identical with *v*, which also changed to β; *c* and *g* before front vowels were palatalized and were then subject to further alterations; *h* was silent; *m* and *n* became silent at the end of a word, and *n* ceased to be sounded before *s*. The voicing of intervocalic surds began during the Vulgar Latin period.

The consonants will now be considered in detail, first the native Latin, next the Greek, lastly the Germanic; the Celtic need not be separately studied. The Latin consonants will be taken up in the following order: aspirate, gutturals, palatals, dentals, liquids, sibilants, nasals, labials.

1. LATIN CONSONANTS.
a. ASPIRATE.

249. *H* was weak and uncertain at all times in Latin, being doubtless little or nothing more than a breathed on-glide: S. 255-256. Grammarians say that *h* is not a letter but a mark of aspiration: S. 262-263. There is no trace of Latin *h* in the Romance languages. Cf. G. Paris in *Rom.* XI, 399.

250. It probably disappeared first when medial: S. 266. Quintilian commends the spelling *deprendere:* S. 266. Gellius says *ahenum, vehemens, incohare* are archaic; Terentius Scaurus calls *reprehensus* and *vehemens* incorrect, and both he and Velius Longus declare there is no *h* in *prendo:* S. 266. Probus states that *traho* is pronounced *trao:* Lindsay 57. Cf. *App. Pr.,* "*adhuc* non *aduc.*" In inscriptions we find such forms as *aduc, comprendit, cortis, mi, nil, vemens:* S. 267-268.

251. Initial *h* was surely very feeble and often silent during the Republic. In Cicero's time and in the early Empire there was an attempt to revive it in polite society, which led to frequent misuse by the ignorant, very much as happens in Cockney English to-day: for the would-be elegant *chommoda, hinsidias,* etc., of "Arrius," see S. 264.

Quintilian says the ancients used *h* but little, and cites "*ædos irco*sque": S. 263. Gellius quotes P. Nigidius Figulus to the effect that "rusticus fit sermo si aspires perperam"; but speaks of bygone generations—i.e., Cicero's contemporaries—as using *h* very much, in such words as *sepulchrum, honera:* S. 263-264. Pompeius notes that *h* sometimes makes position, as in *terga fatigamus hasta,* sometimes does not, as in *quisquis honos tumuli:* Keil V, 117. Grammarians felt obliged to discuss in detail the spelling of words with or without *h:* S. 264-265.

H is dropped in a few inscriptions towards the end of the Republic: *arrespex* (for *haruspex*), etc., S. 264. In Rome are found: E[REDES], *C. I. L.* I, 1034; ORATIA, *C. I. L.* I, 924; OSTIA, *C. I. L.* I, 819. In Pompeii *h* is freely omitted; and after the third century it is everywhere more or less indiscriminately used: *abeo, abitat, anc, eres, ic, oc, omo, ora*, etc., *haram, hegit, hossa*, etc., S. 265-266. Cf. *ospitium, ymnus*, etc., *heremum, hiens, hostium*, etc., Bechtel 77-78; *ortus*, etc., *hodio*, etc., R. 462-463.

252. After *h* had become silent, there grew up a school pronunciation of medial *h* as *k*, which has persisted in the Italian pronunciation of Latin and has affected some words in other languages: *michi, nichil*, Bechtel 78, R. 455. Cf. E. S. Sheldon in *Harvard Studies and Notes in Philology and Literature* I (1892), 82-87.

b. GUTTURALS.

253. *C* and *K* did not differ in value except that *C* sometimes did service for *G: App. Pr.*, "*digitus* non *dicitus*"; *dicitos = digitos*, Audollent 536; cf. S. 341-344. There was some confusion, too, of *Q* and *C:* S. 345.

254. *QV* was pronounced *kw:* S. 340-341, 345-346, 350-351. Before *u* and *o*, however, the *kw* was reduced to *k* by the first or second century, probably earlier in local or vulgar dialects: Quintilian VI, iii, records a pun of Cicero on *coque* and *quoque; condam, cot, cottidie*, S. 351-352; *in quo ante = inchoante, quooperta = coperta, secuntur*, Bechtel 78-79. Cf. § 226. Before other vowels the *kw* was regularly kept in most of the Empire, unless analogy led to a substitution of *k*, as in *coci* for *coqui* through *cocus:* see § 226. But in Dacia, southeastern Italy, and Sicily subsequent developments point to a Vulgar Latin reduction of *que* to *ke, qui* to *ki: Lat. Spr.* 473.

In *quinque* the first *w* was lost by dissimilation: CINQVE, Carnoy 221, found in Spain (so CINQV, *Lexique* 93); CINCTIVS, CINQVAGINTA, S. 351. *Laqueus* seems, for some reason, to have become *laceus: Substrate* III, 274.

255. *X* stood for *ks:* S. 341, 346, 352. After a consonant *ks* early tended to become *s:* Piautus uses *mers* for *merx;* Caper, "*cals* dicendum, ubi materia est, per *s*," Keil VII, 98.

By the second or third century *ks* before a consonant was reduced to *s: sestus* is common in inscriptions, cf. Carnoy 170, Eckinger 126 (Σέστος); *destera*, Carnoy 171; *dester*, S. 353; *mextum* for *mæstum*, Audollent 537. So *ex-* > *es-* in *excutere*, *exponere*, etc.: cf. *extimare* for *æstimare*, Bechtel 139. Hence sometimes, by analogy, *es-* for *ex-* before vowels, as in *essagium*, but not in *exire*.

At about the same time final *ks* became *s*, except in monosyllables: *cojus, conjus, milex, pregnax = prægnans, subornatris*, etc., in inscriptions, S. 353 (cf. *xanto*, etc.); *felis*, fifth century, Carnoy 159; *App. Pr.*, "*aries* non *ariex*," "*locuples* non *lucuplex*," "*miles* non *milex*," "*poples* non *poplex*."

In parts of Italy *ks* between vowels was assimilated into *ss* by the first century, but this was only local: ALESAN[DER], S. 353; BISSIT BISIT VISIT = *vixit*, S. 353. For *ks* > χs, see § 266.

There are some examples, in late Latin, of a metathesis of *ks* into *sk: axilla* > *ascella*, Lindsay 102; *buxus* > *buscus; vixit* > VIXCIT (i. e., *viscit*), Carnoy 157. Cf. *Vok.* I, 145. On the other hand, *Priscilla* > PRIXSILLA, Carnoy 158. In northern Gaul apparently *sk* regularly became *ks*, as in *cresco, nasco*, etc.: see *Mélanges Wahlund* 145.

256. The voicing of intervocalic surds doubtless began as early as the fifth century; it is shown by Anglo-Saxon borrowings and by such Latin forms as *frigare, migat* in inscriptions and manuscripts; there are many examples from the sixth century: *Lat. Spr.* 474. A. Zimmermann, *Zs.* XXV, 731, finds in inscriptions some slight evidence of a change of *t* to *d* during the Empire, in some places perhaps as early as the first century. According to Loth 21–26, intervocalic *c, p, t* were voiced in Gaul in the second half of the sixth century. Rydberg, *Franz.* ₂ I, 32, maintains, on the evidence of inscriptions and manuscripts, that $t > d$ in the fifth century and the beginning of the sixth, while $c > g$ at least two centuries earlier. Cf. *Vok.* I, 125 ff.; *immudavit*, 2d century, Carnoy 121; *eglesia, lebra, pontivicatus*, 7th century, Carnoy 123; *negat, pagandum*, etc., *sigricius = secretius*, etc., Haag 27; *cubidus, occubavit*, etc., *stubri*, etc., Haag 27–28; *cataveris = cadaveris*, etc., Haag 28–29. Some of the above examples show that consonants followed by *r* shared in the voicing, at least as early as the seventh century.

Voicing was not general, however, in central and southern Italy, Dalmatia, and Dacia.

257. Initial *c* and *cr*, in a few words, became *g* and *gr:* **gaveola;* **gratis; crassus + grossus > grassus*, found in the 4th century. Cf. Densusianu 111–112.

(1) C AND G BEFORE FRONT VOWELS.

258. Before the front vowels *e* and *i* the velar stops *k* and *g* were drawn forward, early in the Empire or before, into a mediopalatal position—*k', g'*. *G* seems to have been attracted sooner than *k*: in Sardinian we find *k* before *e* or *i* preserved as a stop while *g* is not—*kelu, kena, kera, kima, kircare, deghe* < *decem, nŏghe* < *nucem*, but *reina*, etc.

In Central Sardinia, Dalmatia, and Illyria *k'* went no further, and in Sicily, southern Italy, and Dacia the *k'* stage was apparently kept longer than in most regions: *Lat. Spr.* 472.

259. *G'* by the fourth century had become præpalatal and had opened into *y*, both in popular and in clerical Latin: *Gerapolis* for *Hierapolis, Per.* 61, 3; *"calcostegis* non *calcosteis," App. Pr.;* CON.GI.GI = *conjugi*, S. 349; *geiuna = jejuna*, Stolz 275, Neumann 5, *Lat. Spr.* 473; GENVARIVS, S. 239; GENARIVS, Pirson 75; *agebat = aiebat, Ienubam = Genavam, ingens = iniens*, Bon. 173; *agebat = aiebat, agere = aiere*, Sepulcri 205; *Gepte, Tragani, Troge*, Haag 33; *iesta*, D'Arbois 10. Before this happened, *frĭgĭdus* in most of the Empire had become *frigdus* (*App. Pr., "frigida* non *fricda"*), *vĭgĭlat* had become *viglat, and *dĭgĭtŭs* in some places had become *dĭctus* (*Franz.* ⸘ I, 15–16): cf. § 233.

This *y*, when it was intervocalic, fused, in nearly all the Empire, with the following *e* or *i* if this vowel was stressed: *magĭster* > *mayister > *maester;* so **pa(g)é(n)sis, re(g)ina, vi-(g)ínti*, etc.; similarly perhaps the proclitic *ma(g)is*. Cf. *Agrientum*, βειεντι = *viginti*, μαειστρο, etc., *Vok.* II, 461 (cf. *maestati, Vok.* II, 460); *trienta*, S. 349, Pirson 97; *quarranta = quadraginta*, Pirson 97; *æliens, colliens, diriens, negliencia*, Haag 34; *recolliendo*, etc., F. Diez, *Grammaire des langues romanes* I, 250. After the accent, and after a consonant, the *y* regularly remained, except when analogy forced its disappearance (as in *colliens* through *colliente, etc.): *légit, léges, plángit, argéntum*. But sometimes it fused with a following *i* in proparoxytones: *roitus* (= *rógitus* = *rogátus*), *Vok.* II, 461.

Spain, a part of southwestern Gaul, and portions of Sardinia, Sicily, and southwestern Italy remained at the *y* stage; elsewhere the *y* developed further in the Romance languages. Cf. *Lat. Spr.* 473.[1]

---

[1] Some light is thrown on the later *clerical* pronunciation by a statement in a fragment of a tenth century treatise on Latin pronunciation, Thurot 77, to the effect *g* has "its own sound" (i. e., that of English *g* in *gem*) before *e* and *i*, but is "weak" before other vowels.

260. *K'* as early as the third century must have had nearly everywhere a front, or præpalatal, articulation: *k'ęntu, duk'ere.* The next step was the development of an audible glide, a short *y*, between the *k'* and the following vowel: *k'yęntu, duk'yere.* By the fifth century the *k'* had passed a little further forward and the *k'y* had become *t'y: t'yęntu, dut'yere.* Through a modification of this glide the group then, in the sixth or seventh century, developed into *t's'* or *ts: t's'ęntu* or *tsęntu.*

Speakers were apparently unaware of the phenomenon until the assibilation was complete. There is no mention of it by the earlier grammarians: S. 340. In the first half of the third century some writers distinguish *ce, ka,* and *qu,* apparently as præpalatal, mediopalatal, and postpalatal; in the fifth century we find BINTCENTE, INTCITAMENTO: P. E. Guarnerio in *Supplementi all' Archivio glottologico italiano* IV (1897), 21–51 (cf. *Rom.* XXX, 617). S. 348 cites FES[IT], PAZE (6th or 7th century). Cf. *Vok.* I, 163. Frankish *tins* (German *zins*) is from *census,* borrowed probably in the fifth century: F. G. Mohl, *Zs.* XXVI, 595.[1]

Sc was palatalized also: *crēscĕre, co(g)nōscĕre, fascem, nascĕre, pĭscem,* etc. Cf. CONSIENSIA, SEPTRVM, S. 348.

261. For a discussion of the subject, see H. Schuchardt, *Vok.* I, 151, and *Ltbl.* XIV, 360; G. Paris in *Journal des savants,* 1900, 359, in the *Annuaire de l'École pratique des Hautes-Études,* 1893, 7, in the *Comptes rendus des séances de l'Académie des Inscriptions,* 1893, 81, and in *Rom.* XXXIII, 322; P. Marchot, *Petite phonétique du français prélittéraire,* 1901, 51–53; W. Meyer-Lübke in *Einf.* 123–126, in *Lat.*

---

[1] In the school pronunciation of the seventh and eighth centuries *c* before *e* and *i* was probably *ts.* In the treatise cited in the preceding note, Thurot 77, it is stated that *c* has "its own sound" before *e* and *i,* and is almost like *q* before other vowels.

Spr. 472, in *Bausteine zur romanischen Philologie* 313 ff.; Carnoy 155–160 (who puts the assibilation in the sixth century and earlier). For a possible indication, through alliteration, of a local assibilation of *c* as early as the second century, see *Archiv* XV, 146.

262. For *c̨e*, *c̨i*, see Palatals below.

(2) C AND G BEFORE BACK VOWELS.

263. *K* and *g* before vowels not formed in the front of the mouth usually remained unchanged: *canis, gustus, pacare, negare.* See, however, § 256. Inasmuch as *a* had in Gaul a front pronunciation (§ 194), *ka, ga* in most of that country became *k'a, g'a*, probably by the end of the seventh century, and then developed further: *carum* > Fr. *cher, gamba* > Fr. *jambe.*

Intervocalic *g* before the accent fell in many words in all or a part of the Empire, and apparently remained — perhaps under learned or under analogical influence — in others: AVSTVS from the second century on, Carnoy 127 (cf. AVSTE, S. 349); FRVALITAS, S. 349; so *leālis, *liāmen, *reālis (for *realis* in *Gl. Reich.*, see *Zs.* XXX, 50); so, too, the proclitic *eo* for *ego*, found about the sixth century, *Vok.* I, 129 (other examples in manuscripts, *Franz.* 2 II, 242–243). But *ligāre, něgāre, pagānus.*

(3) C AND G FINAL AND BEFORE CONSONANTS.

264. At the end of a word the guttural seems to have been regularly preserved in Vulgar Latin: *dīc, dūc, ecce hīc, eccu'hāc, fac, hŏc, sīc;* cf. Italian *dimmi* (< *dīc mī*), *fammi* (< *fac mī*), *siffatto* (< *sīc factum*).

Occasionally, however, the *c* must have been lost, — mainly, no doubt, through assimilation to a following initial consonant: FA for *fac*, *Zs.* XXV, 735. In late texts *nec* is often written *ne* before a consonant, and there is a confusion of *si* and *sic: Franz.* ? II, 215-224, 236-240.

265. Before another consonant *k* and *g* were for the most part kept through the Vulgar Latin period: *actus, oclus; frigdus,* *viglat (§ 233).

For *kw = qu*, see § 254. For *ks = x*, see § 255.

266. *Kt* in some parts of Italy was assimilated into *tt* by the beginning of the fourth century, in the south even in the first century: FATA, OTOGENTOS, in Pompeii, *Lat. Spr.* 476; AVTOR, LATTVCÆ (301 A. D.), OTOBRIS (380 A. D.), PRÆFETTO, etc., S. 348; *App. Pr.*, "*auctor* non *autor*"; Festus, "*dumecta* antiqui quasi *dumecita* appellabant quæ nos *dumeta*," S. 348.

The Celts perhaps pronounced the Latin *ct* as χ*t* from the beginning, inasmuch as their own *ct* had become χ*t* (e. g., Old Irish *ocht-n* corresponding to Latin *octo*, Windisch 394, 398-399); and likewise substituted χ*s* for *ks:* *faχtum > Fr. *fait*, *eχsīre > Pr. *eissir.* Cf. *Einf.* § 186, *Gram.* I, § 650. The resultant phenomena can, however, be explained otherwise: Suchier 735.

267. *Nkt* became *ŋt*, which seems to have been assimilated into *nt* in parts of the Empire, probably by the first century. *defuntus, regnancte, sante, Lat. Spr.* 472; *santo*, S. 278; *cuntis, santus*, Carnoy 172.

There is reason to believe, however, that the *ŋ* was retained very generally in Gaul and perhaps some other regions, and subsequently drawn forward to the præpalatal position—*n':* *sanctum* > Fr., Pr. *saint, sanh*, etc.

268. *Gm* became *um: fraumenta, fleuma, Lat. Spr.* 472; *App. Pr.* "*pegma* non *peuma*" (i.e., πῆγμα); St. Isidore, "*sagma* quæ corrupte vulgo *sauma* [or *salma*] dicitur" (i.e., σάγμα), S. 327. Cf. Italian *sǫma;* and also *salma*, which comes from *sauma* as *calma* from καῦμα. *Soma* occurs in *Gl. Reich.*

269. *Gn* was variously treated in different regions, being preserved in some, assimilated into *n'* or *n* in others, and subjected to still further modifications: *rænante, renum*, Haag 34. Cf. *Lat. Spr.* 476.

In *cognōsco* the *g* generally disappeared, the word being decomposed—after the fall of initial *g* in *gnosco*—into *co-* and *nōsco;* similarly the *g* was sometimes lost in *cognatus: Vok.* I, 115-116, *connato, cunnuscit*, etc.

270. *Gr*, between vowels, in popular words apparently became *r* in parts of the Empire: *fra(g)rare, intĕ(g)rum, nĭ(g)rum, pere(g)rīnum, pĭ(g)rĭtia.*

c. PALATALS.

271. Latin *j* was pronounced *y*, being identical in sound with the consonant that developed out of *ę* and *į* (§ 224): *jam, conjux, cūjus; ęāmus, habęam, tĕnęat, fīlįa, vĕnįo.* Instead of *i* (=*j*) the spelling *ii* was often used: *coiiugi, eiius*, Neumann, *Fortsetzung* 7.

When *y* followed a consonant, that consonant was often more or less assimilated, sometimes entirely absorbed by the *y*. Palatalization was commonest in Gaul, rarest in Dacia.

272. *Dy* and *gy*, in the latter part of the Empire, probably were reduced to *y* in vulgar speech: *deŏrsum, dĭūrnus; adjutare, audįam, gaudįum, hŏdįe, ŏdįum, pŏdįum, vĭdęam; exagįum, fagęus.* Compare OZE = *hodie* (S. 323) and Ζουλεία = *Julia* (Eckinger 80); ZACONVS = *diaconus*, etc. (S. 324) and ZESV = *Jesu*, ZVNIOR = *junior* (S. 239). Cf. *ajutit* = *adjutet*, Pirson 76; *madias* = *maias*, 364 A.D., Stolz 275, Pirson 75, Carnoy

162; *madio = maio*, Haag 34; *magias = maias*, Carnoy 162, S. 349; *juria = jurgia*, Σεριος = *Sergius*, Carnoy 161; *aios* = ἅγιος, *Vok.* II, 461; *Congianus = Condianus*, Carnoy 162; *corridiæ = corrigiæ*, *Remidium = Remigium*, Haag 34; *anoget* = *inodiat, *Gl. Reich*.

Dẹ, dị, however, towards the end of the Empire, had another — doubtless more elegant — pronunciation, which was probably *dz: pŏdium* > It. *pọggio,* but *mĕdium* > It. *mẹzzo.* Servius *in Virg. Georg.* II, 216, says, "*Media, di* sine sibilo proferenda est, græcum enim nomen est," S. 320. St. Isidore writes, "solent Itali dicere *ozie* pro *hodie*," S. 321. The letter *Z* is often used in inscriptions, but we generally cannot tell whether it means *dy, y,* or *dz* (cf. § 339): zes = *dies,* S. 323; ζιε = *die*, Audollent 537; zogenes, S. 324; cf. *sacritus* = διάκριτος, Waters Ch. 63.

In most words the vulgar *y* prevailed, in others — especially in Italy — the cultivated *dz;* from *radius* Italian has both *raggio* and *razzo.* The *dz* pronunciation was especially favored after a consonant: *hŏrdeum* > It. *ọrzo, prandium* > It. *pranzo.*

273. It appears that the labials were not regularly assimilated in Vulgar Latin: *sapiam* > It. *sappia,* Pr. *sapcha,* etc. But through the analogy of *audio* > **auyo, video* > **veyo,* etc., and perhaps through slurring due to constant and careless use, *habeo, dēbeo* often became **ayo,* **deyo:* cf. It. *aggio, deggio,* beside *abbio, debbio.* The reduced forms generally prevailed, but not everywhere. For *plŭvia* a form *plŏja was substituted in most of the Empire: cf. §§ 169, 208,(4).

274. *Ly, ny,* between vowels, probably became *l', n'* before the end of the Empire: *fīlius, fŏlia, mĕlius, palea, tĭlia; Hispania, tĕneat, vĕniam.* This palatal pronunciation may be represented by the spellings *Aureia, Corneius, fiios,* etc., S. 327

Lly, *ll'g'*, *l'g'* were probably reduced to *l'* somewhat later: *allium, malleus; cŏllĭgit; ex-ēlĭgit.*

Oleum, from ἔλαιον, is an exception: cf. It., Sp. *olio*, Pg. *oleo*, Pr. *oli*, Fr. *huile;* the foreign words borrowed from Latin *oleum* indicate the same irregularity.

For *ry*, see § 296.

275. *Sy*, between vowels, doubtless became during the Vulgar Latin period *s'*, a sound similar to English *sh* in *ship: basium, caseus, mansiōnem*, etc.

Ssy, *scy*, *sty* were generally assimilated later: **bassiare, fascia, pŏstea*. Cf. *consiensia*, Pirson 72.

For the confusion of *sy* and *ty*, see § 277.

276. *Cy* and *ty*, in the second and third centuries, were very similar in sound, being respectively *k'y* and *t'y* (cf. Fr. *Riquier* and *pitié* in popular speech), and hence were often confused: Ἀρονκιανός = *Aruntianus*, 131 A.D., Eckinger 99; TERMINA-CIONES (2d century), *concupiscencia* (an acrostic in Commodian), *justicia* (in an edict of Diocletian), many examples in Gaul in the 5th century, *Lat. Spr.* 475; *defeniciones* (222-235 A.D.), *ocio* (389 A.D.), *staacio* (601 A.D.), *tercius*, S. 323; *oracionem* (601 A.D.), *tercia*, Pirson 71; *mendatium, servicium*, etc. Bon. 171; especially common in Gallic inscriptions of the seventh century, Stolz 51. Cf. *Vok.* I, 150 ff.; Densusianu 111.

In later school pronunciation *cy* and *ty* were sounded alike. According to Albinus (S. 321) "*benedictio* et *oratio* et talia *t* debent habere in pænultima syllaba, non *c*." In the treatise published by Thurot (see footnote to § 259), p. 78, we are told that *ti*, unless preceded by *s*, is pronounced like *c*, as in *etiam, prophetia, quatio, silentium; ti*, furthermore, is confused with *ci*, the spelling *c* being prescribed in *amicicia, avaricia, duricia, justicia, leticia, malicia, pudicicia*, etc., also in *nuncius, ocium, spacium, tercius*. Cf. *Gl. Reich.: audatia, speties, sotium; ambicio, inicio, spacio, tristicia*, etc.

This similarity or identity of sound led, in some cases, either locally or in the whole Empire, to the substitution of suffixes and to other permanent transfers of words from one class to the other: cf. Carnoy 151-154. Hence arose numerous double forms: *condicio conditio, solacium solatium;* later *avaritia –cia,* **cominitiare –ciare, servitium –cium*, etc.; so many proper names, *Anitius –cius*, etc., S. 324. Cf. A. Horning in *Zs.* XXIV, 545. This explains such seemingly anomalous developments as *exquartiare > It. *squarciare,* *gutteare > It. *gocciare*, etc. A number of words evidently had a popular pronunciation with *t'* and a school pronunciation with *k'*, or *vice versa:* cf. It. *comenzare cominciare*, etc.[1]

277. *T'y* developed sporadically in the second century, regularly by the fourth, into *ts* (cf. § 260): CRESCENTSIAN[VS], 140 A. D., S. 323; MARSIANESSES = *Martianenses*, 3d century, Carnoy 154; ZODORYS = *Theodorus*, etc., S. 324, *Vok.* I, 68; *ampitzatru, Vincentzus,* Audollent 537. Servius *in Don.* (S. 320) says, "Iotacismi sunt quotiens post *ti–* vel *di–* syllabam sequitur vocalis, et plerumque supradictæ syllabæ in sibilum transeunt." Papirius, cited by Cassiodorus (S. 320): "*Justitia* cum scribitur, tertia syllaba sic sonat quasi constet ex tribus litteris, *t, z,* et *i*"; he goes on to state that it is always so when *ti* is followed by a vowel other than *i* (as in *Tatius, otia,* but not in *otii, justitii*), except in foreign proper names or after *s* (as in *justius, castius*). Pompeius says the same thing at considerable length, adding (S. 320), "si dicas *Titius*, pinguius sonat et perdit sonum suum et accipit sibilum." Consentius

---
[1] For a different explanation of the Italian and Rumanian developments, see S. Puşcariu, *Lateinisches ti und ki im Rumänischen, Italienischen und Sardischen.* 1904; reviewed in *Ltbll*. XXVII, 64.

mentions the assibilation in *etiam*, St. Isidore in *justitia:* S. 320–321. Welsh words borrowed from Latin before the fourth century show no assibilation; but names in *–tiacum*, carried into Brittany in the second half of the fifth century, are assibilated (e.g., *Metiacus* > *Messac*).

At an intermediate stage between *ty* and *ts* — say *t′s′y* — the group, if the *t′* was rather weak, was easily confused with *sy*. Examples are very numerous: OBSERVASIONE, 5th century, S. 323, Pirson 71; *diposisio = depositio*, *hocsies*, *sepsies*, 6th century, S. 323; *tersio*, Pirson 71; cf. *Vok.* I, 153. Clerical usage for a while doubtless favored *sy* for *ty*, and many words have preserved it in various regions, especially in suffixes: *palatium –sium*, *pretium –sium*, *ratio –sio*, *statio –sio*, *servitium –sium*, etc.; hence Italian *palagio* beside *palazzo*, etc., and *–igia* beside *–ezza* from *–ĭtia*. Cf. *Ltblt.* XXVII, 65; *Rom.* XXXV, 480.

278. *K′y* was assibilated sporadically in the third century, but not regularly until the fifth or sixth, after the assibilation of *t′y* was completed: Μαρσιανός = *Marcianus*, 225 A. D., Eckinger 103; *judigsium*, 6th century, Carnoy 154; so *facio, glacies, placeam*, etc. The resulting sibilant was different from that which came from *t′y: faciam* > It. *faccia*, *vĭtium* > It. *vezzo*. But the intermediate stages were similar enough to lead to some confusion, and the ultimate products have become identical in many regions.

279. For *k′, g′*, not followed by *y*, see Gutturals.

d. DENTALS.

280. The dentals were pronounced with the middle of the tongue arched up and the tip touching the gums or teeth, as in modern French, and not as in English: S. 301–302, 307.

281. *D* regularly remained unchanged: *dare, perdo, modus, quid.*

Oscan and Umbrian had *nn* corresponding to Latin *nd:* Sittl 37. There is some indication that this pronunciation was locally adopted in Latin: AGENNÆ, VERECVNNVS, etc., S. 311–312; "*grundio* non *grunnio*," *App. Pr.* If this was the case, the central and southern Italian *nn* for *nd* (as *quannu* for *quando*) may go back to ancient times: *Lat. Spr.* 476.

(1) Occasionally *d* > *l:* old *dacruma* > *lacrima; App. Pr.*, "*adipes* non *alipes*." Cf. Liquids. Cf. § 289, (3).

(2) In a few words *d* > *r: medidies* by dissimilation > *meridies;* ARVORSVM = *adversum*, S. 311; Consentius blames "*peres* pro *pedes*," S. 311. The cases seem to be sporadic and due to different special causes.

282. At the end of a word there was hesitation between *d* and *t; d* may have been devocalized before a voiceless initial consonant, and possibly at the end of a phrase: APVD APVT, S. 365; *capud* in Gregory the Great; FECIT FECED, etc., S. 365; INQVID, SET, etc., S. 366–367; *aput, quot, set*, Carnoy 180. Some of the confusion was doubtless due to the fall of both *d* and *t:* see § 285.

In proclitics assimilation naturally went further, as we may infer from the treatment of the prefix *ad*–*:* people probably said not only *at te* (cf. *attendere*) but sometimes *ar Romam (cf. *arripere*). So the final consonant eventually often disappeared. Cf. S. 358–359. Grammarians warn against the confusion of *ad* and *at*, etc., S. 365–366. Cf. *ad eos* and *at ea*, etc., Carnoy 179–180; *id it, quid quit*, Carnoy 180; *a, quo* and *co*, Haag 29.

Illud, through the analogy of other neuters, became *illum*: Haag 29, *illum corpus*, etc.

283. Intervocalic *d*, perhaps at the end of the Vulgar Latin period, became *ð* in Spain, Gaul, Rætia, northern Italy, and a part of Sardinia: *vĭdēre* > *veðere. Similarly intervocalic *dr*,

either at the same time or later, became ðr in Spain and Gaul: *quadro* > *quaðro.

In *quadraginta*, *dr* > *rr*: *quarranta*, Pirson 97.

284. *T* usually remained unchanged: *těneo*, *sĭtis*, *partem*, *facit*.

Tl, however, seems to have regularly become *cl*: *astŭla* > Pr. *ascla*; *stloppus* > *scloppus > It. *schioppo*; *ustulare* > Pr. *usclar*. Cf. SCLIT· and SCLITIB· (from *stlis stlitis*), S. 312–313; Caper, "*Martulus* ... non *Marculus*," "*stlataris* sine *c* littera dicendum," Keil VII, 105, 107; *App. Pr.*, "*capitulum* non *capiclum*," "*vetulus* non *veclus*," "*vitulus* non *viclus*." For –*tulus* > –*clus*, cf. § 234.

Between *s* and *l* a *t* developed: Caper, "*pessulum* non *pestulum*" (hence Italian *pestio*, etc.), S. 315. So probably *insŭla* > *isla > *istla > *iscla > It. *Ischia*.

285. Final *t* fell in Volscian (*fasia* = *faciat*), often in Umbrian (*habe*), occasionally in Faliscan: Hammer 5, 7, 8. In early dialects we find such forms as CVPA, DEDE: S. 367. In Latin, final *t* disappeared early in the Empire in southern Italy, and during the Empire in most of Italy and Dacia; Rumanian, Italian (except Sardinian), and also Spanish and Portuguese show no trace of final *t* except in monosyllables. Cf. Hammer 28–32. The first sure examples of the fall in Latin are found in Pompeii; others appear later in the inscriptions in Christian Rome and northern Italy, as *ama*, *peria*, *relinque*, *valia*, *vixi*, etc.: S. 367–368, *Lat. Spr.* 472. Gaul, Rætia, and Sardinia kept the *t* late; but forms without the consonant (as *audivi*, *posui*) — possibly due to Italian stonecutters — occur in Gallic inscriptions. Fredegarius wrote *e* for *et*: Haag 29.

Final *nt* perhaps lost its *t* before consonants: *Lat. Spr.*

473–474. The Romance languages show forms with *nt*, with *n*, and without either consonant. *Nt*, in general, is preserved in the same regions as *t*. In inscriptions we find: *dedro* and *dedrot*, in Pisaurum, S. 365; *posuerun, restituerun*, Lat. Spr. 473–474. Cf. Lindsay 124.

Final *st*, likewise, may have lost its *t* before consonants — as *post illum* but *pos' me, est amatus* but *es' portatus: Lat. Spr.* 473. *Pos* is very common in inscriptions, and *es* is found: S. 368. Cf. *pos, posquam* in R. 470. According to Velius Longus, Cicero favored *posmeridianus;* Marius Victorinus preferred *posquam:* S. 368. Both *st* and *s* are represented in the Romance languages.

For the confusion of final *d* and *t*, see § 282: *capud, feced, inquid* are found. When *t* did not fall, it was doubtless often voiced, inside a phrase, before a vowel or a voiced consonant.

Caput became *capus* (Pirson 238) or *capum. Fredegarius uses *capo:* Haag 29.

286. Intervocalic *t* was voiced to *d* in Spain, Gaul, Rætia, and northern Italy probably in the fifth or sixth century: cf. § 256. Inscriptions show a few such forms as *amadus*, S. 309. Such a spelling as *retere* for *reddere* (S. 309) may indicate uncertainty in the use of *d* and *t*.

Later this $d > ð$ in northern Gaul and Spain. In Gaul and Spain, moreover, $tr > dr > ðr$. Cf. § 283.

e. LIQUIDS.
(1) *L*.

287. *L* had a convex formation, like *d* and *t* (cf. § 280): S. 306–307, 309.

288. Priscian I, 38 (S. 324) writes: "*L* triplicem, ut Plinio videtur, sonum habet: exilem, quando geminatur secundo loco posita, ut *il-le*, *Metel-lus;* plenum, quando finit nomina vel syllabas et quando aliquam habet ante se in eadem syllaba consonantem, ut *sol, silva, flavus, clarus;* medium in aliis, ut *lectus, lectum*." Consentius distinguishes the "sonus exilis," which he ascribes to initial and double *l* (as in *lana, ille*), from the "pinguis," heard *before* a consonant (as in *albo, alga*, etc.): S. 326. Other grammarians blame, in obscure terms, a faulty pronunciation of *l* particularly prevalent in Africa or Greece: S. 325–326. See also *Zs.* XXX, 648.

It is likely that *l* before or after another consonant had a thick sound caused by lifting the back of the tongue. *Before* consonants, this formation led in some regions, sporadically by the fourth century but regularly not until the eighth and ninth and later (*Lat. Spr.* 476), to the vocalization of *l* into *u:* κανκουλατῳ in an edict of Diocletian, 301 A.D., Eckinger 12; *cauculus* in manuscripts, *Vok.* II, 494. *After* consonants, this elevation, shifted forwards, brought about the palatalization of *l* in Spanish and Italian: *clavem* > *kl'ave* > Sp. *llave*, It. *chiave*.

According to H. Osthoff, *Dunkles und helles* l *im Lateinischen* in the *Transactions of the American Philological Association* XXIV, 50, intervocalic *l*, except before *i*, also had the thick sound — as in *famulus* (but not in *similis*): thus is explained the different fate of *a* in *calēre* > Old Fr. *chaloir* and *gallīna* > Old Fr. *geline*, etc.

289. During the Latin period *l* regularly remained unchanged: *lūna, altus, mīlle, sōl.* It seems to have fallen in *tribūnal.*

For *ll* > *l*, see § 161. For *ly*, see § 274. For *sl* > *stl, skl,* see § 284.

(1) Metathesis occurs occasionally: Consentius (S. 327) blames "*coacla* pro *cloaca*," "*displicina* pro *disciplina*": cf. *fabŭla* > **flaba* > It. *fiaba*, etc.

(2) There are sporadic examples of the dissimilation of two *l*'s:

App. Pr., "*flagellum* non *fragellum*," "*cultellum* non *cuntellum*"; cf. MVNTV for *multum*, *C. I. L.* IV, 1593. Cf. S. 327.

(3) Marius Victorinus (Keil VI, 8) says: "Gn. Pompejus Magnus et scribebat et dicebat *kadamitatem* pro *calamitate*." Cf. § 281, (1).

(2) *R*.

290. *R* in Classic and Vulgar Latin was probably a gingival or præpalatal trill: S. 307, 309, 328. It generally resisted change: *rīdet, carrus, cŭrsus, pater*.

291. In many words, however, *rs* > *ss*. The principle seems to have been that original *rs* remained, while old *rss*, coming from *rtt*, was early reduced to *ss*: *Lat. Spr.* 471. Velius Longus says (S. 330): "*Dossum* per duo *s* quam per *r* quidam ut lenius enuntiaverunt, ac tota *r* littera sublata est in eo quod est *rusum* et *retrosum*." *Russum rusum, susum* occur in early writers; *dextrosus, introsus, rúsus, suso, susum*, etc., in inscriptions: S. 330. *App. Pr.* has *pessica; Gl. Reich.* has *iusū* = *deorsum*. The assimilation was not consistently carried out everywhere, being probably somewhat hindered by school influence. It took place in the whole territory in *deōrsum* and *sūrsum;* in most of the Empire in *dŏrsum;* in about half the Empire in *pĕrsĭca;* locally in *aliōrsum, retrōrsum, revĕrsus, vĕrsus*.

After long vowels the *ss* > *s* (see § 161); so *sūssum* > *sūsum*, while *dŏssum* remained unchanged: *susum*, Waters Ch. 77; *suso susu susum*, Bechtel 83; *susum* very common, R. 460–461; *diosum*, R. 460. Cf. Corssen I, 243.

292. Moreover, there was a strong tendency to dissimilate two *r*'s, although it was only sporadically carried out: in Old Latin, *-aris* after *r* > *-alis*, as in *floralis; App. Pr.*, "*terebra* non *telebra*"; in inscriptions we find repeatedly *pelegrinus*

(Sittl 74), also *ministorum, perpenna = Perperna, propietas, propio,* S. 329; *albor, coliandrum, criblare, flagrare, meletrix, plurigo* are attested likewise, *Lat. Spr.* 477. Pompeius (S. 329) says: "Barbarismus, quando dico *mamor* pro eo quod est *marmor.*" Cf. Italian *propio, dietro drieto.*

293. Velius Longus (S. 329) tells us that in elegant speech *per* before *l* was pronounced *pel*, as in *pellabor, pellicere.* Cf. PELLIGE, etc., S. 329. So Italian *per lo > pello, averlo >* (in Old It.) *avello*. This assimilation was probably not widespread in Latin; it has left very few traces in the Romance languages. Cf. Italian *Carlo, merlo, orlo, perla,* etc.

294. Metathesis is not uncommon: S. 330–331. Consentius mentions "*perlum* pro *prælum*," S. 330. *Crocodilus* appears as *corcodilus, cocodrilus, corcodrillus,* S. 331; cf. Italian *coccodrillo.* S. 330 notes PRANCATI. For *quatro,* **sempre,* etc., see § 245.

An intrusive *r* is found in *culcitra*, Waters Ch. 38.

295. Final *r*, except in monosyllables, fell, probably before the end of the Vulgar Latin period, in most of Italy and Dacia: *sŏror >* It. *suora*, Rum. *soaru*. Sittl 11 mentions an early fall of final *r* among the Falisci and the Marsi, as in *mate, uxo;* cf. FRATE, MATE.

296. *Ry* was probably preserved through the Vulgar Latin period, although it may have been reduced to *y* in parts of Italy: *cŏrium >* *cọryu and possibly *cọyu (cf. It. *cuọio*).

f. SIBILANTS.

297. *S* seems to have been dental, with the upper surface of the tongue convex (cf. § 280): S. 302, 304, 307–308.

The old voiced *s* having become *r* (S. 314–315), Classic Latin *s* was probably always voiceless and remained so in

Vulgar Latin (S. 302-304): this is indicated by the fact that intervocalic *s* is still generally surd in Spanish (*casa*, etc.) and in most popular words in Tuscan (*naso*, etc.); corroborative evidence, as far as it goes, is furnished by such spellings as *nupsi, pleps, urps*, also *maximus, rexi*, etc., and the development of a *p* in such words as *hiemps, sumpsi*. At the very end of the Vulgar Latin period, however, intervocalic *s* may have become voiced in some regions (cf. § 256): *causa, mīsi*, etc.[1]

Classic Latin *s* was generally preserved: *sĕx, ŏssum, cŭrsus, ĭste*.

298. Final *s* often fell in Umbrian (*kumate*), and occasionally in Faliscan: Hammer 5, 8. Cf. Sittl 27, who cites Umbrian PISAVRESE. In early Latin final *s* was very weak after *ŭ* and *ĭ*, and often was not written. Cicero (*Lat. Spr.* 471) says the loss of *-s* is "subrusticum, olim autem politius." Quintilian also (S. 361) notes the omission of *-s* by the ancients. Ennius and his followers down to Catullus did not count *-s* before a consonant in verse: S. 355-356. Cf. Pompeius (Keil V, 108): "*S* littera hanc habet potestatem, ut ubi opus fuerit excludatur de metro." In the older inscriptions *-s* is freely omitted, but later it is in the main correctly used until the second century of our era: *Lat. Spr.* 471. The omission is commonest in nominative *-ŏs* or *-ŭs*, but occurs also in *-ĭs* and *-ăs*, rarely in *-ās*: *bonu, Cornelio, nepoti, pieta, Terentio, unu*, etc., and *matrona* for *matronas*, S. 361-362. According to *Chronologie* 175-186, the nominative singular without *s* (as *Cornelio, filio*) predominated in central Italy until the time of Cæsar, when *-s* was partially restored; but by 150 to 200 A. D. the forms without *s* became common

---

[1] In the previously cited Latin treatise (see footnote to § 259), Thurot 77, *s* between vowels is described as "weak," except in compounds, such as *resolvit*. This evidently indicates a voicing in late school pronunciation.

again, and prevailed in central Italy in the third century (*eio* for *ejus*, *liberio*, etc.). Cf. *morbu* = *morbus*, etc., Audollent 539, 540; *filio* = *filios*, *C. I. L.* IX, 1938. In most of Italy, and probably in Dacia, final *s* disappeared for good from the common pronunciation in the second and third centuries, (except in monosyllables)(*Lat. Spr.* 471): *amātis* > It. *amate*, *sĕntīs* > It. *senti*, *tĕmpus* > It. *tempo*; but *das* > It. *dai*, *tres* > Old It. *trei* (later *tre*). Cf. Hammer 19-28, Densusianu 122-123.

In Gaul, Spain, and some other regions, *-s*, probably owing to the previous linguistic habits of the natives, was strongly pronounced and therefore preserved. Carnoy 185-206 records the omission of *-s* in many inscriptions, but notes that as this nearly always happens at the end of a line it is doubtless only a conventional abbreviation.

299. According to Velius Longus (S. 316), *trans-* became *tra-* before *d, j*, and sometimes before *m* and *p*: *traduxit*, *trajecit*; *tra(ns)misit*, *tra(ns)posuit*; *transtulit*. We sometimes find, however, *transduco* and *transjicio*. Both forms occur before *l* and *v*: *tra(ns)luceo*, *tra(ns)veho*.

Italy generally favored *tra-* (but *trasporre*), Gaul and Spain usually preferred *tras-* (but *traduire*, *traducir*).

300. In *presbÿter*, a new nominative constructed from πρεσ-βύτερος, the *s* fell in Italy and elsewhere through the substitution of the prefix *præ-* (as in *præbĭtor*) for the unusual initial *pres-*: hence It. *prete*, Pr. *preveire* (< *præbÿtĕrum*).

301. For prosthetic *i* or *e* before *s* + consonant, see § 230. In Old French *pasmer* (from *spasmus*) the *s* was lost probably through confusion with *es-* coming from the prefix *ex-*.

302. For *ss* > *s*, see § 161. For *sy*, see § 275. For assibilation, see Gutturals and Palatals. For *z*, see § 246 and Greek Consonants.

g. NASALS.

303. *N*, like *d* and *t* (§ 280), was dental or gingival, with an arched tongue: S. 269–270.

M and *n*, initial and intervocalic, regularly remained unchanged: *mĕus, nŏster, amat, vĕnit*. For the reduction of *mĭnus–* to *mis–*, see § 245. There was a dissimilation of two *n*'s in *Bononia* > It. *Bologna*.

304. *M* and *n*, final or followed by a consonant, were obscure and weak in Classic Latin; the preceding vowel must have been partly nasalized, and the mouth closure incomplete. According to Priscian (S. 275), "*m* obscurum in extremitate dictionum sonat, ut *templum*, apertum in principio, ut *magnus*, mediocre in mediis, ut *umbra*." Terentianus Maurus (S. 275) says that for *n* the air comes through both nose and mouth. So Marius Victorinus (S. 275): "*N* vero sub convexo palati lingua inhærente gemino naris et oris spiritu explicabitur." The same author describes (S. 275) a sound between *m* and *ṅ*: "Omnes fere aiunt inter *m* et *n* litteras mediam vocem quæ non abhorreat ab utraque littera sed neutram proprie exprimat." Cf. S. 276.

305. In Classic Latin the nasal naturally took before labials the form of *m;* before dentals, *n;* before *f* and *v*, probably first *m*, then *n*, as the pronunciation of these fricatives changed from bilabial to dentilabial (cf. § 320); before gutterals, *ŋ: combura, immitto, imperio; conduco, contineo, innocens; comfluo confluo, comvenio convenio; anguis, inquit, uncus* (cf. IVNCXI, NVNCQVAM, S. 278). Cf. S. 270, 279–280. The *ŋ* — or "*n* adulterinum"— is described by Nigidius (in Gellius), and also by Priscian, as between *n* and *g* (S. 275); cf. S. 269–270, 272. Before liquids the nasal was assimilated (*colligo, corrigo*, etc.), before *s* it was silent (*cosul*, etc.: cf. §§ 171, 311).

Final nasals seem to have been adapted, like medial nasals, to a following consonant: *nom paret, cun dūce, nom* or *non·fēcit, iŋ carne; nol lĕgo, cur rēgibus, i senātu.* Cicero advocated *cun nobis;* Servius, *cun navibus: Lat. Spr.* 476. In inscriptions we find *cun, locun sanctum, nomem, quan floridos, quen,* S. 364; cf. *forsitam mille,* Bechtel 81 (*forsitam,* Carnoy 220).

306. In the vulgar speech of the Empire the sound before labials seems to have been indistinct, and even before dentals not always clear (S. 271–272); before *f* and *v* there was great uncertainty (cf. §§ 171, 311), and there was apparently some doubt before *gu* and *qu* (S. 272): this is indicated by such spellings as *senper, quamta, nynfis, nunquam,* S. 276–277; *conplere, decemter,* Carnoy 176; *tan mulieribus,* Carnoy 220. Cf. Carnoy 176–177. In both old and late inscriptions the nasal is often omitted altogether before a consonant: *Decebris, exeplu, occubas,* etc., *innoceti, laterna, secudo,* etc., *iferos,* etc., *defuctæ, pricipis, reliquat,* etc., S. 273, 281–285. For the change of *ŋkt* to *ŋt,* then to *nt,* see § 267: *santa,* etc., Pirson 92; *santo,* etc., frequent, S. 278.

The hesitation and inconsistency in spelling are certainly due in part to imperfect articulation, largely to mere carelessness in cutting, but in great measure also to the mistaken efforts of later writers to restore a real or hypothetical earlier orthography: compare the treatment of prefixes, § 32.

In late Vulgar Latin *m, n, ŋ* must have been reinforced, as there is little trace of confusion in the Romance languages.

307. *Mn* seems at one time to have been pronounced *m:* Quintilian (S. 286) says: "*Columnam* et *consules* exempta *n* littera legimus." Cf. Priscian (S. 275): "*N* quoque plenior in primis sonat et in ultimis partibus syllabarum, ut *nomen,* *stamen;* exilior in mediis, ut *amnis, damnum.*" Carnoy 166 has *Interamico,* for *-amn-,* from the first century.

Late inscriptions, on the other hand, show a fondness for such spellings as *calumpnia, dampnum* (cf. Bon. 189, *calumpnia, dampnare,* etc.); and *mpn* is common in the early Romance languages. It is likely that this orthography indicates a conscious and painful effort to articulate clearly. Toward the end of the Empire fashion evidently prescribed a distinct pronunciation of *mn,* counteracting a previous tendency to slur the group.

The Romance languages point to the preservation of *mn,* although it was probably assimilated into *nn* in central and southern Italy before the Empire was over (*Lat. Spr.* 476): *Interanniensis,* Carnoy 166.

308. Between *m* and *s* or *t* a *p* generally developed in Latin — that is to say, the latter part of the *m* was unvoiced and denasalized before the surd that followed; this *p* was not always written: *sum(p)si, sum(p)tus,* etc. Cf. S. 298.

309. Final *m* often fell in Umbrian (as in *puplu*), occasionally in Faliscan: Hammer 5, 8. In Old Latin it was weak: S. 356. It is often omitted in inscriptions down to 130 B. C., and again in late plebeian inscriptions; in the last century of the Republic and the first two centuries of the Empire the traditional spelling is carefully observed: early and late such forms as *dece, eoru, mecu, mense, septe, unu* are very common, and conversely forms with a superfluous *m,* S. 363-364; cf. Audollent 539-540, abundant examples; *App. Pr., ide, numqua, oli, passi, pride.* The omission of *-m* and the wrong use of it are very frequent in the *Per.: que ad modum, terra,* Bechtel 79; *jacente,* etc., *accedere,* etc., Bechtel 80; *dormito* for *dormitum,* Bechtel 91; cf. Bechtel 107. So R. 462,

ardente lucernam, etc. According to Quintilian (S. 362), Cato said *dice hanc;* he adds that there is scarcely any *m* audible in *tantum ille, quantum erat.*

Final *m* before vowels seems to have been, from early times, only a weak nasal glide: in *circueo* it disappears (S. 274), in poetry it may be disregarded (cf. *audiendu'st*, etc., S. 361). Before consonants it was assimilated (cf. TAN DVRVM, etc., S. 361): see § 305. Cf. S. 356–358, 360. Carnoy 206–221, who notes the omission of –*m* in many inscriptions under all possible conditions, reaches the conclusion that it became silent at the end of polysyllables by the first century, having disappeared very early before vowels, next before spirants and at the end of a phrase, then (by assimilation) before other consonants.

In the opinion of Schuchardt, *Vok.* I, 110–112, the preceding vowel was nasalized. The contrary view is maintained by Seelmann, 288–292. As the fall of *m* seems to have been due primarily to a failure to close the lips completely between two vowels, it is likely that the nasalization was slight.

The Romance languages point to a loss of –*m* in all words but monosyllables: *damnu(m), pŏssu(m), tĕnea(m)*; *cŭm, jam, quĕm* (*quen*, Audollent 537). Cf. Hammer 32–41.

310. Final *n* must have been indistinct (S. 358), but it seems to have been reinforced in Classic speech (S. 286). The prefix *con–* became *co–* before vowels, as in *coactum, cohærere, cohors, coicere:* S. 274, 282. Before *gn*, too, the final *n* of prefixes fell very early, as in *cognatus, cognosco, ignotus:* S. 274. Otherwise there is no sure proof of the fall of –*n* in Latin (S. 364–365), but there is abundant evidence of its assimilation to a following labial (IM BELLO, etc., S. 361): see § 305; cf. *Lat. Spr.* 473. For further assimilation, cf. Caper (Keil VII. 106), "*in Siciliam* dicendum, non *is Siciliam*": see § 311.

§ 311]   AN INTRODUCTION TO VULGAR LATIN.   131

The Romance languages indicate the disappearance of $-n$, except in monosyllables: *nŏme(n)*, *sēme(n)*; *ĭn*, *nōn*. It probably fell late, after the Vulgar Latin period: *Lat. Spr.* 473. For final *nt*, see § 285.

311. Before fricatives or spirants *n* regularly fell, probably through nasalization of the preceding vowel: see § 171. This phenomenon was only partially recognized by Classic authority: *–ensĭmus > –ēsĭmus*, *–iens > –iēs*, *–onsus > –ōsus*, as in *vicesimus*, *toties*, *formosus* (S. 273); *ns*, however, was kept in participles, as *videns*, *mansus;* both forms were used in *–ē(n)sis* (according to Velius Longus, Cicero preferred *foresia*, *hortesia*, S. 287). Charisius (S. 286) records that "*mensam* sine *n* littera dictam Varro ait." Cf. Quintilian (S. 286), "*consules* exempta *n* littera legimus."

In popular speech the fall was probably constant from early times: *cesor*, *cojux*, *cosol*, *coventionid*, *iferos*, *infas*, *libes*, etc., S. 274, 281–285; Stolz 243 ff. Plautus repeatedly uses *mostrare*, Stolz 243. Terence seems to intend a rhyme in "neque pes neque mens," *Eunuchus* 728. Such forms are frequent in inscriptions: *cofecisse*, *cojectis*, *cojugi* (very common), *covenimus*, *ifer* (Capua, 387 A. D.), *iferi*, *ifimo*, *ifra*, *iventa*, *resurges* (on a coin of Vespasian's reign), S. 274, 281–285. So in Greek-letter inscriptions: κλήμης, κόζοῦς, etc., Eckinger 80, 113–115. Cf. Audollent 538, *iferi;* Carnoy 177, *cojugi*, etc., *mesis*, etc.; Pirson 94, *infas*, *remasit; App. Pr.*, "*ansa* non *asa*"; R. 461–462, *prægnas* repeatedly, *mesor messor = mensor*. Conversely, with a superfluous *n: fidens = fides*, *quiensces*, etc., S. 274, 285; *thensaurus*, Stolz 243; "*Hercules* non *Herculens*," "*occasio* non *occansio*," *App. Pr.; locuplens*, *occansio*, *thensaurus*, etc., R. 459.

Before *f*, *j*, *v*, the *n* was generally restored by analogy (see § 171); such words as *conjux*, *convenio* are really new formations: S. 274. The only sure Romance traces of the loss of *n* before these consonants in Latin are Italian *fante* and French *couvent*, although at a later date *nf* became *f* in Rætia and much of southern France.

Before *s*, the fall of *n* was permanent, and the only Romance words containing *ns* are learned terms or new formations: *mesa, mesis, pesat, sposus, tosus;* but *pensare*.

h. LABIALS.
(1) *P*.

312. *P* regularly remained unchanged: *pater, ŏpus, cŏrpus*.

(1) There was some sporadic confusion of *p* and *b*: BVBLICÆ, SCRIPIT, S. 299; *App. Pr.,* "*plasta* non *blasta*," "*ziziber* non *ziziper*"; *cannabis* and It. *canapa*.

313. In Italy and perhaps elsewhere there was a tendency to drop *p* between a consonant and an *s* or *t: redemti*, etc., Pirson 93; *scultor*, etc., S. 299.

In a part of Italy *ps* became *ss* as early as the first century: *isse* for *ipse* is found in Pompeii, and is attested by Martial and possibly by the *icse* for *ipse* mentioned by Suetonius, *Lat. Spr.* 476.

In central and southern Italy *pt* became *tt* probably early in the Empire: *scritus*, etc., S. 299; *settembres*, 7th century, Carnoy 165. In a part of Gaul *captīvus* seems to have been pronounced **caχtīvus:* it may be that in Gallic speech the *pt* of this word became χ*t*, as was the case with Celtic *pt* (Dottin 100; cf. Old Irish *secht-n* = *septem*, Windisch 394); or perhaps *captīvus* became first *cactīvus, under the influence of Celtic *cactos (Welsh *caeth*) = Latin *captus* (Loth 35).

314. Intervocalic *p* probably became *b* in the fifth and sixth centuries in Spain, Gaul, Rætia, and northern Italy: see § 256. Cf. Pirson 60–61: *labidem*, etc. *Pr* likewise became *br: Abrilis*, Pirson 61; *lebræ*, Bon. 160; *stubrum*, Haag 862.

In northern Gaul intervocalic *p* and *pr*, even in clerical Latin, developed through *b* and *br* into β and β*r* by the seventh century: *rivaticus*, 629 A. D., *Vok.* I, 128; *cavanna, Gl. Reich.*

For *pe̥, pi̥*, see § 273.

(2) *B*.

315. When *b* was not intervocalic, it usually remained unchanged: *bĕne, blĭtum, oblītus*.

Mb, as in Oscan and Umbrian, became *mm* in Sicily and southern and central Italy, the *mm* being found in inscriptions as far north as Rome: *Lat. Spr.* 476. Cf. *nd*, § 281.

Before *s* or *t* it is likely that *b* regularly became *p* in Latin, although it was often written *b: absens apsens, ab– apsolvere, plebs pleps, scribsi scripsi, scribtum scriptum, trabs traps, urbs urps; App. Pr., "celebs* non *celeps," "labsus* non *lapsus."*

Final *b* must have been often assimilated to a following consonant: *sud die*, 601 A. D., Carnoy 165.

316. In the Empire, especially in the second century, initial *b* and *v* were much confused in inscriptions (cf. *V*): *biginti, bixit, botu, vene*, etc., S. 240; *Baleria, Balerius, Beneria, Beneti, Betrubius, Bictor, bos, valneas*, Audollent 536; African *birtus, bita, boluntas, Vok.* I, 98; *bivere*, very common, Carnoy 140; *baluis*, Bechtel 78; *vibit*, etc., R. 456; *bobis* in Consentius, *Vok.* III, 68.

In the Romance languages there are few, if any, traces of such an early interchange. Probably the confusion was mainly or wholly graphic, being due to the identity in sound of *b* and *v* between vowels (§ 318): *Lat. Spr.* 473; cf. *Einf.*, § 120. The Spanish levelling of initial *b* and *v* does not go back to Vulgar Latin (Carnoy 139–141); the confusion is far commoner in Italian inscriptions than in Spanish or Gallic (Carnoy 142–146). We find also a change of initial *v* to *b* in north Portuguese, Gascon, south Italian, and Old Rumanian.

317. After liquids, too, there was a confusion of *b* and *v* in inscriptions, *b* being substituted for *v* much oftener than *v* for *b: Nerba, salbum, serbus, solbit*, etc., S. 240; *berbex*, Waters Ch. 57; *solbere*, repeatedly, Carnoy 140; *solbere*, etc., R. 455; *App. Pr.*, "*alveus* non *albeus*."

In all probability *v* really changed to *b* after liquids: see *V*. *B* remained unchanged.

318. Intervocalic *b* opened into *β;* the development apparently began in the first century, was well along in the second, and was completed, at least in Italy, in the third: Οὐιουία = *Vibia*, Rome, Eckinger 95; DEVERE, DEVITVM, PROVATA, etc., S. 240. As *v* also was pronounced *β*, a confusion in spelling resulted, *b* and *v* being used indiscriminately: CVRABIT, IVBENTVTIS, NOBE, etc., S. 240; IVVENTE = *jubente*, 2d century, *Einf.* 127, § 120; *cabia* = *cavea, Danuvium, Dibona, iubenis, vovis*, etc., Audollent 536–537; *devitum* (6th century), *lebis, redivit, vibi*, Carnoy 134–135; *annotavimus, lebat*, Bechtel 78; *devetis, habe* = *ave, rogavo, suabitati*, etc., R. 455–456; cf. Stolz 51, Pirson 61–62, Carnoy 134–136. Cf. *V*.

When this *β* became contiguous to a following consonant, it was vocalized into *u:* *faula, *paraula, *taula, etc. Cf. *V*.

Intervocalic *br*, perhaps not until the end of our period, became *βr* in northern Gaul, Rætia, part of northern Italy, and Dacia.

(1) In the early stages of clerical Latin intervocalic *b* was pronounced *β*, as in popular speech: *faβula, *taβula, etc. Later, perhaps by the seventh century, it was sounded *b*.

(2) In *App. Pr.* we find "*sibilus* non *sifilus*," and Priscian (S. 300) mentions "*sifilum* pro *sibilum*"; cf. French *siffler*. Perhaps the form with *f* comes from some non-Latin Italic dialect: cf. *bubulcus* = It. *bifolco*, and a few other words.

(3) For *habēbam* > *aβęa, see § 421.

319. *Bę, bị* probably remained unchanged, at least in most of the Empire: *rabies, rŭbeus,* etc. For the analogical change of *habeo* to **ayo, dēbeo* to **deyo,* see § 273.

(3) *F.*

320. *F* was originally bilabial (S. 294–295), but became dentilabial by the middle of the Empire (S. 295): cf. § 305. It is the old *f,* apparently, that is described by Quintilian (S. 296–297); a plain description of the dentilabial *f* is given by Terentianus Maurus and Marius Victorinus (S. 296).

(1) Grammarians speak of an alternation of *h* and *f: fœdus > hœdus, fasena > harena, fircum > hircum, habam > fabam,* etc., S. 300. The *f* and the *h* doubtless belonged to different dialects in early Latin; according to Varro, *Ling. Lat.* 5, § 97, the *f* for *h* was Sabine. This phenomenon can have no connection with the change of initial *f* to *h* in Spanish and Gascon.

321. It is probable that intervocalic *f* became *v* at the end of the Vulgar Latin period (cf. § 256): *alevanti = elephanti, paceveci = pacifici, pontevecem = pontificem,* Haag 32–33.

(4) *V.*

322. The letter *v* was doubtless originally pronounced *w;* but, losing its velar element, the sound was reduced, probably early in the Empire, to the bilabial fricative β. During the Empire Greek-letter inscriptions have ου or β for *v* (Νερουα or Νερβα): Ούιουία = *Vibia,* Rome, Eckinger 95; β for *v* is common from the first century on, Eckinger 85–91. Velius Longus, in the middle of the second century, says that the *u* in *ualente* is pronounced "cum aliqua aspiratione": S. 232.

Hence arises a complete confusion of intervocalic *b* and *v* (cf. *B*): CVRABIT, IVBENTVTIS, etc., S. 240; *jubari* for *juvari* in Gregory the Great. This leads to a graphic confusion of initial *b* and *v* in inscriptions: BIGINTI, BIXIT, BOTV, etc. (so INBICTO), S. 240.

Later the bilabial β became dentilabial *v* in most of the Empire: cf. § 305.

For the substitution of *w* for β or *v* in a few words, see Germanic Consonants.

323. After liquids β seems to have closed regularly into *b;* this state was preserved in Rumanian (Densusianu 97, 103-105), but elsewhere the β or *v* was partially restored by school influence: CERBVS, CORBI, CVRBATI, FERBEO, NERBA (about 100 A.D.), SERBAT, SOLBIT, E. G. Parodi in *Rom.* XXVII, 177, cf. § 317. So *vervex* became *verbex, then *berbex*: Waters Ch. 57; BERBECES, 2d century, *Einf.* 127, § 120 (also in *Gl. Reich.*).

Hence came hesitation in spelling (*ferveo, ferbui*, etc.) and inconsistent results in the Romance languages: *cŏrvus* > It. *corbo corvo*, Fr. *corbeau;* *cŭrvus* > Old Fr., Pr. *corp*, Sp. *corvo;* *nĕrvus* > It. *nerbo*, Fr. *nerf;* *servare, servire* > It. *serbare, servire*.

324. Intervocalic *w* or β had a tendency in older Latin, as in Umbrian, to disappear between two like vowels: *divīnus* > *dīnus* (cf. Umbrian *deivina* > *deina*, Sittl 26), *obliviscor* > *obliscor, si vis* > *sīs*. Cf. Lindsay 52. Also, at all times, before or after *o: bŏvis* > *bōs; devorsum* > *deōrsum; faor*, Pirson 63; *moere*, Audollent 539; Νοεμβριος, *Vok.* II, 479; NOEM[BRIS], S. 241; "*pavor* non *paor*," *App. Pr.;* cf. late *noembris, noicius*, Lindsay 52. "*Favilla* non *failla*" in *App. Pr.* seems to be isolated.

In the above cases the fall apparently was only sporadic. But before an accented *o* or *u*, the *w* or β fell regularly in most of the Empire: *aunculus*, *Vok.* II, 471 (cf. *auncli*, Pirson 63); FLAONIVS, S. 241; **paōnem;* *paōrem.

Furthermore, intervocalic *w* or β regularly disappeared in popular speech before any *u*, probably towards the end of the Republic (when *-vos* > *-vus*): FLAVS, vIvs, S. 241 (cf. *flaus* in

App. Pr., vius in Pirson 63); *oum, Vok.* II, 472 (cf. *oum* in Probus, Keil IV, 113); *nous*, Audollent 539 (cf. *noum*, Pirson 63); *gnæus*, Lindsay 52; *datius*, Carnoy 128; *primitius*, Pirson 63; *aus, rius, App. Pr.* Often, however, the *v* was restored, after the analogy of a feminine or a plural form: *ovum* (beside *oum*) through *ova*, *rivus* (beside *rius*) through *rivi*, etc. Cf. § 167.

(1) In inscriptions -VS is common in place of -VVS; in most cases this is probably only graphic: Carnoy 128-131. The ÆVM of *C. I. L.* I, 1220, cited by Schuchardt (*Vok.* II, 471) and others as *æum*, is evidently intended for *ævum*.

325. When intervocalic *w* or *β* became contiguous to a following consonant, it was vocalized into *u* (cf. *B*): Classic *claudo, naufragus,* etc.; Vulgar *aucella, triumphaut,* etc.

(5) *U*.

326. *U* in hiatus which had not already become *w* (§§ 223-224) probably took that sound by the end of the Vulgar Latin period: *eccu' hīc* > **eccwic, eccu' ista* > **eccwista, nŏcui* > *nǫcwi, placuit* > *placwit.* Before this, the original Latin *w* (spelled *v*) had become *β*: § 322.

2. GREEK CONSONANTS.

327. In Greek the surd and the sonant stops must have been less sharply differentiated than in Latin; the sonants were perhaps not fully voiced, and the surds doubtless had a weak, voiced explosion: so they were not always distinguished by the Latin ear. The Greek liquids, nasals, and sibilants usually remained unchanged in transmission.

328. Single consonants sometimes became double in Latin, and Greek double consonants sometimes became single: νόμος > *nummus;* ἐκκλησία > *ec(c)lesia.* Cf. Claussen 847-851.

(1) Β, Γ, Δ.

329. Β, γ, δ regularly remained *b*, *g*, *d:* βλαισός > *blæsus;* γάρον > *garum;* δέλτα > *delta*. Sometimes, however, they were unvoiced into *p*, *c*, *t:* Ἰάκωβος > **Jácopus* (also **Jácomus*); γόγγρος > *conger gonger*, σπήλυγγα > *spelunca;* κέδρος > *citrus*. Cf. Claussen 833–838.

Γμ > *um* (cf. § 268): σάγμα > *sagma sauma*.

(2) Κ, Π, Τ.

330. Κ, π, τ generally remained *c*, *p*, *t:* κόλαφος > *colaphus;* πορφύρα > *purpura;* τάλαντον > *talentum*.

Κ, however, often became *g;* π sometimes became *b;* of a change of τ to *d* there is no example, although κάνδιτος for *candidus* (Eckinger 98) seems to point in that direction: Ἀκράγας > *Acragas Agragas*, κάμμαρος > *cammarus gammarus*, κόμμι > *gummi*, κυβερνᾶν > *gubernare*, κωβιός > *gobius;* cf. EGLOGE, PROGNE, S. 346; *App. Pr.*, "*calatus* non *galatus*" (= κάλαθος); the confusion is mentioned by Terentius Scaurus and others, S. 347; — πύξος > *buxus*, πυρρός > *burrus*, cf. *bustiola* in *Gl. Reich.*

Κν > *cin* in κύκνος > *cicinus* > Old. It. *cecino*.

331. After nasals, κ, π, τ regularly came to be pronounced *g*, *b*, *d* in Greek: ἀνάγκη > *anángi*, λαμπρός > *lambrós*, ἄντρον > *ándron*. This late Greek pronunciation perhaps accounts for such cases as καμπή > Lat. *gamba*, τύμπανον > Fr. *timbre*, σάνταλον > Fr. *sandal*. Cf. Claussen 838–841.

(3) Θ, Φ, Χ.

332. The explosives θ, φ, χ became in Old Latin *t*, *p*, *c* (S. 252–253): πορφύρα > *purpura;* old inscriptions, *Pilipus*, etc., S. 259; later inscriptions, *Teodor, nimpæ, Cristo*, etc., S. 259–260. From the middle of the second century B. C. we find the spellings TH, PH, CH: Claussen 823–833. People of fashion undoubtedly tried to imitate the aspirates (Lindsay 54), but popular speech kept the old *t, p, c*, for new words as well as for old: σπαθή > *spatha = spata;* κόλαφος > *colaphus = colapus,* συμφωνία > It. *zampogna,* φάλαγξ > It., Sp. *palanca,* φαντασία > Pr. *pantaisar;* χορδή > *chorda = corda.*

Quintilian (S. 256) says there were no aspirate consonants in older Latin. Cicero (S. 256) speaks of using the old, unaspirated pronunciation (as *pulcros, triumpos*) in order to be better understood. The proper spelling is discussed by grammarians: S. 257–258.

The letter *h* is occasionally misused, as in PHOSIT, PACHE, etc.: S. 260. It is transposed in *Phitonis, phitonissæ,* Bonnet 141, 218; cf. *Fitonis, Fitones* in *Gl. Reich.*

333. In φάλλαινα > *ballæna,* and some other early adoptions, φ > *b;* perhaps the reason is to be sought in a Greek dialect pronunciation: Claussen 829–831. In δοχή > *doga,* etc., χ > *g:* Claussen 831. In θεῖος > It. *zio* we have a late development of θ; cf. *App. Pr., "Theophilus* non *izofilus":* Claussen 833.

(1) Evidence of a late school pronunciation of θ as *ts* is to be found in Thurot 78, 79 (cf. footnote to § 259): " *T* quoque, si aspiretur, ut *c* enuntiatur, ut *æther, nothus, Parthi, cathedra, catholicus, etheus, Matheus*"... " In principio inquam dictionis nulla prescripta causa variari compellitur, ut *thiara, Thiestes, Thestius, Thescelus, Theos.*"

334. By the first century A. D., φ had developed into *f* in some places (S. 261): DAFNE occurs in Pompeii, Claussen 828; *f* is common later in southern Italy, S. 261. Certainly as early as the fourth century (Lindsay 58) *f* came to be the standard pronunciation: *App. Pr., "amfora* non *ampora," "strofa* non *stropa";* Bechtel 79, *neofiti;* so ὀφήκιον for *officium,* etc., Eckinger 97. In late words φ regularly appears as *f:* φάσηλος > *phaselus faselus;* κέφαλος > It. *cefalo;* etc.

(4) LIQUIDS, NASALS, AND SIBILANTS.

335. The liquids regularly remained unchanged: λαμπάς > *lampas;* ῥήτωρ > *rhetor.* *Rh* in common speech was doubtless pronounced like *r.*

In σέλινον > It. *sẹdano,* and a few other words, we probably have to do with a late Greek change of λ to δ.

336. The nasals, too, regularly remained unchanged: μαῦρος > *maurus;* νομή > *nome.* There are, however, some indications that they were weak before consonants: βόμβος > Pr. *bobansa,* etc. Cf. Claussen 845.

337. Of the sibilants, σ and ξ were regularly unchanged: σίναπι > *sinapis;* ἔξοδος > *exodus.* In ὀσμή? > It. *orma,* σ has probably become *r.* For πρεσβύτερος > *prebiter,* see § 300.

The unfamiliar combination ψ lent itself readily to metathesis: ψάλλειν > *psallere spallere.*

For ζ, see below.

(5) Z.

338. Z doubtless had several pronunciations in Greek. In early Latin it was represented by *ss* or *s:* μάζα > *massa,* ζώνη > *sona* (Plautus). From Sulla's time on it was written *z* in Latin: Claussen 841–843. The grammarians throw no light on the Latin pronunciation. Quintilian refers only to the Greek letter and the lack of a corresponding Latin one; Velius Longus discusses *z* at length, as a simple sound, but seems to be referring only to Greek speech: S. 308. Priscian (Keil II, 36) says that ζ is sounded *sd,* but was often replaced, among the ancients, by *s, ss,* or *d*—as in *Saguntum, massa, Medentius.*

339. Judging from inscriptions, it was pronounced in Vulgar Latin *dy,* later *y* (cf. § 272), and subsequent developments confirm this view: *baptizare* was equivalent to *baptị(d)yare,* *zelosus* to (*d*)*yelọsus*. The ending –*ị*(*d*)*yare* became very common: see § 33.

The spelling *di* for *z* occurs repeatedly: *baptidiare* is found several times in *Per.* (90, 22, etc.; cf. Bechtel 79), and is common in inscriptions (cf. *baptidiatus*, Carnoy 163); *oridium* for ὄρυζα, *Lat. Spr.* 473. Conversely, *z* is often used for *di*: ZABVLLVS, *Vok.* I, 68; *zabulus, zacones*, Koffmane 38; *Lazis = Ladiis, zabulus, zaconus, zebus, zeta = diæta, zosum = deorsum*, R. 457–458.

In late inscriptions *z* for *j* is common: *zerax* = ἱεραξ (202 A. D.), *zanuari, Vok.* I, 69; ZESV, ZVNIOR, S. 239; Ζουλεία = *Julia*, κόζους = *conjux*, Eckinger 80. Cf. *septuazinta*, Carnoy 163.

3. GERMANIC CONSONANTS.

340. Most of the consonants offer no peculiarities, being treated as in Latin. A few, however, had no Latin equivalents: *ð, þ, h*, and *w*. Furthermore, *b* and *k* came in after the corresponding Latin sounds had undergone some modification.

341. *B* between vowels, occurring apparently only in words adopted after Latin intervocalic *b* had become β (§ 318), remained a stop: *roubôn* > It. *rubare*, *strîban > Pr. *estribar*.

G, although it can scarcely have come in time to share in the early palatalization of Latin *g* before front vowels (§§ 258 ff.), seems to have followed a similar course, and to have participated also in the later Gallic palatalization of *g* before *a* (§ 263): *gilda* > It. *geldra*, *gíga > Pr., It. *giga, geisla* > Pr. *giscle; garba* > Fr. *gerbe, garto* > Old Fr. *jart*.

K resisted front vowels: *skëna* > Sp. *esquena, skërnôn* > It. *schernire;* so *rîk-ĭtia > Pr. *riqueza*, etc. *Franko* seems to have been an early acquisition, and its derivatives palatalized their *k* before *e* and *i*: *frank-ĭscus* > It. *Francesco*, etc. In the regions where Latin *c* was palatalized, in the seventh century and later, before *a* (§ 263), Germanic *k* was modified in the same way before all front vowels (including *a*): cf. Old Fr. *eschine, eschernir, richesse;* so *blank-a* > Fr. *blanche* (but It. *bianca*).

342. The spirants *ð* and *þ* were replaced in Latin by the corresponding stops, *d* and *t: wiðarlon* > It. *guiderdone; haunipa* > Fr. *honte, pahso* > It. *tasso, parrjan* > Fr. *tarir, prèscan* > Pr. *trescar.* Cf. Kluge 500.

343. Germanic *h* appeared when Latin *h* had long been silent in popular speech.

At the beginning of a word it kept its sound in northern Gaul, but apparently was neglected in the rest of the Empire: *hanca* > Fr. *hanche*, Sp. *anca; hapja* > Fr. *hache*, Pr. *apcha; hardjan* > Fr. *hardir*, It. *ardire; hëlm* > Old Fr. *helme*, It. *elmo.* Bon. 445 notes that *ab*, rather than *a*, is used before initial *ch: ab Chilperico*, etc.

Intervocalic *h* disappeared in most words, but in a few — perhaps borrowed at a different date — it seems to have been sounded *kk* in the greater part of the Empire: *fëhu* > Fr., Pr. *feu*, It. *fio; skiuhan* > Fr. *esquiver*, It. *schivare; spëhôn* > Old Fr. *espier*, Pr. *espiar;* — *jëhan* > Old Fr. *jehir*, Pr. *gequir*, It. *gecchire*, Old Sp. *jaquir.*

Hs, ht were generally treated like Latin *ss, tt: pahso* > It. *tasso;* — *slahta* > Old Fr. *esclate*, Pr. *esclata*, It. *schiatta; slëht* > Pr. *esclet*, It. *schietto.* But *wahta*, doubtless adopted at a different time, became Old Fr. *gaite*, Pr. *gaita;* cf. It. *guatare.*

344. Germanic *w* was a strong velar and labial fricative, at a time when original Latin *w* (spelled *v*) had become the purely labial fricative *β* (§ 322). It was nearer in sound to Latin *u̯:* see § 326. In the *Gl. Reich.* we find it represented by *uu*, in *uuadius, reuuardent*, etc. Bon. 167 records *Euua, wa* (the interjection), *Waddo, walde, Wandali*, etc. It is generally written *w* in Fredegarius, but *Wintrio* is spelled *Quintrio:* Haag 38.

In extreme northern and eastern Gaul, in northwestern Italy, and in Rætia this *w* apparently remained unchanged in the Vulgar Latin period; elsewhere, through a reinforcement of its velar element, it became *gw: warjan* > **warire guarire, wërra* > *werra guerra, wîsa* > **wisa guisa*.

Through association with Germanic words, the β of some Latin words was changed to *w: vadum + watan* > **wadum, vastare + wost–* > **wastare*, etc.

See E. Mackel, *Die germanischen Elemente in der französischen und provenzalischen Sprache*, 1884; W. Waltemath, *Die fränkischen Elemente in der französischen Sprache*, 1885; W. Bruckner, *Charakteristik der germanischen Elemente im Italienischen*, 1899.

IV. MORPHOLOGY.

A. NOUNS AND ADJECTIVES.

1. GENDER.

345. The three genders of Latin were not, in the main, dependent on sex or lack of sex. They were grammatical distinctions, whose observance was a matter of outward form. If words lost their differentiating terminations, confusion of gender ensued.

a. MASCULINE AND FEMININE.

346. Between masculine and feminine there was not much confusion, but there were some important shifts:—

(1) Feminines of the second declension nearly all became masculine: *fraxĭnus*, etc.; cf. *castaneus* for *castanea*, Bon. 194. Feminines of the fourth declension varied (*Gram.* II, 461): *dŏmus, fīcus, manus*.

(2) In Gaul, abstract nouns in *–or*, through the analogy of the great majority of abstract terms, became feminine (Bon. 503–504): *color, honor, Lat. Spr.* 483; *dolor, timor*, Bon. 504.

(3) Nouns that had a proparoxytonic accusative in *–erem, –icem, –inem, –orem*, or *–urem* were of uncertain gender (*Gram.* II, 464–467): *carcĕrem, pulĭcem, margĭnem, lepŏrem, turtŭrem*.

(4) There were some sporadic changes: *duos arbores*, Pirson 157; *cucullus* and *cuculla*, G. 293; *fons* feminine in late Latin, *Lat. Spr.* 483; *grex* became feminine.

(5) See also § 351.

b. MASCULINE AND NEUTER.

347. In Classic Latin a number of neuters became masculine: *balteum –us, caseum –us, cornu –um –us, frenum –i, nasum –us, tergum –us, vadum –us;* cf. *collus –um, lectus –um*.
In popular and late Latin this tendency was strong: ante-Classic, m. *papaver;* Plautus, m. *guttur, dorsus* (*Mil. Glor.* II, 4, 44), *lactem* (*Bacch.* V, 2, 16); Varro, m. *murmur;* Petronius, *balneus, cælus, fatus, lactem, vasus –um, vinus,* etc., Waters Ch. 39, 41, 42, 57, Densusianu 129, 132; *collus, me[nt]us,* etc., Audollent 545; MARIS, MAREM, Densusianu 132; *castellus, fænus, lignus, signus, templus, verbus, vinus,* etc., R. 266; *sulphurem,* G. 293; *frigorem, maris* nom. sg., *marmorem, pectorem, roborem,* Bon. 348; *incipit judicius,* etc., D'Arbois 135. Beside *lūmen, nōmen, pĭper* there must have been **lūmĭnem, *nōmĭnem, *pĭpĕrem*.
Conversely we find *cĭnus,* n., for *cĭnis, cĭner,* m.; there must have been a **pŭlvus,* n., beside *pŭlvis,* m. and f. (*Lat. Spr.* 483); Petronius has *thesaurum,* Waters Ch. 46. Cf. *gladium, laqueum, puteum, thesaurum,* etc., R. 270–272.
Cf. Bon. 345–349, 507–509. For the confusion of masculine and neuter in Africa, see *Archiv* VIII, 173.

348. The transition from masculine to neuter was facilitated by the fall of final *m* (§ 309), and also by the fall of final *s* in the regions where that phenomenon occurred (§ 298). These changes reduced considerably the distinguishing marks of the two genders: —

filiu(s)	*foliu*	*come(s)*	*corpu(s)*
filii	*folii*	*comiti(s)*	*corpori(s)*
filio	*folio*	*comiti*	*corpori*
filiu	*foliu*	*comite*	*corpu(s)*
filio	*folio*	*comite*	*corpore*
filii	*folia*	*comite(s)*	*corpora*
filioru	*folioru*	*comitu*	*corporu*
filii(s)	*folii(s)*	*comitibu(s)*	*corporibu(s)*
filio(s)	*folia*	*comite(s)*	*corpora*
filii(s)	*folii(s)*	*comitibu(s)*	*corporibu(s)*

In the second declension the only difference is in the nominative singular and the nominative and accusative plural; and in Italy and Dacia the distinction disappears even in the nominative singular. In the third declension the genders are distinguished only in the accusative singular and the nominative and accusative plural.

349. Thus the masculine and neuter inflections came to be fused, the characteristic neuter plural –*a* being regarded as an alternative masculine plural ending: Petronius writes *nervia* for *nervi*, Waters Ch. 45; cf. *rivus rivora*, Zs. XXX, 635. So *lŏcus*, *mūrus*, for instance, give in Italian: sg. *luogo*, *muro;* pl. *luoghi luogora*, *muri mura*. Cf. § 351.

Nearly all neuters became masculine: *os locutus est*, R. 266; *donum cælestem*, etc., R. 277; *hunc sæculum*, *hunc stagnum*, *hunc verbum*, *hunc vulnere*, Bon. 386, 348. *Mare*, however, perhaps influenced by *terra*, generally became feminine: *maris*, m. and f., Densusianu 132; *mare*, f., Haag 48. Greek neuters in –*ma*, if popular, generally became feminine: *cyma*, *sagma*.

The loss of the neuter gender for nouns was probably not complete until early Romance times. Cf. *Archiv* III, 161.

350. Among pronouns, the neuter forms were kept to express an indefinite idea: *hŏc*, *id ĭpsum*, *ĭllud* or *ĭllum*, *quĭd*, *quŏd*.

Neuter adjective forms were used for a similar purpose: in the early stages of the Romance languages we find phrases pointing to such Vulgar Latin constructions as **mihi est grave quod ille non veniat*, etc.

c. FEMININE AND NEUTER.

351. Classic Latin often used not only the singular for the plural in a collective sense (as *eques*, *miles*, etc., in Livy: cf. Draeger I, 4), but also the collective plural for the singular (as *frigora, marmora, rura:* cf. Draeger I, 5-9; *Archiv* XIV, 63). So the neuter plural forms in *-a* were preserved in their collective use after the neuter singular forms had disappeared.

This formation in *-a* was extended to many masculine (cf. § 349) and even to some feminine nouns: *digita, fructa, fusa, grada* occur in late Latin, *Lat. Spr.* 482. Cf. Old Fr. *crigne* < ? *crinea = *crines;* It. *dita, frutta,* etc.; Sardinian, Apulian, Rumanian *frunza* < ? *frondia = *frondes.*

352. In late Latin and early Romance this collective plural in *-a* came to be taken for a feminine singular: *tribula* sg., R. 269; *gaudia* sg., Bon. 351; *ligna ... ardet* (cf. *rama*), *Gl. Reich.; hic est iesta,* D'Arbois 10; cf. *ne forte et mihi hæc eveniat,* etc., R. 435. The feminine character of such words was doubtless reinforced by the use, for instance, of an *illæ pectora to match *quæ pectora: Chronologie* 199. Conversely, *palpebrum* for *palpebra* occurs, R. 270.

Hence arose such feminine singular forms as **brachia,* **folia, gaudia, gesta, ligna,* etc., for which a new plural was created: *brachias,* Audollent 548; *armentas, membras, Gl. Cassel; ingenias, simulachras, Gl. Reich.*

In most of the Romance territory the *-a* forms were kept only as feminine singulars, but many were preserved as plurals in central and southern Italy and Rumania.

353. Aside from these, few neuter nouns became feminine: *marmor,* f., occurs in late Latin, *Lat. Spr.* 483. For *mare* and Greek neuters in *-ma,* see § 349. For *cinus* = *cinis,* *pulvus = *pulvis,* see § 347.

2. DECLENSION OF NOUNS.

354. For the use of cases, see §§ 85-100. By the end of the Vulgar Latin period the cases were generally reduced,

except in Dacia, to two,—a nominative and an accusative-ablative,—the plural following the analogy of the singular. In Dacia the dative singular was to some extent preserved also: § 91. Cf. K. Sittl in *Archiv* II, 550.

355. The number of declensions was reduced to three, the fourth and fifth being absorbed by the others.

(1) The transfer from the fourth to the second began in Classic Latin and continued in vulgar and late speech: *dŏmus, fīcus,* so *frŭcti, senāti; gustus* in Petronius; *manos,* Audollent 544; *jusso, passos,* Bechtel 86; *cornum, fructo fructos, gelus, genum, gradus, senatus, spiritus,* etc., R. 260–262, 270; *lacus, mercatus,* G. 282–283; *jusso, lucto,* etc., Bon. 135. All the fourth declension eventually went over. One result of the intermediate confusion was an accusative plural spelling *-us* for *-os,* which was very common in Gaul: Bon. 337–338.

(2) The transfer of nouns in *-ies* from the fifth to the first declension began also in Classic Latin: *effigies -ia, luxuries -ia, materies -ia. Acia, facia, glacia, scabia* are attested later: Densusianu 133, *Lat. Spr.* 482. All passed over in the greater part of the Empire; but *-ies* was kept in the Spanish peninsula, in southern Italy and Sardinia, and occasionally in southern Gaul, being assimilated to the third declension: cf. Sp. *haz,* Pr. *glatz,* etc. *Dies* maintained itself, as a third declension noun, beside *dia.*

Fifth declension nouns not in *-ies* went into the third: *res rem, spes spem,* etc. There was also an inflection *spes spene(m),* whence Italian *spene* (cf. SPENI): W. Heræus in *Archiv* XIII, 152.

356. The other declensions generally held their own, but there were a few shifts:—

(1) For an inflection *mama mamāne(m),* etc., see § 359.

(2) For an inflection *Bellus Bellōne(m)*, etc., see § 362. Beside *ervum ervi*, there was an *ervus ervoris: Lat. Spr.* 483. *Fīmus fīmi*, under the influence of *stĕrcus*, apparently became *fĕmus* (*Gl. Reich.*) **fĕmŏris*: cf. Old Fr. *fiens*, Pr. *femps*. *Fŭndus fŭndi* perhaps became *fŭndus* **fŭndŏris*: Old Fr. *fonz*, Pr. *fons*, Fr. *effondrer*. Beside *termĭnus –i*, there was a *termen termĭnis*.

(3) On the other hand, *ŏs > ŏssum* (R. 259-260), *vas > vasum vasus* (Waters Ch. 57); so apparently *ros > *rōsum* (cf. Fr. *arroser*, It. *rugiada*, etc.); beside *coclear* there was *coclearium*. *Caput* became *capus* (Pirson 238) and **capum –i:* cf. *Ltblt.* XXVII, 367. *Corpo* for *corpore* occurs in the *Per.:* Bechtel 86.

Greek nouns of the third declension sometimes passed into the first: *absis > absida*, G. 280; *lampas > lampada*, R. 258-259, G. 280, Dubois 258; *pyxis > *buxida; siren > sirena*, G. 280. So a few Latin nouns: *juventus* or *–tas > juventa*, likewise *tempesta* (*Gl. Reich.*) and probably **potesta;* but the old forms were retained also. *Puulva* for *pŭlvis* is recorded by Audollent 416.

a. FIRST DECLENSION.

357. In countries which did not lose final *s* (§ 298), the accusative plural form came to be used as a nominative plural. This use was due in the main to the analogy of the singular, where there was only one form, and of feminine nouns of the third declension, which had only one form in the plural: *filia filia(m)*, *matres matres*, hence *filias filias*. So *linguas*, Audollent 546. It probably was not common until late Vulgar Latin or early Romance times.

In Italy and Dacia, where the fall of *–s* made the accusative plural identical with the singular, the nominative plural was kept instead.

(1) According to Mohl, *Chronologie* 205–209, the nominative plural in –*as* was probably old in some parts of Italy: SCALAS, nom., 57 B.C.; LIBERTI LIBERTASQVE, Dalmatia; HIC QVESCVNT DVS MRES DVAS FILIAS, Africa. M. Bréal, *Journal des savants* 1900, Feb., p. 70, affirms that there was a feminine in –*a* with a plural in –*as* in Oscan, and also in Latin down to the second century B. C.; Celtic, too, had a similar plural. D'Arbois 21–24 assumes Celtic influence: *hic sunt cartas*, etc. No foreign influences are needed to explain the practice, but they may have helped its diffusion.

358. An ablative in –*abus* is occasionally found: *Cassiabus, feminabus, filiabus, pupillabus, Archiv* VIII, 171; *deabus, filiabus*, etc., Pirson 115–116; *animabus, famulabus, filiabus, villabus*, Bon. 331. This form left no traces in Romance.

359. Feminine proper names and words denoting persons often developed, rather late, an inflection in –*ánis*, etc., or –*énis*, etc., probably under the influence of the consonantal declension of Greek names that was in vogue in schools. Pupils were taught to inflect *Glaucé Glaucénis, Nicé Nicénis*, etc. (R. 264); cf. Dante's *Semelé*, etc.: hence arose *Anna Annánis* or –*énis, mamma mammánis, amita *amitánis* (so *Juliana Julianenis* in Pirson 143), cf. W. Heræus in *Zs. fr. Spr.* XXV, ii, 136. Some masculine person-names in –*a* had the same declension (*Einf.* 150, § 153): *barba barbani, sacrista *sacristanis* (cf. It. *sacristano*), *scriba *scribanis* (cf. It. *scrivano*). Both *mamani* and *tatani* are found in the third century: W. Heræus in *Archiv* XIII, 152–153. See G. Paris, *Les accusatifs en* –ain, *Rom.* XXIII, 321; E. Philipon, *Les accusatifs en* –on *et en* –ain, *Rom.* XXXI, 201; W. Meyer-Lübke in *Ltblt.* XXV, 206; G. Salvioni in *Rom.* XXXV, 198. In *Lat. Spr.* 483, Meyer-Lübke expresses doubt whether the feminine –*a* –*anis* is connected with masculine *tatani*, etc.

This feminine inflection left some traces in Gaul, Rætia, and Italy: Fr. *nonnain, putain*, etc.; Lombard *madrane*, etc., *Rom.* XXXV, 207.

(1) G. Salvioni, *La declinazione imparisillaba in* -a -áne, -o -óne, -e éne -íne, -i íne -éne, *Rom.* XXXV, 198, shows that these forms of declension were very common in the mediæval Latin documents of all parts of Italy, from 750 on: *amitane*, 218; *Andreani*, 216; *barbane*, 214-215; *domnani*, 219; *Joanneni*, 250; etc. *Attane, barbane* still exist at both ends of Italy. According to Salvioni, the starting-point of all this inflection was *bárba barbánis*, from which it was extended to other nouns of relationship and to proper names; *bárba barbánis* itself he would ascribe to the influence of the synonymous *bárbo**barbónis. A Germanic origin is postulated by J. Jud, *Recherches sur la génèse et la diffusion des accusatifs en* -ain *et en* -on, 1907; also in *Archiv für das Studium der neueren Sprachen* XXIV, 3-4, 405.

(2) A. Zimmermann, *Zs.* XXVIII, 343, shows that there was also an inflection in *-átis*, *-étis*, and *-ótis: Aureliati, Agneti*, etc. Cf. *Eugeneti* from *Eugenes*, R. 264, Dubois 250; *Andreate, Rom.* XXXV, 216; also *Joannentis, Rom.* XXXV, 250.

360. In general, at the beginning of the Romance period, the first declension was reduced to this pattern:—

luna	facịa	*folịa
luna	facịa	folịa
lune lunas	facịe facịas	folịe folịas
luna(s)	facịa(s)	folịa(s)

In Dacia the dative singular (*lune*, etc.) was kept also.

b. SECOND DECLENSION.

361. As neuter nouns became masculine, they assumed, partly in Vulgar Latin but mostly in Romance, the masculine inflection in those countries where the masculine and neuter differed: *vinus*, etc. Cf. §§ 347-349.

The plural in -*a*, however, was retained to a considerable extent, especially in southern and central Italy and Dacia. Some masculines took this -*a*, by the analogy of *bracchia*, etc.: *botella, **botula, digita, fructa, rama*, etc. Cf. §§ 349, 351-352.

362. From the seventh century on,—perhaps under Germanic influence combined with the analogy of the Latin type

gúlo gulónis, etc.,—there developed in Gaul, Rætia, Italy, and possibly Spain, a declension *–us* (or *–o*) *–ónis* for masculine proper names: *Húgo Húgon* was Latinized into *Húgo Hugóne*(*m*) (cf. § 152); *avus avi* > *avo avonis*, attested in Lucca in 776 (*Rom.* XXXV, 204); hence *Pétrus* or *Pétro Petróne*(*m*), *Paulus* or *Paulo Paulóne*(*m*), etc. Cf. Pirson 133: *Bellus Belloni, Firmus Firmonis*. See E. Philipon in *Rom.* XXXI, 201; G. Salvioni in *Rom.* XXXV, 198.

Traces of this inflection are to be seen especially in French and Provençal proper names: *Foucon, Huon*, etc. So perhaps Italian *Donatoni, Giovannoni*, etc., and possibly Corsican *baboni, suceroni: Rom.* XXXV, 212–213.

363. In general, at the beginning of the Romance period, the second declension followed this pattern:—

annu(*s*)	*faβe*(*r*)	*vinu*(*s*)	*bracciu *–us*	*fructu*(*s*)
annu –o	*fabru –o*	*vinu –o*	*bracciu –o*	*fructu –o*
anni	*fabri*	*vini*	*braccia –i*	*fructi –a*
anno(*s*)	*fabro*(*s*)	*vino*(*s*)	*braccia –o*(*s*)	*fructo*(*s*) *–a*

The letters enclosed in parentheses were silent in Italy and Dacia. In Gaul the accusative plural ending was often spelled *–us:* Bon. 337–338; cf. § 355, (1).

c. THIRD DECLENSION.

364. In the ablative there was considerable confusion of *–ī* and *–ĕ* in Classic Latin: *marī marĕ, turrī turrĕ*, etc. This was carried further in common speech: cf. *Vok.* II, 85, 87. The ablative in *–ĕ* finally triumphed, but there are some traces of *–ī:* It. *pari*, etc.

365. In the accusative plural there was still greater confusion of *–īs* and *–ēs* (*nubēs nubīs*, etc.), both in Classic and in Vulgar Latin: cf. *Vok.* I, 247–249. Apparently *–ēs* crowded out the rarer *–īs*, which left no sure traces.

Italian *pani*, etc., Rumanian *pînĭ*, etc., are best explained, as by Tiktin 565–566, through the analogy of the second declension: see § 368. Cf. *folli* for *folles* in *Gl. Reich.*

366. In the nominative singular the common -*ĭs* largely displaced the less frequent -*ēs*: *Vok.* I, 244–247, III, 116; Caper, "*fames* non *famis*," Keil VII, 105; *App. Pr.*, "*nubes* non *nubis*"; *ædis, famis, nubis*, etc., R. 263; *famis*, etc., Sepulcri 220. As -*ēs* and -*ĭs* came to be pronounced alike before the end of the Vulgar Latin period (cf. §§ 174, 243), it is futile to trace the Romance forms phonetically to one source rather than the other.

367. Nouns which added a syllable in the genitive, without a change of accent, tended in popular speech to use for the nominative a form in -*is*, -*es*, or -*e* fashioned on the model of the oblique cases: so *sæps* > *sæpes*, *stips* > *stipes*; *Jovis*, nom., in Ennius, Varro, Petronius (Waters Ch. 47); *lacte* in Ennius, Plautus, Petronius (Waters Ch. 38), Apuleius, Aulus Gellius; *bovis* in Varro, Petronius (Waters Ch. 62); *carnis* in Livy; *stirpis* in Livy, Prudentius; *suis* in Prudentius (F. D'Ovidio in *Raccolta di studii critici dedicata ad Alessandro D'Ancona* 627); *lentis* in Priscian; *calcis* in Venantius Fortunatus; *divite*, etc., Audollent 545–547; "*grus* non *gruis*," *App. Pr.*; *principens* (= *principis*), R. 263; *antestetis, superstitis, Vok.* III, 9; *urbis*, Haag 45; *pedis, travis* (three times), *Gl. Reich.*; cf. *Chronologie* 203, *Lat. Spr.* 481. These forms prevailed in Romance, perhaps in late popular Latin.

In Vulgar Latin this formation was extended to words with a shift of accent: *excellente* for *excellens* in Petronius, Waters Ch. 45, 66; *audace, castore, latrone, victore, voluntate*, etc., Audollent 545–547; *heredes*, R. 263; *cardonis, papilionis* (cf. *aculionis* for *aculeus*), *Gl. Reich.*; *heredes*, etc., D'Arbois 85–88.

These forms, too, prevailed in Romance, except for names of persons, which, being used mainly in the nominative and vocative, retained and generally preferred the old nominative form: *hŏmo*, *sŏror*, etc.; *cantātor*, *servītor*, etc. But names of persons in *-ans* and *-ens* usually made over the nominative: *parentis*, etc. (also *presentis*, etc.), D'Arbois 85-88; so, no doubt, *amantis, etc. (also *clamantis, etc.), but *infans* (also *prægnans*).

368. In most of the Romance languages (but not Spanish), masculine nouns made over their nominative plural on the model of the second declension, which was regarded as the normal masculine type: *fīlii*, hence **patri;* *lŭpi*, hence **cani;* *anni*, hence **mē(n)si*.

The process may have begun in the Vulgar Latin period, but there is virtually no evidence that it started so early: in late Latin, however, *elifanti* is common, according to Bon. 367; *parentorum* is frequent in charters; in the *Gl. Cassel*, made in Italy in the eighth or ninth century, we find *sapienti*.

369. Neuters in *-n* and *-s* regularly kept their nominative-accusative singular, as *nōme(n)*, *cŏrpus cŏrpu(s);* for **lūmĭne(m)*, **nōmĭne(m)*, beside the old forms, see § 347. For the nominative-accusative plural, however, they constructed, probably in late Vulgar Latin or early Romance, new forms on the masculine pattern, as *nōmes **nōme(s)*, *cŏrpes **cŏrpe(s);* but in Italy and Rumania the old ones, especially those in *-ŏra*, were kept also (*Lat. Spr.* 482). In these countries *-ora* was used as a plural ending (It. *cǫrpo*, *cǫrpi cǫrpora;* Rum. *timp*, *timpurĭ*), and was extended in Old Italian to the second, in Rumanian to both the second and first declensions: cf. Tiktin 566.

Neuters in *-r*, which apparently became masculine or

feminine earlier than the others, often developed an accusative singular in –*e*(*m*) as well as a nominative-accusative plural in –*es: marmorem*, Bon. 348, Zauner 30; *papaverem*, Plautus, *Pœn.* I, 2, 113; **piperem; sulphurem*, G. 293; cf. § 347. But *marmor*, etc., were kept also. *Cŏr* apparently made its plural *cŏres instead of **cŏrdes:* according to Mohl, *Lexique* 21–38, the word shows no trace of *d* in any of the Romance languages, except Spanish *cuerdo*, and so probably goes back to an Old Latin *cōr *cōris = κῆρ κῆρος; the open *o* would possibly be explained as due to a cross between this *cōr and the Classic *cŏr*.

Caput became *capu(*m*) or *capus* (Pirson 238), and passed into the second declension: cf. § 356, (3).

370. A few feminines in –*is* apparently became neuters in –*us*, but the original forms were kept also: *cĭnis cĭnus; pŭlvis* *pŭlvus, whence Sp. *polvo*, Old Fr. *pols* (It. *pŏlve* may come from *pŭlver*).

Incus, incūdis > *incūdo, incūdĭnis: Lat. Spr.* 483.

Sanguis, sanguĭne(*m*) also *sangue*(*m*).

371. In general, at the beginning of the Romance period, the third declension must have gone about as follows (–*ĭs* and –*ēs* having coincided in the pronunciation –*es*):—

(1) No Change of Accent.

NO CHANGE OF STEM.

THINGS.			PERSONS.	
cane(*s*)	*fine*(*s*)	*res*	*pate*(*r*)	*mate*(*r*)
cane	*fine*	*rem re*	*patre*	*matre*
cane(*s*)	*fine*(*s*)	*res*	*patre*(*s*)	*matre*(*s*)
cane(*s*)	*fine*(*s*)	*res*	*patre*(*s*)	*matre*(*s*)

CHANGE OF STEM.

THINGS.			PERSONS.	
pede(s)	*arte(s)	*corpu*(s)	*come*(s)	*vergo*
pede	*arte*	*corpu*(s)	*cómite*	*vírgine*
pede(s)	*arte*(s)	*corpe(s) *córpora*	*cómite*(s)	*vírgine*(s)
pede(s)	*arte*(s)	*corpe*(s) *córpora*	*cómite*(s)	*vírgine*(s)

(2) Change of Accent.

THINGS.		PERSONS.		
*sermóne(s)	*ratióne(s)	*amáto*(r)	*soro*(r)	*parente*(s)
sermóne	*ratióne*	*amatóre*	*soróre*	*parente*
sermóne(s)	*ratióne*(s)	*amatóre*(s)	*soróre*(s)	*parente*(s)
sermóne(s)	*ratióne*(s)	*amatóre*(s)	*soróre*(s)	*parente*(s)

Letters enclosed in parentheses were silent in Italy and Dacia.

d. LOSS OF DECLENSION.

372. In Italy and Dacia, through the dropping of final *r* and *s*, declension nearly disappeared before the end of the Vulgar Latin period: cf. Audollent 545–547, nom. *alumnu*, *Glaucu*, *Romanu*, etc. It was probably lost altogether soon after, although a few double forms still remain: e. g., It. *ladro*, *ladrone*.

It disappeared early in Spain also. In most of Gaul it lasted through the twelfth century and later.

373. In Gaul and Spain the forms preserved were the accusative singular and the accusative plural. In Italy and Rumania, for phonetic reasons, the surviving cases are the accusative singular and the nominative plural.

There are, however, not a few examples of the nominative singular of names of persons.

3. DECLENSION OF ADJECTIVES.

374. Adjectives were declined after the same model as nouns. As neuter nouns assumed masculine endings (§ 347), the neuter adjective forms were less and less used; the neuter singular, however, was kept to represent a whole idea (cf. § 350), and the neuter plural (as *omnia*) was doubtless employed from time to time as an indefinite collective.

375. The principal types are:—

(1) THREE GENDERS.

-us -a -um		
bonu(s)	*bona*	*bonu*
bonu –o	*bona*	*bonu –o*
boni	*bone –as*	*bona*
bono(s)	*bona(s)*	*bona*

So superlatives, as *optĭmus, –a, –um*.

-er -a -um		
liβe(r)	*libra*	*libru*
libru –o	*libra*	*libru –o*
libri	*libre libras*	*libra*
libro(s)	*libra(s)*	*libra*

So *æger, ægra, ægrum*.

-er -is -e		
ace(r)	*acre(s)*	*acre*
acre	*acre*	*acre*
acre(s)	*acre(s)*	*acria*
acre(s)	*acre(s)*	*acria*

(2) TWO GENDERS.

triste(s)	*triste*
triste	*triste*
triste(s)	*tristia*
triste(s)	*tristia*

(3) Originally ONE GENDER in the Nominative Singular.

*felíce(s)	félis	*prudénte(s)	prúde(s)
felíce	félis	prudénte	prúde(s)
felíce(s)	felícia	prudénte(s)	prudéntia
felíce(s)	felícia	prudénte(s)	prudéntia

(4) COMPARATIVES apparently did not reconstruct the Nominative Singular:—

mélio(r)	méliu(s)
melióre	méliu(s)
melióre(s)	melióra
melióre(s)	melióra

376. There was a good deal of confusion of types in Latin times: beside *alacer*, m. and f., there was *alacris*, m. and f., and there was probably also a feminine *alacra and *alecra. *Pauper* early developed a feminine *paupera* and later a neuter *pauperum: paupera, pauperum, pauperorum*, R. 275 (cf. *pauperorum*, Waters Ch. 46). *Macer, miser, sacer* passed into the –*us* –*a* –*um* class, Densusianu 142; so *tæter* > *tetrus, App. Pr. Declīvis, effrēnis, imbecillis* also assumed the –*us* –*a* –*um* inflection in the Latin period; so *trīstis* > *tristus, App. Pr.* Cf. *celerus, gracilus, præstus, sublimus*, etc., and conversely *benignis, infirmis*, etc., R. 274. *Præcox* developed a feminine *præcoca:* Neue II, 162.

In the Romance languages more adjectives went over to the –*us* –*a* –*um* type: Pr. *comuna, doussa*, etc.

4. COMPARISON.

377. For the new method of comparison, see § 56. The Romance type, not completely evolved in Vulgar Latin, was:—

$$carus \quad \begin{Bmatrix} plus \\ magis \end{Bmatrix} carus \quad ille \begin{Bmatrix} plus \\ magis \end{Bmatrix} carus$$

However, the Classic Latin comparatives of many common adjectives remained: *altior, grandior, gravior, grevior, grossior* (G. 285), *levior, longior, major, melior, minor, pejor;* also **bellatior.* So the adverbs: *longius, magis, melius, minus, pejus, sordidius, vivacius,* etc. The old superlatives remained to a considerable extent, in the clerical language, as intensives: *altissimus, carissimus, pessimus, proximus, sanctissimus.*

5. NUMERALS.[1]

378. *Unus* was probably declined like *bonus.* It was used also as an indefinite article (§ 57) and an indefinite pronoun (cf. § 71).

Dŭo came to be replaced by *dŭi,* attested in the third century: *Archiv* IX, 558 (cf. II, 107). Its inflection at the end of the Vulgar Latin period was probably: —

| dui doi (duo?) | due doe duas doas | dua doa |
| duo(s) | dua(s) doa(s) | dua doa |

In early Romance there was doubtless much confusion of the forms.

379. The numbers between two and twenty were as follows: —

Trēs probably developed a nominative **trei,* on the model of *dui.*

Quattuor became *quattor* (*Archiv* VII, 65), also *quatro* (Carnoy 221), **quattro.*

Quīnque, by dissimilation, became *cīnque* (*Archiv* VII, 66); so *cinquaginta* (*Archiv* VII, 70). Cf. § 254.

Sĕx, sĕpte (and **sĕtte*), *ŏcto* (and **ŏtto*), *nŏve, dĕce* offer no peculiarities Cf. *Archiv* VII, 68.

Beside *ūndĕce* there seems to have been **ŭndĕce.*

For *dōdĕce,* see § 225.

Trēdĕce is regular.

---

[1] See M. Ihm, *Vulgärformen lateinischer Zahlwörter auf Inschriften* in *Archiv* VII, 65.

160   AN INTRODUCTION TO VULGAR LATIN.   [§ 381

Quattuordĕcim regularly became *quattōrdĕce (cf. § 225), but also
*quattŏrdĕce.

Quīndĕce is regular.

Beside *sēdĕce* there was *dĕce et (or *ac*) *sĕx*.

Septendĕcim, etc., went out of use; also *unus de vīginti*, etc.: G. 400.
Priscian (Keil III, 412) mentions *decem et septem*. Beside this *dĕce et sĕpte*
there was **dĕce ac sĕpte;* so *dĕce et (or *ac*) *ŏcto*, *dĕce et (or *ac*) *nŏve*.

380. The tens, beginning with 20, are irregular: cf. § 142.

Vīgĭntī, trīgĭnta regularly became *vii̯nti, trii̯nta* (§ 259):
βειεντι occurs in a sixth century document of Ravenna, *Vok.*
II, 461; *trienta, Archiv* VII, 69. These forms easily contracted into *vi̯nti, tri̯nta* (*vinti, trinta: Archiv* VII, 69), which
account in general for the Italian, Provençal, and French
words; Rumanian has new formations. But beside these we
must assume for Spanish something like **vi̯inti*, **tri̯inta*, with
an opening of the first *i* and an early shift of accent, probably
anterior to the fall of the *g; trĭ́ginta* is, in fact, mentioned as a
faulty pronunciation by Consentius, Keil V, 392. Cf. G. Rydberg in *Mélanges Wahlund* 337.

This change of accent apparently occurred everywhere for
the subsequent tens: *quadráinta, *cinquáinta, *sexáinta,
*septáinta *settáinta, *octáinta *ottáinta, *nonáinta **nováinta;*
the *septua–* and the *octo–* of 70 and 80 were made to conform
to the type of the others. Outside of the Spanish peninsula
–áinta apparently became *–ánta*. Furthermore the *dr* of
*quadráinta became *rr: quarranta* is found in an inscription,
perhaps of the fifth century (Pirson 97; *Zs. fr. Spr.* XXV, ii,
136; *Archiv* VII, 69).

381. *Cĕntu* was regular. For *ducĕnti, trecĕnti*, etc., there
were probably new formations, such as *dŭi cĕntu, etc.

Mille was regular. For its plural it had *dŭi mīlle or **dŭi
mīl(l)ia*, etc.

382. The ordinal numerals, after 5th, were probably not very commonly used: the Romance languages show many new formations; in northern Italian, Provençal, and Catalan the distributive ending *-ēnus* was employed (*septēnus* for *sĕptĭmus*, etc.).

Prīmus, secŭndus, tĕrtius, quartus, quīntus were generally kept, inflected like *bŏnus;* but some languages have new formations even for these.

The ordinals were best preserved in Italy.

B. PRONOUNS AND PRONOMINAL ADJECTIVES.

383. The nominative and accusative remained; and the dative was preserved in personal, demonstrative, relative, and interrogative pronouns. The ablative gave way to the dative and accusative. The genitive was usually lost; but *cūjus* was kept, and so was the genitive singular and plural of *ille, ĭpse,* and *iste.*

1. PERSONAL PRONOUNS.

N. B. — For the *use* of personal pronouns, see § 60.

384. As the pronouns came to be expressed more and more, *ille* and also *hīc, ĭpse,* and *is* were used to supply the lacking pronoun of the third person: cf. §§ 60, 67. Examples occur as early as the second century: *Franz.* ? II, 262. *Hŏc* served as an indefinite neuter. *Inde* assumed the function of an indefinite genitive: *nemo inde dubitat,* Regnier 110.

385. *Ego* lost its *g* in all the territory, but probably not until the end of the Vulgar Latin period. According to Meyer-Lübke, *Lat. Spr.* 484, *eo* occurs in manuscripts of the sixth century.[1] See § 263.

---

[1] But his reference to *Vok.* I, 242 is incorrect.

In the last syllable of *tĭbĭ*, *sĭbĭ* the short *i* prevailed, and was carried into *nōbīs*, *vōbīs*. On the pattern of *mī* < *mihi*, there were formed *tī*, *sī* beside *tĭbĭ*, *sĭbĭ*; these are found, according to *Lat. Spr.* 484, from the sixth century on; cf. *Franz.* ₂ II, 243–244.

386. The inflection was probably reduced to: —

ẹo	nọs	tụ	vọs		
mį	nọβe(s)	tį tẹβe	vọβe(s)	sį sẹβe	sį sẹβe
mẹ	nọs	tẹ	vọs	sẹ	sẹ

2. POSSESSIVES.

387. *Mĕus, tŭus, sŭus* were declined like *bŏnus; nŏster, vŏster*, like *līber*. But *mī* was used, beside *mĕus, mĕa*, as a masculine and feminine vocative (G. 281–282); *mi domina* is common, G. 282, Dubois 261–262. For the plural of the third person, *illōru* came, in the Romance languages except Spanish, to replace *sŭus*, etc.

By the analogy of *mĕus*, there was a *seus: C. I. L.* XII, 5692, 9; cf. *siæ*, IX, 3472.

Sous is found in Gaul, *Zs. fr. Spr.* XXV, ii, 135: perhaps it is only a phonetic spelling of *sọus* < *suus*, but it may represent a pronunciation *sọus* with an *o* opened by dissimilation (cf. § 167). There doubtless was a **tọus* also.

Vester disappeared. Vulgar Latin *vŏster* may be a survival of the Old Latin *vŏster*, or a reconstruction on the model of *nŏster:* cf. § 199, (1).

388. In archaic and popular Latin there was a short *sus sa sum*, probably used originally in the unaccented position: *sas, sīs* occur in Ennius, *sam* in Festus; *so* is found in *C. I. L.* V, 2007. There must have been similar short forms for the first and second persons singular: *mīs*, indeed, is used by Ennius.

The full inflection is found in the sixth century: *Franz. ℈ II*, 244.

These forms survived in Romance: Old It. *fratelmo, madrema*, etc.

3. DEMONSTRATIVES.

N. B. — For the *use* of demonstratives, see §§ 61-68. For their function as definite articles and personal pronouns, see §§ 60, 67-68, also § 392.

389. When *ille* and *iste* had a really demonstrative force, they came to be compounded usually with the prefix *ecc'* or *eccu'*: see § 65. Cf. *Franz. ℈* II, 283-304.

390. The inflection of *ille* developed considerably in popular speech. *Ipse* and *iste* followed a similar course; we find, however, the special forms *ipsus* for *ipse* and *ipsud* for *ipsum*, R. 276; *Franz. ℈* II, 274.

Ille, nom. sg. m., was partially replaced, probably in the second half of the sixth century, by *illī*, framed on the model of *quī*: Bon. 114, *illi = ille, ipsi = ipse*; cf. *Franz. ℈* II, 246-260.

Through the analogy of *cūjus, cūi*, the m. *illīus* gave way to *illūjus*, and the dat. sg. m. *illī* was replaced in part by *illūi*. The former, however, subsequently went out of use, and the latter is not found in Calabria, Sicily, Sardinia, and the Spanish peninsula. *Illius* (*ipsius, istius*), having become archaic in popular speech, sometimes occurred as a dative: *Franz. ℈* II, 277-279. There was another dative form, *illo*, used by Apuleius and others (Neue II, 427; R. 275; Quillacq 83); but it disappeared from late Latin, being confused with the ablative and the accusative. The Old Latin genitive *illī* (*ipsi, isti*), was abandoned: cf. *Franz. ℈* II, 273, 275.

In the dat. sg. f., beside *illī*, there was *illæ* (or *ille*), used by Cato and others (Neue II, 427; R. 275; Audollent 302); and from that, on the model of *illūi* (and perhaps of *quei*), was made *illæi* (*illei*), which was used beside *įllī* and *įllæ*. In the genitive, on the same pattern (influenced perhaps by *quejus*), was constructed *illæjus* (*illejus*), which crowded out *illīus*.

Illujus, illui, illejus, illei are found from the sixth century on: *Zs.* XXVI, 600, 619. Cf. *Lat. Spr.* 484: *illujus, illui, illejus, illæ, ille; ipsujus, ipseus.*

Illōrum displaced the f. *illārum*. It came, furthermore, to be used, in Romance, for the dat. m. and f. *įllīs*, which, however, did not entirely disappear. In parts of northern Spain and southwestern France *illōrum* seems to have become *illūrum, through the analogy of *illūjus, illūi*.

The neuter *įllud* was replaced by *įllum*: Neue II, 426; R. 276.

391. The popular inflection, at the end of the Vulgar Latin period, was something like this (brackets indicating forms not kept in Romance): —

ęlle ęllį	ęlla	ęllu
[ellujus]	ellejus	
ęllį [ęllo] ellui	ęllį ęlle ellęi	ęllį
ęllu ello	ęlla	ęllu ęllo
ęllį	ęlle	ęlla
elloru elluru?	[ellaru] elloru elluru?	
ęllį(s) elloru	ęllį(s)	
ęllo(s)	ęlla(s)	ęlla

392. When unaccented, these words tended to lose their first syllable (see § 157): *tū įllam vįdēs* > **tu 'la' vęde(s); vįdēs tū įpsam clavem* > **vęde(s) tu 'sa' clave'*? *Lui* and *lei* are found after the seventh century: *Franz.*₂ II, 281–283.

Ille and *ipse* were used freely as definite articles from the fourth century on: Densusianu 177. *Ille* prevailed, except in Sardinia, Majorca, a part of Catalonia and Gascony, and some dialects on the south shore of France. Cf. *Franz.*₂ II, 271–272.

4. INTERROGATIVE AND RELATIVE PRONOUNS.

N. B. — For the *use* of these pronouns, and the substitution of *qui* for feminine *quæ*, see §§ 69–70.

393. In Christian inscriptions from the fifth century on, *quī* takes the place of *quĭs*, and also of the feminine *quæ*. Beside *cūjus*, *cūi* is found a corresponding feminine *quejus*, *quei*: see Mohl in *Zs.* XXVI, 619.

The combined inflection of *quī* and *quĭs*, by the end of the Vulgar Latin period, was probably reduced, in common speech, to something like this: —

quị	que	quị	cǫd quẹd
cuju(s)	queju(s)	cuju(s)	cuju(s)
cuị	queị	cuị	cuị
que	qua	que	cǫd quẹd
cǫ?	qua	cǫ?	cǫ?
quị	que	quị	que
cǫs?	quas?	cǫs?	que

The genitive was probably not used everywhere; perhaps it was kept only in Spain. *Unde* and *d'ŭnde*, 'whence,' took the meaning 'of which': Bon. 580.

394. *Qualis*, inflected like *trīstis*, was used as an interrogative pronoun and adjective. In the Romance languages (*ĭl*)*le* + *qualis* came to be employed as a relative pronoun.

5. INDEFINITE PRONOUNS AND ADJECTIVES.

395. For these, see § 71. *Alter, nūllus, sōlus, tōtus, ūnus* doubtless developed an inflection like *bŏnus*: gen. *nulli*, etc., R. 276; dat. *solo, toto, uno*, etc., R. 276–277. *Alter*, however, assumed a dative **altrūi*, on the model of *illūi*, etc.

C. VERBS.

1. THE FOUR CONJUGATIONS.

396. There was some confusion of conjugations; the first and fourth were least affected. In the *Peregrinatio* the second decidedly preponderates over the third (Bechtel 87); in other texts the third gains at the expense of the second.

The second gained most in Spain, the third in Italy, the fourth in Gaul. Eventually Spanish and Portuguese discarded the third, Sicilian and Sardinian the second.

New formations went into the first and fourth.

a. FIRST CONJUGATION.

397. The first conjugation generally held its own, defections being few and partial.

Beside *do, dant* and *sto, stant* there came into use **dao, *daunt* and **stao, *staunt:* Rum. *daŭ, staŭ;* Old It. *dao;* Pr. *dau, daun, estau, estaun;* Pg. *dou, estou*. Mohl, *Lexique* 47, would connect these forms with Umbrian *stahu*, but it seems more likely that they were late Latin formations due to an effort to keep the root vowel distinct from the ending. Cf. Probus, "*adno* non *adnao*," *Lexique* 47.

In northern Gaul there may have developed with **stao* a **stais* and a **stait*, on the analogy of (**vao*), **vais, *vait* (see § 405): cf. *Lexique* 47–54.

The Italian present subjunctive *dia* from *dare* is associated by Mohl, *Lexique* 47 and *Pr. Pers. Pl.* 30, with Umbrian *dia*. It is entirely possible, however, that the form is a later, Italian development due to the analogy of *sia:* see § 419, (2).

398. For new formations, — such as *abbreviare, follicare, werrizare*, etc., — see §§ 33–35. Germanic verbs in *–on* and in

-*an* (but not -*jan*) regularly went in the first conjugation: *roubôn* > It. *rubare, witan* > It. *guidare*. Cf. § 36.

b. SECOND CONJUGATION.

399. Even in Classic Latin there was some confusion between the second conjugation and the third: *fervĕre, tergĕre*. In Vulgar Latin the second lost some verbs to the third in most of the territory: **ardĕre,* **lucĕre, lugĕre* (R. 283), *miscĕre* (R. 284), **mordĕre,* **nocĕre,* **ridĕre, respondĕre* (Bechtel 88: *responduntur*), *tondĕre,* *torcĕre (for *torquēre*). Other verbs passed over locally or occasionally: *seditur,* Bechtel 88.

400. Some verbs went into the fourth, probably through the pronunciation of –*eo* as –*io* (see § 224): **complīre, florīre* (R. 284), **implīre,* **lucīre, lugīre* (R. 284), *putrīre. The inchoative –*ēscĕre* then became –*īscĕre:* **florīsco, lucīsco,* *putrīsco.

Habēre, at least in Italy, sometimes became *habīre: Vok.* I, 266 ff.; *havite, C. I. L.* V, 1636; *habibat, Itala,* Luke VI, 8; *avire* in many Italian dialects in which *e* does not phonetically become *i*, and even in early Tuscan (cf. E. Monaci, *Crestomazia italiana dei primi secoli* I, p. 20, l. 1c, etc). According to Mohl, *Lexique* 108–109, this is a peculiarity of ancient Umbrian.

401. While retaining *habeo, habes, habet, habent,* the verb *habēre*, under the influence of *dare* and *stare*, adopted the forms *ho or **hao,* **has,* **hat,* *hant or *haunt.

c. THIRD CONJUGATION.

402. The third conjugation gave a few verbs to the second, perhaps beginning with those that had a perfect in –*ui*, such as *cadere* **cadui, capere* **capui, sapere sapui: sapere* was influenced, especially in Italy, by *habēre; capere* may easily have imitated *sapere*, and *cadere* may have followed *capere*.

In Spain all the third conjugation verbs eventually passed into the second. This transition was probably helped by a partial fusion of *ěsse* and *sedēre*.

403. The anomalous *pŏsse pŏtui, vĕlle vŏlui* naturally went over to the second conjugation, assumed the infinitive forms *potēre,* *volēre, and conformed their inflection more or less to the regular type. *Vĕlle*, however, was discarded in Spain and Sardinia.

(1) *Potere, potebam* occur repeatedly in the sixth century (*Pr. Pers. Pl.* 24), *potebo* is found in the *Gl. Reich.*, *potebas* in Fredegarius (Haag 60). *Posso* for *pŏssum* is used by Gregory and Fredegarius (*Pr. Pers. Pl.* 24), *poteo* is attested in 745 A.D. (*Pr. Pers. Pl.* 25). The present indicative must have been inflected something like this:—

pǫssu pǫsso pǫtęo *pǫssęo	**potęmu(s)*
pǫte(s)	*potęste(s)* **potęte(s)*
**pǫte(t)*	*pǫssun(t)* **pǫten(t)*

The present subjunctive must have had corresponding forms.

(2) *Volimus* is found in the sixth century (*Lat. Spr.* 478), *volemus* in the seventh (*Pr. Pers. Pl.* 21); *voles* is found in the *Gl. Reich*. *Volestis*, framed on the pattern of *potestis*, is twice used by Fredegarius (*Pr. Pers. Pl.* 21). The present indicative forms must have been something like this:—

*vǫlęo	*vǫlimu(s) volęmu(s)*
vǫle(s)	*voleste(s)* **volęte(s)*
**vǫle(t)*	**vǫlen(t)*

The present subjunctive must have been similarly inflected.

404. Beside *facĕre* there doubtless existed *fare (*Facere* 48), strongly influenced by *dare* and *stare*. *Dare* and *facere* were associated in old formulas: *Lexique* 53. Furthermore, a suggestion of shortening existed in the monosyllabic imperative

§ 405] AN INTRODUCTION TO VULGAR LATIN. 169

fac (also *fa: Zs.* XXV, 735), which must have led to *fate beside *facĭte*. The present indicative certainly had several sets of forms, one series being on the pattern of the first conjugation, but the present subjunctive retained its old inflection (see *Facere* 72, 121; *Zs.* XVIII, 434): —

facįo	*fao	*fo	fácimu(s)	*fáimus	*famu(s)
face(s)	*fais	*fas	fácite(s)	*fáitis	*fate(s)
face(t)	*fait	*fat	facįun(t)	*faunt	*fant

There was also a rare infinitive *facire*, which occurs several times in the sixth and seventh centuries: *Facere* 13.

405. *Vadēre* supplied its missing past tenses from *īre* and other verbs. These other substitutes, whose origin constitutes one of the most discussed problems in Romance philology, resulted — to cite only the principal types — in the verbs *allare or *alare* (used in northern Gaul), *annare (used in southern Gaul), *andare (used in Spain and Italy). It is now generally thought that *allare and *annare developed in some peculiar way (perhaps through distortion in military commands) from *ambŭlare*, which is very common in late Latin in the sense of 'march' or 'walk.' *Andare is commonly traced to *ambĭtare, coming either from *ambĭtus* or, more probably, from *ambŭlare* with a change of suffix. C. C. Rice, in the *Publications of the Modern Language Association of America* XIX, 217, argues that the three verbs sprang from Latin *annare* (= *adnare*) and its derivatives *annŭlare, *annĭtare. For a bibliography of the subject, see Körting. Cf. also A. Horning in *Zs.* XXIX, 542; H. Schuchardt in *Zs.* XXX, 83; *Lexique* 56–78. Both *ambulare* and *alare* occur in the *Gl. Reich*. *Amnavit* is found on a sixth century African vase: see F. Novati in *Studi Medievali* I, 616–617.

Ire and the other substitutes were introduced also into the present. The present indicative, moreover, was influenced by *facere fare*: —

vado	*vao	*vo	vádimu(s)	ímu(s) etc.
vade(s)	*vais	*vas	vádite(s)	íte(s) etc.
vade(t)	*vait	*vat	vadun(t)	*vaunt *vant

406. Verbs in *-io* tended to pass into the fourth conjugation (see, however, § 416): **capīre*, beside **capēre; cupīre*, Lucretius (*Lat. Spr.* 477), Densusianu 148, Bon. 426; *fodīri*, Cato; *fugīre*, St. Augustine (*Lat. Spr.* 477), common in the Vulgate (R. 285), Sepulcri 229, Bon. 427, Haag 60, *Gl. Reich.*; *morīri*, Plautus, and **morīre*.

Some others went over, at least locally: **fallīre; gemire*, Pirson 148; *occurire*, Pirson 148; **offerīre, *sofferīre*, by the analogy of *aperīre* (*sufferit*, R. 286; cf. *deferet*, *offeret*, Bechtel 90; *offeret*, first half of the 7th century, Carnoy 112); **sequīre*, beside **sĕquĕre*.

Dicĕre, probably in the Vulgar Latin period (cf. *Lexique* 62), developed a form **dīre*, doubtless suggested by *dīc* (cf. *fac* and **fare*, § 404) and helped by the analogy of *audīre*.

d. FOURTH CONJUGATION.

407. The fourth conjugation usually held its own, and gained some verbs from the others.

For new formations, — such as **abbellīre, ignīre*, — see § 34. Germanic verbs in *-jan* regularly went into the fourth conjugation in Latin (Kluge 500): *furbjan* > It. *forbire;* *marrjan* > Fr. *marrir;* *parrjan* > Fr. *tarir;* *warnjan* > It. *guarnire.* Cf. § 36.

For the intrusion of the inchoative *-sc-* into this conjugation, see § 415.

2. FUNDAMENTAL CHANGES IN INFLECTION.

408. Of the personal forms of the verb there remained in general use in Romance only the following tenses of the active voice, the entire passive inflection having been discarded: the indicative present, imperfect, perfect, pluperfect, and in some regions the future perfect; the subjunctive present, pluperfect, and in some regions the perfect; the imperative present. For instance: *amo, amabam, amavi, amaram, (amaro); amem, amassem, (amarim); ama.* See Syntax.

Of the impersonal forms of the verb there remained: the present active infinitive, the present participle, the perfect participle, the gerund (especially the ablative case), and probably in some standing phrases the gerundive. For instance: *amare, amans, amatus, amando, (amandus?).* The supine fell into disuse from the first century on. See Syntax.

409. The entire passive inflection came to be replaced, towards the end of the Vulgar Latin period, partly by active and reflexive constructions but mainly by a compound of the perfect participle with *ĕsse* (in northern Italy *fĭĕri*): *līttĕra scrībĭtur > littera scripta est* (or *fit*).

Deponent verbs became active: *mentire, operare,* etc., R. 298; cf. R. 297-302, 388-389. Conversely, some writers substituted the deponent for the active inflection of a few verbs: Petronius, *rideri,* etc., R. 304; cf. R. 302-304.

Cf. §§ 112-114.

410. The Latin perfect was kept in its preterit sense. In its perfect sense it was replaced, in the Vulgar Latin period, by a compound of *habēre* and the perfect participle — in the case of neuter verbs, *ĕsse* and the perfect participle: *fēci > habeo factum; reverti > reversus sum,* R. 289. Similar compounds replaced the pluperfect and the future perfect. See §§ 121-124.

The old pluperfect indicative (*amāram, audīram*) was kept, as a preterit or a conditional, in various regions: see § 124. In the subjunctive the pluperfect was used instead of the imperfect, which disappeared everywhere but in Sardinia (*facheret*, etc.): *amārem*>*amāssem, audīrem*>*audīssem;* cf. §118.

The old future perfect — *amā(vĕ)ro* — fused with the perfect subjunctive — *amā(vĕ)rim* — and apparently remained more or less in use, as a future indicative or subjunctive, in all regions except Gaul and Rætia. It is best preserved in Spanish and Portuguese, but is found also in Old Rumanian and Macedonian. There are traces of it in Old Italian, sometimes confused with the pluperfect indicative and later sometimes with the infinitive (*ápriro, póteri, crédere*, etc.): see C. De Lollis in *Bausteine* 1; V. Crescini in *Zs.* XXIX, 619.

411. The old future, with the exception of *ĕro*, was crowded out by the present and by new formations, especially by the infinitive combined with the present indicative of *habēre* (*amābo*>*amar' habeo*): see §§125–129. In this compound all the various forms of the present indicative of *habēre* were used (see §§273, 401): **amar' –ábeo, –áyo, –áo, –ó;* **amar' –ábe(s), –ás;* **amar' –ábe(t), –át;* **amar' ában(t), –áunt, –ánt.* In the first and second persons plural, *habēmus* and *habētis* eventually, as they came to be regarded as mere endings, were reduced to *–ẹmu(s), –ẹte(s)*, to correspond to the dissyllabic or monosyllabic *–áyo, –ábe(s), –ábe(t), –ában(t)* and *–ó, –ás, –át, –ánt:* **amar' –ému(s),* **amar' –éte(s).*

On the model of this new future, an imperfect of the future, or conditional, came to be made, in late Vulgar Latin and Romance, from the infinitive combined with the imperfect or the perfect of *habēre* (see §130): **amar' –abẹ(b)a(m)* or **amar' –abu̯i.* In these formations the unaccented (*h*)*ab-* disappeared, as in the first and second persons plural of the future: **amar' –é(b)a,* **amar' –ísti*, etc.; but **amar' ábui*, etc. In Italian we find, beside *–ía* from *habēbam* and *–ábbi –ébbi* from *habŭi*, a form in *–éi* (*ameréi*), which has prevailed in the modern language, while in Old Italian the *ei* was sometimes detached and used as a preterit of *avere:* it is probably due to the analogy of the first person singular of the weak preterit (*credéi*, hence *crederéi*), cf. § 426.

412. The imperative disappeared, except the present, second person singular and plural: *ămā, amāte; tĕnē, tenēte; crĕdĕ, crēdĭte; audī, audīte.* The first and third persons were supplied from the present subjunctive. In some verbs the present subjunctive was used instead of all imperative forms. See § 115.

Instead of the plural form, the second person plural of the present indicative came to be used: *adferte > adferitis,* R. 294. For the monosyllabic *dic, duc, fac,* writers sometimes employed *dice, duce, face:* R. 294.

3. INCHOATIVE VERBS.

413. The Latin inchoative ending *-sco* was preceded by *ā-, ē-, ī-,* or *ō-*. The types *-āsco* and *-ōsco* were sparingly represented and were not extended in late and popular Latin; they have bequeathed but few verbs — such as Pr. *iráisser < irāscĕre, conóisser < co(g)nōscĕre* — to the Romance languages. The types *-ēsco* and *-īsco* — as *parēsco, dormīsco* — were extended in the third century and later, and lost their inchoative sense.

414. There is some evidence of a confusion of *-ēsco* and *-īsco* in Latin. Virgilius Grammaticus (Sepulcri 194) mentions double forms of inchoative verbs, such as *calesco calisco,* etc. *Clarisco, erubisco,* etc., are common in Gregory the Great: Sepulcri 193. Cf. *criscere,* etc., in *Vok.* I, 359 ff.

In Veglia, the Abruzzi, Sardinia, and a part of Lorraine neither of these two endings left any trace. Only *-ēsco* survived in the Tyrol, the Grisons, French Switzerland, Savoy, Dauphiné, Lyons, the Landes, Béarn, and Spain — Sp. *parecer,* *florecer;* *-esco* was preferred also in Rumanian. Elsewhere, although there are traces of *-ēsco,* *-īsco* prevailed — Fr. *il fleurit,* It. *fiorisce.* For Pr. *despereissir,* etc., see E. Herzog in *Bausteine* 481.

415. The ending *-īsco* eventually entered into the formation of the present stem of fourth conjugation verbs. There is no direct evidence of this in Latin, nor are there any traces of it in Spanish, Portuguese, Sardinian, or southern Italian; but in the earliest texts of France, northern and central Italy, Rætia, and Rumania we find a type

*finịsco	finịmu(s)
*finịsce(s)	finịte(s)
*finịsce(t)	*finịscun(t)

The *-sc-* then generally disappeared from the infinitive — It. *fiorire.* Later, in some regions, the *-sc-* was carried throughout the present indicative (Fr. *finissons, finissez*); it also penetrated the present subjunctive (Fr. *finisse*), and in some districts eventually the present participle and the imperfect indicative (Fr. *finissant, finissais*).

See *Archiv* I, 465; *Zs.* XXIV, 81; *Rom.* XXX, 291–294; *Lat. Spr.* 478.

4. PRESENT STEMS.

416. Many verbs in *-io* dropped the *i̯* whenever it was followed by another vowel. In the present participle this was a regular phonetic development (see § 225): *audientem* > **audente, facientem* > **facente, partientem* > **partente, sentientem* > **sentente.* Hence forms without the *i̯* were introduced more or less into the indicative and subjunctive: *audio* **audo,* **dŏrmo, partiunt* **partunt, sĕntiam* **sĕntam,* etc.

By the analogy of these, the *e̯* was occasionally lost in the second conjugation: *vĭdeo* **vĭdo.* On the other hand, by the analogy of *capiunt, faciunt*, etc., the second conjugation admitted such forms as *habeunt, *vĭdeunt, etc., beside the regular *habent, vĭdent*, etc.

417. The verbs *struĕre, trahĕre, vehĕre* developed infinitive forms *strúgere, trágere, végere (*tragere* and *vegere* are used by Fredegarius, Haag 34) and a whole present and imperfect inflection with –g–, as *trago, *tragam, *tragēbam. The guttural was derived from the perfect indicative and the perfect participle — *struxi structus, traxi tractus, vexi vectus* — on the analogy of *ago actus, figo fixi, lego lectus, rego rexi rectus, tego tectus*, and also *fingo finxi fictus, tango tactus*, and probably *cingo cinxi cinctus, jungo junxi junctus, pango panxi panctus, plango planxi planctus, ungo unxi unctus*, etc.

There may have been also *strúcere, *trácere, *vécere, based on the analogy of *dico dixi dictus, duco duxi ductus*.

Cf. *Substrate* VI, 131.

418. The verbs *dare, debēre, dīcĕre, facĕre, habēre, pŏsse, stare, vadĕre, vĕlle* underwent considerable changes in the present: see §§ 273, 397, 401, 403–406, 412, 416.

419. *Esse* was made into *ĕssĕre, to bring it into conformity with the usual third conjugation type. Considerable alterations were made in the present indicative and subjunctive. For the use of *fĭĕri* for *ĕsse*, see § 409. The Spanish use of *sedēre* for *ĕsse* is probably later than our period.

(1) The present indicative shows some signs of a tendency to normalize its erratic inflection by making all the forms begin with *s*. The old *esum* cited by Varro (*Pr. Pers. Pl.* 128) went out of use. Italian *sei* and Rætian *šeš* point to a *sĕs beside *ĕs;* Italian *siete* and Rætian *siede*, etc., indicate a *sĕtis for *ĕstis*, while there is some evidence of an alternative *sŭtis on the model of *sŭmus;* Old Italian *se* for *è*, Provençal *ses* for

es, usually understood as reflexive forms, may go back to *sĕt and *sĕst for *ĕst*. In the first person plural *sŭmus* became *sŭmus* and *sĭmus* (see § 220); *sŭmus*, the usual Classic form, was preferred in Spain, Portugal, northern Gaul, and the Tyrol (Sp. *somos*, Old Fr. *sons*, etc.); *sĭmus*, which was used, according to Suetonius, by Augustus, and by various purists of the Augustan age (Stolz 58), prevailed in southern Gaul, Italy, Dalmatia, and Dacia (Pr. *sem*, Old It. *semo*, etc.): cf. *Lat. Spr.* 479; *Pr. Pers. Pl.* 130; *Rom.* XXI, 347. Provençal *esmes* < *ĕsmus seems to be a new formation on the analogy of *ĕstis;* Mohl, *Pr. Pers. Pl.* 135, would derive it from old *esĭmus*, which existed with *esum*. The present indicative inflection was doubtless something like this: —

```
sǫm                    sǫmu(s)   sęmu(s)   *ęsmu(s)
ęs    *sęs             ęste(s)   *sęte(s)  *sǫte(s)?
ęst   *sęt?  *sęst?    sǫnt
```

(2) In the present subjunctive the analogy of other third conjugation verbs tended to introduce the characteristic vowel *a*. It is likely, too, that from early times there was a reciprocal influence of *fiam*, etc., and the Old Latin optative *siem*, etc. (cf. *Lexique* 51): *fiet* is common for *fit*, Pirson 150; *fiam* replaces *sim* in northern Italy and Dacia. Hence comes an alternative inflection *sĭam, etc., which ultimately prevailed: —

```
sęm   *sęa              sĭmu(s)   siámu(s)
sįs   *sęa(s)           sįte(s)   *siáte(s)
sęt    sęa(t)           sęnt      *sęan(t)
```

For *sĭat*, see *sead* in *Vok.* II, 42. *Siámus*, according to *Lat. Spr.* 478, occurs in Italian documents of the eighth century.

5. IMPERFECT.

N. B. — For the loss of the imperfect subjunctive, see § 118.

420. The endings were *–ābam*, *–ēbam*, *–iēbam*, *–ībam*. In the third conjugation *–iēbam* regularly developed into *–ēbam*, just as *-ientem* > *-entem* (see §§ 225, 416): *faciēbam* > *facēbam. In the fourth conjugation *-iēbam* and *-ībam* existed side by side from early times (Neue II, 445), *-ībam* — as in *munībam* — being common in early Latin and recurring at later periods (Lindsay 491); *-ībam*, which stressed the characteristic vowel of the fourth conjugation, prevailed in popular speech, and *-iēbam* disappeared: *vestibat*, etc., Dubois 277–278.

421. *Habēbam*, pronounced *aβεβa* (cf. § 318), developed another form, *aβεa, probably through dissimilation. Hence came an alternative ending *-ea* for *-eβa*, which in Romance was widely extended, affecting all the conjugations but the first: It. *vedéa, credéa, sentía*. It is common to nearly all the Romance territory except Rumania: *Lat. Spr.* 479.

6. PERFECT.

422. We must distinguish two types, the weak and the strong: the weak comprises the *v-* perfects in which the *v* is added to a verb-stem (*-āvi, -ēvi, -īvi*), the strong includes all others. Verbs of the first and fourth conjugations generally had weak perfects, those of the second and third had mostly strong. Only six verbs — all of the second conjugation and most of them rare — regularly had a perfect in *-ēvi: deleo, fleo, neo, -oleo, -pleo, vieo; silevit* for *siluit* occurs also, R. 287.

All first and fourth conjugation verbs with strong perfects probably developed a weak one in Vulgar Latin: *præstiti* > *præstavi*, R. 289; *salui* > *salivi*. For further encroachment of the weak type on the strong, see § 426.

a. WEAK PERFECTS.

423. A tendency to keep the stress on the characteristic vowel, and also a general inclination to omit *v* between two *i*'s (see § 324), led early, in the fourth conjugation, to a reduction of *–īvĭstī* to *–īstī* and *–īvĭstis* to *–īstis*, which brought about, still early, the further reduction of *–īvī* to *–īi* and *–*ĭi*, *–īvĭt* to *–ĭt* and *–*ĭit*, *–īvĕrunt* to *–ierunt*, and, later, the reduction of *–īvĭmus* to *–īmus* and probably *–*īmmus* (the lengthening of the *m* being due to compensation and also, perhaps, to a desire to distinguish the perfect from the present). For *–ĭit*, as in *leniit*, see Servius *ad Aen.* I, 451; for *–ierunt*, see Neue III, 452–454; for *–īmus*, as in *repetīmus*, etc., see Neue III, 449.

Then a contraction of the two vowels gave, in the first and third persons singular and the third person plural, *–ī, –it*, *–*ĭrunt: audī*, Neue III, 434 (cf. S. 241: 65–121 A.D.); *petīt*, etc., Neue III, 446–448; "*cupit* pro *cupivit*," Priscian XII, 17 (Keil II, 587); *perīt, petīt, redīt*, Bayard 60; *perit*, etc., Bon. 440.

A contraction without the fall of *v*, in the third person singular, gave rise, locally, to an alternative form, *–*īut:* It. *servio*, etc.

424. The loss of *v*, carried into the first conjugation, gave rise early to a reduction of *–āvĭstī, –āvĭstis, –āvĕrunt* to *–āstī, –āstis, –ārunt*. Much later *–āvī* > *–āi, –āvit* > *āit* and *–āt*, *–āvīmus* > *–āmus* and probably *–*āmmus: calcai* (Probus), *edificai, probai* (Probus), *Vok.* II, 476; σεγναι, Densusianu I, 152; — *laborait, C. I. L.* X, 216; *speclarait, Vok.* II, 476; *dedicait, Lexique* 46; "*fumât* pro *fumavit*," Priscian XII, 17 (Keil II, 587); *denumerat, judicat*, Fredegarius (Haag 55); — *cœlebramus, memoramus, vocitamus*, Gregory of Tours (Bon. 440); *speramus*, Fredegarius (Haag 55). The third person singular in *–ait* is found in Old Sardinian: *Lat. Spr.* 479.

A contraction without the fall of *v* gave rise, in the third person singular, to *–aut;* and, in the first person plural, probably to *–*aumus: triumphaut* in Pompeii, Densusianu I, 152. This *–aut* prevailed in Romance: It. *amò* and *amáo*, etc. The

§ 426] AN INTRODUCTION TO VULGAR LATIN. 179

*-aumus is preserved in some Old French dialects near Douai: Rom. XXX, 607.

425. The forms in the first and fourth conjugations, therefore, were: —

-ávi̯	-ái̯			-i̯vi̯	*-i̯i̯	-ii̯ -i̯
-ásti̯				-ísti̯		
-áve(t)	-áut	-áit	-át	-i̯ve(t)	*-i̯ut	*-i̯it -iit -i̯t
-ávimu(s)	-ámu(s)	*-ámmu(s)	*-áumus	-i̯vimu(s)	-i̯mu(s)	*-i̯mmu(s)
-áste(s)				-iste(s)		
-árun(t)				*-i̯run(t)		

With the exception of -ivi in Old Italian, the forms with v were not preserved in Romance.

Verbs in -ēvī doubtless had a similar inflection: *delēī, delēstī, etc. Some other second conjugation verbs apparently adopted this perfect: silevit, R. 287.

426. Compounds of dare had a perfect in -dĭdī (credĭdī, perdĭdī, vendĭdī, etc.), which in Vulgar Latin became -dḝdi (see § 139): perdedit, etc., Audollent 544. This -dedi was extended to many other verbs in -d-: prandidi, Keil IV, 184; descendidi, respondidi, Lat. Spr. 479, 480; ascendiderat, descendidit, incendederit, odedere, pandiderunt, prendiderunt, videderunt (cf. edediderit with an extra -de-), R. 288.

Through the analogy of -āi, *-ēi, *-īi, helped by dissimilation, this -dedi became *-dei. Hence arose eventually an inflection *-dei̯, *-desti, *-det, *-dem(m)u(s), *-deste(s), -derun(t), from which there came a set of endings *-ei̯, *-esti, etc., corresponding to the -ai -asti, etc., and the -ii, -isti, etc., of the first and fourth conjugations: so caderunt, Gl. Reich. In some of the Romance languages these endings were carried into other verbs of the third and even the second conjugation (It. battéi, Pr. cazét); in Provençal they invaded the first also (améi). In Dacia, on the other hand, they apparently did not develop at all. In Italy, under the influence of *stetti* < *stĕtŭi*, *dare* had (beside *diẹdi* < *dĕdi*) a perfect *dẹtti*, whence arose an inflection *–dẹtti*, etc., and a set of endings *–ẹtti*, etc., beside *–dẹi* and *–ẹi*.

Through these endings the weak type encroached somewhat on the strong. In Italy all strong verbs except *esse* introduced weak endings in the second person singular and the first and second persons plural: It. *presi, prendesti*, etc.; cf. *plaudisti* for *plausisti*, R. 286, also *vincisti*, *Gl. Reich*. In Rumania, where there was no *–dẹi*, the *–ui* and *–si* types were extended.

A few weak verbs adopted strong inflections: *quæsīvi* > *quæsi, sapīvi* > *sapui*.

b. STRONG PERFECTS.

427. There are three types — those that add *u* to the root, those that add *s*, and those that have nothing between the root and the personal endings: *plac-u-i, dīc-s-i* = *dīxi, bĭb-i*. In the first class the *u* lost its syllabic value and became *w* (cf. § 326): *placwi*, etc.

428. The *–ui* type, according to Meyer-Lübke, *Gram*. II, 357, included from the start not only perfects of the *placui* sort, but also all perfects in *–vi* not made from the verb-stem (cf. § 422), — such as *cognōvi, crēvi, mōvi, pāvi*, — this ending being pronounced *wui*, but written *vi* to avoid the doubling of the *v*. At any rate, the development of the *vi* indicates that it was sounded *wui, wwi*, or *βwi* in Vulgar Latin: cf. It. *conọbbi, crẹbbi*, etc.; Pr. *mọc*, etc.

This perfect disappeared from the first and fourth conjugations: *crepui* > **crepavi, necui* > *necavi*, etc.; *aperui* > *aperii **apersi, salui* > *salivi salii* *salsi, etc   In the second and third conjugations it maintained itself very well: *cognovi, crevi,* *gemui*(?), *messui*(?), *molui, movi, pavi, tenui, texui*. It lost *posui* (>*posi*), *silui* (>*silevi*), and possibly a few others. On the other hand it received many additions: *bĭbi* > *bĭbui; cĕcĭdi* > *cadui* *cadedi; cēpi* > *capui*, Haag 56, *Lat. Spr.* 479 (so *recĭpui*); *expavi* > *expabui, Lat. Spr.* 479; *lēgi* > *lēgui *lĕxi: natus sum* > *nacui; peperci* > *parcui*, R. 288; *sapivi* > *sapui; sēdi* > *sēdui; stĕti* > also *stĕtui; sustŭli* >*tolui* *tolsi; texi* > *texui, Lat. Spr.* 479; *vēni* > also *vēnui; vīci* > also *vĭncui* *vĭnsi; vīdi* > also *vīdui* *vĭdui; vīxi* > also *vīscui;* etc. Cf. A. Zimmermann in *Archiv* XIII, 130; *Zs.* XXVIII, 97.

429. Of the *–si* class, — which comprised perfects in *–si*, *–ssi*, and *–xi*, — some thirty-five were preserved: *arsi, cinxi, clausi, coxi, divisi, dixi, duxi, excussi, finxi, fixi, frixi, junxi, luxi, mansi, mīsi* (also *mĭssi*, perhaps on the model of *mĭssus*, cf. § 163), *mulsi, pinxi, planxi, pressi, rasi, rexi, risi, rosi, scripsi, sparsi, –stinxi, strinxi, struxi, tersi, tinxi, torsi, traxi, unxi, vixi. Sensi*, however, became *sentii*.

In Vulgar Latin there were perhaps some thirty or more new formations: *abscō(n)si*, Keil VII, 94; *accē(n)si; *apĕrsi; *attĭnxi; *copĕrsi; *cŭrsi; *defe(n)si; *ērsi* from *ērĭgo; *franxi; *fūsi; *impĭnxi; *lĕxi; *mŏrsi; *occīsi; *offĕrsi; *pē(n)si; pĕrsi, Lat. Spr.* 480; *pŏsi*, R. 288; *prē(n)- si; *pŭnxi; *quæsi; *redĕmpsi; *respō(n)si; *rōsi; *salsi; *sŏlsi; *sŭrsi; *taxi, *tanxi; *tē(n)si; *tŏlsi; *vĭnsi; *vŏlsi*. Some of these — *defensi, *fusi, *morsi, *occisi, *pensi, *prensi, *responsi, *rosi, *tensi* — assumed the *s–* perfect through having an *s* in the perfect participle.

Cf. *Einf.* § 165.

430. Among the *–i* perfects, the reduplicative formations were discarded in Vulgar Latin, with the exception of *dĕdi* and *stĕti* (also *stĕtui*), whose reduplicative character was no longer apparent; compounds of *dare* usually formed their perfect like the simple verb (cf. § 426; but *circumdavit* in *Gl. Reich.*), while compounds of *stare* tended to follow the regular first conjugation model (*præstĭti* > *præstavi*, R. 289). *Cĕcĭdi* became *cadui or **cadedi; fefelli* > **falii; peperci* > *parcui*, R. 288. The other reduplicative perfects either disappeared or passed into the *–si* class: *cucurri* > **cŭrsi; momordi* > **mŏrsi; pependi* > **pē(n)si; pupŭgi* > **pŭnxi; tetendi* > **tē(n)si; telĕgi* > *taxi *tanxi.

The other *–i* perfects were greatly reduced in number in Vulgar Latin. Some simply disappeared, some became weak, some went over to the *–ui* or the *–si* type: *ēgi, vĕrti; fūgi* > **fugii; bĭbi* > **bĭbui, cēpi* > *capui, lēgi* > **lēgui, sēdi* > **sēdui; accendi* > **accē(n)si, defendi* > **defē(n)si, frēgi* > **franxi, fūdi* > **fūsi, lēgi* > **lĕxi, prendi* > **prē(n)si, solvi* > **sŏlsi, vīci* > **vīnsi, volvi* > **vŏlsi.* There were no additions. Two of the old perfects maintained themselves intact, and two more were kept beside new formations: *fēci, fui; vēni* **vēnui, vīdi* *vĭdui.

431. In *fui* the *u* was originally long, but it was shortened in Classic Latin; Vulgar Latin seems to show both *ū* and *ŭ*. In an effort to keep the accent on the same syllable throughout (cf. §§ 423–424), *fuĭsti* > **fusti, fuĭstis* > **fustis;* then *fuĭmus* generally became **fum(m)us, fuit* was often shortened to *fut, and *fuĕrunt* became *furunt. There may have been also, through dissimilation, a form *fŏrunt.

The prevailing inflection, with some variations, was probably something like this: —

fu̦i fo̦i	**fo̦m(m)u(s)*
**fo̦sti̦*	**fo̦ste(s)*
fo̦e(t) fu̦e(t) **fo̦t* **fu̦t*	**fo̦run(t)* **fu̦run(t)* **fo̦run(t)?* *fo̦erun(t)?*

7. PLUPERFECT AND FUTURE PERFECT.

432. When preserved at all, these tenses followed the old types: *plácuĕram* (cf. § 137), *placuíssem, plácuĕro; díxĕram, dixíssem, díxĕro; fécĕram, fecíssem, fécĕro*. In formations from weak perfects only the contracted forms were used: *amāram, amāssem, amāro; delēram, delēssem, delēro; audī(e)ram, audīssem, audī(e)ro;* cf. *alaret, ortaret* in *Gl. Reich.* Bayard 60–61 notes that St. Cyprien employed only the shortened forms — *petisset*, etc. — before *ss*.

433. In some regions a tendency to keep the accent on the same syllable throughout the pluperfect subjunctive led to a change of *–assēmus, –assētis*, etc., to *–*ássĭmus,* *–*ássĭtis*, etc.: It. *amássimo amáste*, Sp. *hablásemos hablásies;* but Pr. *amessém amessétz*, Fr. *aimassións aimassiéz.*

8. PERFECT PARTICIPLE.

434. Verbs which had no perfect participle were obliged to form one in order to make their passive and their perfect tenses: *fĕrio,* **fĕrītus.*

435. In the first conjugation *–ātus* was preserved and was extended to all verbs: *frictus > fricatus; nectus > necatus; sectus > secatus;* so the new *alatus, Gl. Reich.* The ending *–ĭtus*, in the first conjugation, generally fell into disuse: *crepitus >* **crepatus; domitus > domatus*, R. 295; *plicitus > plicatus; sonitus >* **sonatus; tonitus >* **tonatus; vetitus > vetatus*, R. 296. Nevertheless there were some new formations in *–ĭtus:* **lĕvĭtus, prŏvĭtus, rŏgĭtus, vŏcĭtus;* cf. *Lat. Spr.* 480.

In the third conjugation *–ātus* disappeared: *oblatus > offertus* (*Gl. Reich.*), *sublatus >* *suffertus, by the analogy of *apertus, copertus; sublatus* (from *tollo*) *> tŏllĭtus* (*Gl. Reich.*).

436. In the fourth conjugation –*ītus* was preserved and was extended to nearly all verbs: *saltus*>**salītus; sensus*>**sentītus; sepultus* > *sepelītus*, old and found in all periods, Pirson 152, *Gl. Reich.* *Apertus* and *copertus*, however, were kept; and *ventus* generally became **venūtus*.

In the third conjugation *quæsītus* > **quæstus*.

437. In the second conjugation the rare *–ētus* disappeared as a participial ending: *complētus*, etc., were kept only as adjectives.

438. The ending *–ūtus*, belonging to verbs in *–uere* and *–vere* (*argutus, consutus, minutus, secutus, solutus, statutus, tributus, volutus*), offered a convenient accented form, corresponding to *–ātus* and *–ītus*. It was extended to nearly all the verbs that had an *–ui* perfect: **bibutus, *habutus, *parutus, *tenutus, *venutus, *vidutus*, etc.; but *status*. It did not always, however, entirely displace the old perfect participle: *natus* was kept beside **nascūtus*.

Eventually *–ūtus* was carried further, — as **credutus, *perdutus, *vendutus*, — and in Sicily encroached largely on *–ītus*.

On the other hand, **mŏvītus* and **mŏssus* were formed beside **movutus, *sŏlvĭtus* (or **sŏltus*) beside *solutus, *vŏlvĭtus* (or **vŏltus*) beside *volutus*.

439. The ending *–ĭtus* tended to disappear (cf. § 435): *absconditus* > *absco(n)sus; bibĭtus* > **bibutus; credĭtus* > **credutus; fugĭtus* > **fugītus; molĭtus* > **molutus; parĭtus* > **parutus *parsus; perditus* > **perdutus *persus; submonitus* > **submo(n)sus; vendĭtus* > **vendutus*. A few of these participles, however, remained, and there were some new formations in *–ĭtus: gĕmitus?, pŏs(i)tus, sŏlitus; *lĕvitus, *mŏvitus, prŏvitus, rŏgitus, *sŏlvitus* (or **sŏltus*), *tŏllitus, vŏcitus, *vŏlvitus* (or **vŏltus*).

440. The ending *-tus* was kept for some twenty verbs, occasionally with a change of stem: *cinctus; dictus; ductus; exstinctus; factus; fictus finctus*, R. 295; *fractus *franctus; frīctus; lectus; mistus; pictus *pinctus; punctus; rectus; scriptus; strictus *strinctus; structus; *surtus* for *surrectus; tactus? *tanctus?; tinctus; tortus; tractus.* There were a few new formations in *-tus: offertus, *quæstus, *suffertus, *vīstus;* and perhaps **sŏltus, *vŏltus* (cf. § 439).

About fifteen verbs probably replaced *-tus* by *-ātus, -ītus,* or *-ūtus: captus *capītus; cognōtus > *conovūtus?; crētus > *crevūtus?; fartus > *farcītus* and *farsus, Lat. Spr.* 480; *frīctus > frīcātus; mōtus > *movūtus?* and **mŏssus; nectus > necātus; pastus > *pavūtus?; saltus > *salītus* and **salsus; sectus > secātus; sepultus > sepelītus; tentus > *tenūtus; texus > *texūtus; ventus > *venūtus* and *venītus,* Bechtel 91; *vĭctus > *vincūtus* and **vinctus; vīctus > *vixūtus.*

441. The ending *-sus* was generally kept: *acce(n)sus; arsus; clausus; defe(n)sus; divīsus; excussus; fixus; fusus; ma(n)sus; mīssus,* also perhaps **mīsus* by the analogy of *mīsi; morsus; pe(n)sus; pre(n)sus; pressus; risus; rosus; sparsus; te(n)sus; tersus; to(n)sus; visus,* also probably **vistus.* Several of these developed also a participle in *-ūtus: *pendutus, *vidutus,* etc. *Salsus,* 'salted,' maintained itself beside *salītus.*

A few verbs replaced the old form by one in *-ītus* or *-ūtus: expansus > *expandutus; falsus > *fallītus; fusus > fundutus, Gl. Reich.; gavīsus > *gaudutus; messus > metītus,* Dubois 282; *sensus > *sentītus; sessus > *sedutus.*

On the other hand, there were some new formations in *-sus: absco(n)sus,* Keil VII, 94, *Lat. Spr.* 480, R. 295 (very common); *farsus, Lat. Spr.* 480; **mossus; *parsus; *persus; *salsus; *submo(n)sus.*

9. PERSONAL ENDINGS.

442. For the reduction of *–io* to *–o*, see §416.

443. Meyer-Lübke, *Grundriss* I², 670, assumes that in Italy *–ās* and *–ēs* became *–i*. The evidence, historically considered, does not support this view. Italian *lodi* and Rumanian *lauzi*, from *laudas*, are correctly explained by Tiktin 565–566 as analogical formations.

444. As unaccented *ē*, *ĕ*, and *ĭ* came to be pronounced alike (§ 243), great confusion ensued between *–ēs* and *–ĭs*, *–ĕt* and *–ĭt*. This confusion is very frequent in the *Peregrinatio:* Bechtel 88–89, *colliget*, etc.

445. In southern and to some extent in northern Gaul the first person plural lost its final *s*, perhaps in the Vulgar Latin period: *vidēmus* > Pr. *vezém*. This is not a phonetic phenomenon, as *–s* did not fall in this region. It may be that *–s* was dropped because it was regarded as a characteristic of the second person, as *t* was of the third (cf. *Pr. Pers. Pl.* 73–80):—

ámo	*amámu
ámas	amátes
ámat	ámant

446. According to Mohl, *Pr. Pers. Pl.*, forms like *cánomus, due to Celtic influence, were used in northern Gaul instead of *canĭmus*, etc.; then the accent was shifted to the penult — *canómus, whence came the French *–ons*. This theory has not found acceptance.

447. In strong perfects the first person plural, *–ĭmus*, — through the analogy of *–istis* and *–isti*, and doubtless of weak perfects as well, — tended, perhaps after our period, to stress its penult: *fēcĭmus* > Pr. *fezém*. There are traces of this in inscriptions and elsewhere: S. 47, 53. The shift, however, was not universal, as there are in Italian and French remains of the original accentuation.

448. In the present indicative and imperative, *-ĭmus, -ĭtis, -ĭte* generally became, in the sixth or seventh century, *-ému(s), -éte(s), -éte*, — the penult assuming the accent, to match *-ámu(s), -áte(s), -áte* and *-ému(s), -éte(s), -éte* and *-ímu(s), íte(s), íte* in the other conjugations. The shift was perhaps helped by the analogy of the future — *mittĭmus*, for instance, being attracted by *mittēmus: Pr. Pers. Pl.* 30, 64. Rumanian, however, kept the old accent (Tiktin 596): *úngem, úngeț̦i; víndem, víndeț̦i;* etc. There are some traces of its preservation in southeastern French dialects also. Furthermore, *facĭmus, facĭtis* and *dīcĭmus, dīcĭtis* kept their old forms in many regions.

449. For the reduction of *-iunt* to *-unt*, see § 416. Beside *-ent*, in the second conjugation, there was an ending *-*eunt* (*habeunt, etc.), — due to the analogy of *-iunt*, — which was particularly common in Italy: cf. § 416.

The endings *-ent* and *-unt* came to be very much confused (*credent, *vĭdunt, etc.); their interchange is frequent in the *Peregrinatio:* Bechtel 88–90, *absolvent, accipient, exient, responduntur*, etc. According to Mohl, *Pr. Pers. Pl.* 112, the confusion goes back to early Italic. The Classic distinction was best kept in Gaul and northern Italy; in Spain and Portugal, Sardinia, and a part of southern Italy, *-ent* prevailed; in central and the rest of southern Italy, Rætia, Dalmatia, and Dacia, *-unt* was preferred.

450. In the perfect, the third person plural ending *-ēre* was discarded. The ending *-erunt*, in Classic Latin, sometimes had a short *e* (*ĕ* is common in the comic poets, Virgil wrote *tulĕrunt*, etc.); in Vulgar Latin this vowel was apparently always short: *débuerunt, díxerunt, víderunt.* Cf. § 137.

INDEX.

N. B.— Arabic numerals refer to Paragraphs. Words printed in Roman type belong to ancient, words in *italics* to modern languages.

a 194–5, 228, 229 (1), 231, 240, 243, 244
 accented 39, 194–5
 –arius 39
 ja–> je– 229 (1)
 unaccented 228, 229 (1), 231, 240, 243, 244
–a 37
a 181
ab 14, 77, 92
 before j 222
 before s + cons. 230
ab 78
ab– 26
ab–> au– 236
ab ante 47, 48
abbellire 18, 34
abbio 273
abbreviare 25
abbreviatio 37
abeo = habeo 251
abias 224
abiat 224
abiete 224
–abilis 39
ab intus 47
abitat 251
Ablative 92–7, 383
 abl. absolute 97
 abl. = accus. 94–6
aboculare 26
ab olim 47
abs– 28
absconsus 439, 441

absida 356 (3)
absolvent 449
abyssus 149
ac– 24, 65
accedere(m) 309
accensus 441
Accent 134–58
 primary 135–52
  Greek words 143–50
  other foreign words 151–2
 shift 136–8, 140
  ficatum 141
  nouns 367
  numerals 142
  recomposition 139
  verbs 423–4, 431, 433, 447–8, 450
  vowels in hiatus 136–8
 secondary 153–5
 unstressed words 156–8
Accented Vowels: *see* Vowels
accepere 201
acceptabilis 39
accipient 449
accubitorium 37
–accus 37
Accusative, 82, 94–6, 98–9, 373, 383
 acc. = abl. 94–6
 acc. + infin. 82
 acc. pl. in –us 244, 355 (1)

acer arbor 43
–aceus 37
acia 355 (2)
–acius 37
a contra 47
a(c)qua 164
Acqui 86
Acragas 330
ac si 83
ac sic 24, 47, 84
acua = aqua 223
–aculare 35
aculionis 367
ad 14, 78, 86, 90, 93, 96, 98
ad = at 282
ad– 23, 25
adaptus 23
adcap(i)tare 25
addedi 139
addormire 25
adferitis (**imper.**) 412
adgenuculari 25
ad horam 47
adimplere 30
Adjectives
 comparison 56, 377
 declension 374–9
 numerals 378–82
 unus (**article**) 57
adjutare 34
ad mane 47
adnao 397
adparescere 34
adpetere 32

INDEX.

adpretiare 25
adpropiare 25
ad semel 47
ad sero 47
adsteti 139
ad subito 47
adtonitus 32
ad tunc 47
ad ubi 47
aduc 250
adulescentulus 37
adunare 25
Adverbs 73-5
æ 174, 178, 209-10, 228, 243, 244
  accented 174, 178, 209-10
  unaccented 174, 178, 243, 244
  -æ = -e 174, 244
æcclesia 228
ædis 366
ægis 188
æliens = eligens 259
æques = e- 175
æquus = e- 175, 210
æteneris = itineris 201
Æthiopia 188
æum = ævum 324 (1)
a foras 47
a foris 47
agennæ = -nd- 281
agere = ajere 259
aggio 273
aggravatio 37
Agneti 359 (2)
agnetus = -na- 194
-ago 37
Agragas 330
Agrientum 259
agurium 228
agustas 228
Agustus 228
ahenum 250
ai > æ > e 209
αι 188
Aiax 188, 222
aiglon 37 (-o)
Aiiax 222

aiio 222
-aio 39 (-arius)
aios = ἅγιος 272
Aix 86
ajutit = adjutet 272
-al 37
alacer 195 (1)
alare 405, 435
alauda 19
alaudula 37
alba spina 43
alberca 19
albeus 317
albor = arbor 292
-ale 37
alecer 195 (1)
Alesander 255
alevanti = eleph- 321
Alexander 38, 255
alguem 71
alguien 71
-alia 37
alicer 195 (1)
alicunus 71
alid = aliud 71
alio(r)sum 291
alipes = ad- 281 (1)
aliquanti 71
aliqui 71
aliquis 13, 71
aliquot 71
-alis 39
alium 224
alius 71
allare 405, 435
allegorizare 19
alleviare 34
allium 274
a longe 47
alques 71
alter 71, 233, 395
altiare 34
altior 377
altissimus 377
altitia 37
alto (**adv.**) 40
altra 233
altrui 395

alumnu (**nom.**) 372
am 78
amadus = -t- 286
amantis (**nom.**) 367
amão 424
amaricare 34
ama(t) 285
ambitare 405
ambolare 232
ambulare 10, 232, 405
amei 37
amenus 215
amfora 334
amicicia 276
amido 187
amistat 154
amita 239, 359, 359 (1)
amitane 359 (1)
amitanis 359
amma 16
amnavit 405
amò 424
a modo 47
amourette 37 (-ittus)
ampitzatru 277
ampora 334
amurca 186
amure 203
amygdalum 19
an 11, 14, 83
-an 36
-âν 36
anangi 331
anathema 19
anathematizare 19
anc 40
anc = hanc 251
anca 343
ancilia 187
ancora 150, 187
-ancus 37 (-incus)
-anda 37
andare 405
andata 37 (-ta)
Andreani 359 (1)
Andreate 359 (2)
andron 331
anellus 37, 42

anemis 232
-aneus 39, 42
angelice 40
angelus 19
Angers 86
angliscus 39
angostia 208 (1)
anguil(l)a 163
ang(u)lus 233
angustiare 34
Anicius 276
animabus 358
animalico 37 (-icca)
Anitius 276
Annanis 359
annare 405
annata 37 (-ta)
Annenis 359
annitare 405
annotavimus = -bi- 318
annulare 405
anos = annos 247
-ans 39
anser 13
anta 239
ante 96
antemittere 46
antestetis (**nom.**) 367
-antia 37
anticus 226
antiefne 184
antiphona 184
anus = annos 244
-anus 39, 42
Aorist 124
apcha 343
aperii 428
apersi 428, 429
apertus 436
apotheca 182
apothecarius 39
apparescere 35
appo 78
apprendere 12
ápriro 410
apsens 315
apsolvere 315
apte = -æ 244

apud 14, 78, 282
aput 282
aqua 164, 223
aquilotto 37 (-ottus)
-ar 37
Arbonenca 37 (-incus)
arbor (**masc.**) 346 (4)
arb(o)rem 235
arboricellus 153
ardente(m) 309
ardere 399
ardire 343
-are (**infin.**) 33, 34, 36, 397-8
-are (**nouns**) 37
ares = aries 225
aretem 225
argentum 259
-aria 37
-aricius 39
arida (**noun**) 13
ar(i)dorem 219
ar(i)dus 237
aries 225, 255
ariex = -s 255
-aris 39
-aris > -alis 292
-arius 39
armeise 184
armentas 352
-*aro* 39 (-arius)
Aroncianos 276
arrespex = haruspex 251
Arrius 251
arroser 356 (3)
arsi 429
arsus 441
artemisia 184
artetico 184
arthriticus 184
Article 57, 68, 392
artic(u)lus 234
arvorsum = adversum 281 (2)
arvum > arum 226
-*as* 38
-as > -i 443
ascella = axilla 42, 255

ascendiderat 426
ascetes 182
ascla 284
asculta 228
a semel 47
aspargo 31
aspectare 25
Aspirates 249-52, 265
aspra 233
-asse 161
-assem 161
-ássemus 433
-ássetis 433
Assibilation 277-8, 260-1
Assimilation 229 (3), 255, 264, 265, 267, 269, 282, 293, 307, 310, 315
Asti 86
astula 284
at 11
at = ad 282
-ata 37 (-ta)
-aticum 37
atque- 24, 65
atque ille 24
atque ipse 65
atque is 65
atrium 12
atta 16, 359 (1)
Attane 359 (1)
atticissare 33
attinxi 429
Attitta 37 (-ittus)
-attus 37
at ubi 48
-atus 37 (-ta), 39, 42
participle 435, 440
au 178, 211-3, 228, 229 (7)
accented 178, 211-3
unaccented 228, 229 (7)
au > o 229 (7)
au 189
auca 13, 236
aucellus 13, 325
aucidere 212
audace (**nom.**) 367
audi = audivi 227, 423
audiendu'st 309

aud(i)entem 416
aud(i)o 272-3, 416
audivi(t) 285
audus 236
–aumus = -avimus 424
aunc(u)lus 234, 236, 324
Aureia = -elia 274
Aureliati 359 (2)
aurora 11
aus = avus 241, 324
ausare 18, 34
ausculum = osc- 212
Austus 263
aut 174
aut ... aut 84
-aut = -avit 424
autem 11, 14
Authorities 5
autor 266
autumnal(e) 242
auyo 272-3
av- > au- 236, 241
avaricia 276
avec 78
avello = *averlo* 293
-avi > -ai 424
avica 13, 236
avicella 37, 42, 325
av(i)dere 219
avidus 236
aviolus 13
avis 13
avis struthius 43
avire 400
-avit > -ait -at -aut 241, 424
avo = avus 362
avus 13
ayo = habeo 273

b: see Labials
baboni 362
bac(c)a 163
bacito 37 (-ittus)
bac(u)lus 234
Baiocasses 151
bajulus 233
Baleria = Va- 316

Balerius = Va- 316
bal(i)neum 146, 219
  balneus 347
ballæna 150, 162, 333
balneum 146: balneus 347
balteum -us 347
bannus 19
baplo 235
baptidiare 339
baptisma 149
baptizare 19, 33, 339
baptizatio 19
barba -anis 359, 359(1)
barbane 359(1)
barbar 242
barbo -onis 359(1)
barbutus 42
baro 16
bassiare 275
bas(s)ium 163
basso 40
battalia 16
battei 426
ba(t)t(u)ere 137, 226
Bayeux 151
bel(l)ua 164
Bellus -onis 362
bene 40, 74
bene bene 55
benegnus 172 (2)
bene placitum 43
Beneria = Ve- 316
benignis 376
benivolus 201
berbeces 323
berbex (-ix) 42, 317, 323
bestemmia 182
Betrubius 316
beveire 37 (-tor)
bi- 22
bianca 341
biber 242
biblia 146
bibui 428
bibutus 438, 439
Bictor 316
biduanus 39
bieta 184

bifolco 318 (2)
biginti = vi- 316, 322
-bilis 39
bimaritus 22
bintcente = vincente 260
bis- 22
bisaccium 22
bisacutus 22
bisante 187
bis coctum 43
bis(s)it = vixit 255
bivere = vi- 316
bixit = vi- 316, 322
blæsus 329
blanche 341
blanka 341
blankizare 34
blasphemare 19, 36
blasphemia 146, 182
blasphemus 150
blasta 312 (1)
blitum 184
bobansa 336
bobis = vo- 316
boccone 37 (-o)
bocconi 40
Bodicca 37 (-icca)
boletus 38, 184
Bologna 303
bonatus 37 (-atus)
Bonica 37 (-icca)
bon(i)tatem 231
bonito 37 (-ittus)
Bonitta 37 (-ittus)
Bononia 303
bonu 298
bonus = -os 244
bonus bonus 55
bos = vos 316, 324
botella 361
bottega 182
botu = vo- 316, 322
botula 361
bovis (**nom.**) 367
brac(c)a 163
bracchiale 37
brac(c)hium 163
brachia 352

branca 16
Breaking 177
breviarium 37
brevis 13
Brittanice 40
bruchus 193
buplicæ = pu- 312 (1)
bublus 235
bubulcus 318 (2)
buc(c)a 12, 163
bullicare 35
Buolognino 154
burrus 330
Burrus 187
bursa 187
buscus 255
busta 187
but(t)is 163
butyrum 150
buxida 187, 356 (3)
buxus 187, 330
Byzacinus 42

c: see Gutturals
 c for g 253
 cy 276, 278
-c 40
caballus 12
cabia = cavea 318
cactivus 313
cactos 313
cadedi 428
cadĕre 402
caderunt 426
cadui 428
cælebramus (perf.) 424
cælus 347
Cæseris 233
cæsorium 37
caeth 313
calamarium 37
calamellus 37
calamus 150
calatus = ga- 330
calcai = -avi 424
calcaneum 37 (-ium)
calce pistare 46
calciare 224

calcis (nom.) 367
calcius 224
calcoste(g)is 259
caldo 40
cal(e)facere 219
calefacis 139
calere 288
cal(i)dus 155, 219, 237
calisco 414
calma 268
calotta 187
cals 255
calumpnia 307
calura 42
camel(l)us 42, 150, 163
camera 145
camerlingo 37 (-ing)
caminus 150
camīsia 201 (1)
cammarus 330
canalia 37
cani (pl.) 368
cantare 34
capabilis 39
capĕre 8, 402
capiclus 234, 284
capire 406
cap(i)talis 231
capitanus 39
capitium 37 (-ium)
capitulus 42, 234
capītus 440
capriolus 224
captiare 34
captio 9
captivare 34
captivus 313
capud 282
capui 428
capum 285, 356 (3), 369
capus 285, 356 (3), 369
caput 13, 282, 285, 356 (3), 369
cardonis (nom.) 367
cardu(u)s 226
carissimus 377
caritabilis 39
Caritta 37 (-ittus)

carnis (nom.) 367
carnutus 39, 42
caroneus 39
carrica 11
car(ri)care 18, 33, 231, 239
cartas (nom. pl.) 357 (1)
carum 263
casa 12
Cases 85-100, 354, 372, 383
caseum -us 347; cf. 163
casotta 37 (-ottus)
cas(s)eus 163; cf. 347
Cassiabus 358
cas(s)us 161
castaneus 346 (1)
castellus 347
castius 277
castore (nom.) 367
cata 19, 71
cata unus 71
cataveris = -d- 256
catechizare 19, 33
cat' unus 71
cauculus 288
cauditus 42
caus(s)a 161
cavia 224
-ce 40
cecino 187, 330
cedat = cædat 210
cedo 162
cedrus 182
cefalo 334
celeps 315
celerus 376
-cellus 37
Celtic Words 19
ce(n)sor 311
consus 260
centu 381
ceperint 215
cepi 215
cerasus 38, 195 (3)
cerbus 323
cerebellum 231
cereolus 13
ceresus 195 (3)
ceresus 38, 195 (3)

INDEX.

certitudo 37
cetto 162
-ceus 39
Chairibertus 39 (-arius)
chaloir 288
Change of Meaning 8–10
Change of Suffix 42
chan(n)e 163
chartaceus 39
cher 263
chiaro (**adv.**) 40
chiave 288
Chilperico 343
chiosa 185
Chiusi 86
cholera 145
chommoda 251
c(h)orda 186, 332
Chrestus 184
chrisma 184
C(h)ristus 184, 332
cib 206
cicinus 330
-cillus > -cellus 42
cima 38, 187
cimiterium 192
cinctius 254
cinctus 440
cinqua(gi)nta 254, 379, 380
cinque 254, 379
cinsum = ce- 196
cinus 347, 370
cinxi 429
cip(p)us 163
circa 80, 96
circare 16
circueo 309
circumdavit 430
cis 14
cit(h)era, -ara 38, 233
cito 162
citrus 329
ciurma 191
-cius 39
civ(i)tas 12, 231
clamantis (**nom.**) 367
clarisco 414
Cla(u)dius 211 (1)

claudo 236, 325
clausi 429
clausus 441
clavem 288
clavido 236, 325
Clepatra 191
clerc 154
clergue 154
Clerical Pronunciation 218, 259[1], 260[1], 276, 277, 297[1], 318 (1), 333 (1)
clericatus 37
cler(i)cus 39, 154, 239
Clio 190
Clodius 212
cloppus 16
closa 212
cludo 211 (2)
-clus 234
co = quod 282
coacla 289 (1)
coactum 310
coccodrillo 294
cocens 226
coclearium 356 (3)
coclia 224
cocodrilus 294
cocus 226
coda 212, 213
codex 213
cœmiterium 192
cœpi 72, 124
coexcitare 30
coexercitatus 30
cofecisse 311
cognatus 9, 269
co(g)nosco 43, 197, 269, 310
cognovi 428
cognusco 197
cohærere 310
cohors 12, 310
coicere 310
coiiugi 271; **cf.** 311
cojectis 311
cojugi 311; **cf.** 271
colaphizare 19
col(a)p(h)us 19, 148, 154, 186, 237, 330, 332

colbe 154
coles 213
coliandrum 292
collecta 37 (-ta)
collectus 37 (-ta)
colli(g)ens 259
col(li)gere 31, 139, 259, 272, 305, 444
colliget 444
col(lo)care 9, 31, 231 239
collo 160
collus –um 347
colober 208
colobra 208 (2), 217
colomna 208
coloquinta 187
color (**fem.**) 346 (2)
colp 154
colustra 197
comenzare 276
cominciare 276
cominiciare 276
cominitiare 25, 153, 276
comitem 235
commando 31
comment 41
commixtius 23
comodo = quo– 226
comœdia 192
comparare 8, 12, 231, 233
Comparison 56
comperare 231, 233
complacere 25
complire 400
Compound Words 43–9, 64
comprendit 250
computare 31
computus 235
comuna 376
con– 23, 25
concha 186
concupiscencia 276
condam 254
condedit 139
conder(e) 242
condicio 276
conditio 276
Conditional 124, 130, 411

confessor 18
confortare 25, 34
conger 329
Congianus 272
congigi 259
Conjugation 101-30, 396-450
  Four Conjugations 396-407
    First 397-8
    Second 399-401
    Third 402-6
    Fourth 407
  Fundamental Changes 408-12
  Imperfect 420-1
  Inchoative Verbs 413-5
  Perfect 422-31
    Strong 427-31
    Weak 422-6
  Perfect Participle 434-41
  Personal Endings 442-50
  Pluperfect and Future Perfect 432-3
  Present Stems 416-9
  Use of Forms 101-30
Conjunctions 82-4
co(n)jus 255
co(n)jux 171, 255, 311
conmittere 32
connato 269
conobbi 428
conoisser 413
conopeum 146
conovutus 440
conpendium 32
conplere 306
consacrati 31
conservam(m)us 163
consiensia 260, 275
consili 227
consilium 42
consirier 37 (-erium)
Consonants
  Aspirate 249-52
  Dentals 280-6

Double: see Double Consonants
Germanic: see Germanic Consonants
Greek: see Greek Consonants
  Groups 131-2, 160
  Gutturals 253-70
  Labials 312-26
  Latin 246-8
  Letters 246
  Liquids 287-96
  Nasals 303-11
  Palatals 271-8
  Sibilants 297-302
constare 31
consuere 31, 137
consuetudo 42
co(n)sul 171, 311
conteneo 139
continari 226
contra 96
contra- 26
contrafacere 26
co(n)ventio 171
convitare 25
coperire 225
copersi 429
copertus 436
cophinus 186
coque 254
coraticum 18, 37
corbeau 323
corbi 323
corbo 323
corcodilus 294
corcodrillus 294
cores = corda 369
corium 294
Corneius = -elius 274
Cornelio (nom.) 298
cornicula 42
cornu -um -us 347, 355 (1)
cor(o)nare 231
corp 323
corpes = corpora 369
corpi -ora 369
corpo = corpore 356 (3)

corpo 160
corregia 201
corridiæ 272
corrigo 305
corrotulare 229
cors 12, 310
corso 208
cortem 203, 225
cortensis 39
cortilis 39
cortis 250
corvo 323
corvus 323
cosol 311
costumen 42
cosul 305
cot 254
cotes 212
cotidiæ 244
cot(t)idie 162, 226, 244, 254
couleuvre 208 (2)
court 203
couvent 311
covenimus 311
coventionid 311
covetum = cubitum 208
coxale 37
coxi 429
crebbi 428
credea 421
crededi 31, 139
credens (noun) 13, 39
credentia 37 (-antia)
crédere 410
credutus 438, 439
crepatus 435; crepere 194
crepavi 428
Crescentsianus 277
cresco 255
cresima 184
cresme 184
crevi 428
crevutus 440
criblare 292
crigne 351
c'ritare 229
criz 206
crocitare 35

crocodilus 150, 294
c'rot'lare 229
crucifigere 46
crudilitas 197
-crum 37 (-culum)
crupta 187
crus 13
crust(u)lum 234
crypta 187
cubidus = cupidus 256
cuculla 13; cf. 346 (4)
cucullus -a 346 (4)
cuerdo 369
culcitra 294
-culum 37, 234
-culus > -cellus 42
-c(u)lus 42, 234
cum (conj.) 82, 226
cum (prep.) 14, 78, 95, 305
cumba 187
cun = cum 305
cunnuscit 269
cuntellum = cul- 289 (2)
cuoio 296
cuopre 160
cuore 160, 177
cupa(t) 285
cupire 406
cupít 423
cup(p)a 163
cupressus 150
cur 12, 82
curabit = -avit 318, 322
currens 39
cursi 429
cursorium 37
curvus 323
Cusanca 37 (-incus)
cy 276-8
  cy = ty 277
cycnus 187, 330
cyma 38, 187; (fem.) 349
cymba 187
cymiterium 192
cypressus 150

d: see Dentals
  dy 272

da 48
dacruma 281 (1)
dactylus 19
dad 48
Dafne 334
dai 298
dampnum 307
Danuvium 318
dao 397
dare 397
datíus 324
Dative 90-1, 383
dau 397
daun 397
dave 48
de 14, 48, 77, 88, 92, 95
de- 23, 25
  de- > di- 229 (2)
deabus 358
de ad 48
de ante 48
deaurare 23, 25
debbio 273
debeo 273
debere 10, 72, 117, 126 (4)
debita 37
deb(i)tum 235, 239
decanus 39
dece(m) 309
decem et (or ac) septem 379
dece(m)bris 306
decemter 306
dec(i)mus 239
Declension 85-100, 354-76
  Adjectives 374-6
  Fall of Decl. 100, 372-3
  Nouns 354-73
  Shift of Decl. 355-6, 376
    First 357-60
    Second 361-3
    Third 364-71
  Use of Cases 85-100
declivis 376
de contra 47
decumus 220
dede = dedit 285
de deorsum 47

dedi 430
dedicait 424
ded(i)cavit 231
dedro dedrot 285
deexacerbare 30
deexcitare 30
defeniciones 276
defensa 37 (-ta)
defensi 429
defensorius 39
defensus 441
deferet 406
Definite Article 68, 392
de foris 47, 81
defuntus 267, 306
deggio 273
defna 324
de inter 48
de intro 47
de intus 47, 48
deitas 37
del(i)catus 227
delitus 198
delta 329
de magis 47
de medio 47
deminat 139
Dentals
  d 272, 281-3
    dy 272
    nd > nn 281
  Final 282, 285
  Intervocalic 283, 286
  nd > nn 281
  nt 285
  st 285
  t 284-6
denumerát 424
deo(r)sum 291, 324
deorsum 224
Deponent Verbs 113, 409
de post 48
deprendere 250
de retro 47, 48, 292
Derivation 20-49
descendidi 426
de semel 47
despereisser 414

INDEX. 197

desso 62
dester 255
desto 225
de sub 48
de super 48
de sursum 47
detti 426
de unde 70, 393
deus 167
devere 318
devetis 318
devidere 229 (4)
devinus 229 (4)
devitum 318
dexcito 225; cf. 30
dextro(r)sus 291
deyo 273
dia = dies 355 (2), 397
dia 397
diabulus 38
diaconissa 19
Dialects 2, 3
dibeto 196
Dibona 318
dic 264, 406, 412
dice = dic 412
dice(m) 309
dicere 406
dicimus 448
dicitis 448
dicitus = -g- 253
dictus 166, 440
dictus = digitus 233, 238, 259
–didi > –dei 426
dies 13, 167, 355 (2)
dietro 292
digita 351, 361
digitus 233, 238, 253, 259
dignus 172 (2)
dilevit 229 (2)
diligibilis 39
dimmi 264
dinus = divinus 324
Dionigi 227
Dionysii 227
diosum = deorsum 291
Diphthongization 177

Diphthongs 177, 209–16
  æ 209–10
  au 211–3
  eu 214
  œ 215
  ui 216
diposisio 277
dire 406
directus 229
diri(g)ens 259
dirivare 229 (2)
dis– 23, 25
discere 12
disfacit 139
disfactus 23
dis(je)junare 25, 229
displacet 139
displicina 289 (1)
Dissimilation 167, 195 (6), 229 (4), 254, 289 (2), 292, 303, 421, 426, 431
distinguere 223, 226
dita 351
diu 11, 13
diurnus 13
divisi 429
divisus 441
divite (**nom.**) 367
divota 229 (2)
dixemus 232
dixi 429
dodecim 225
doga 186, 333
dolor (**fem.**) 346 (2)
dolus = dolor 18, 21
domatus 435
domin(i)ca 239
dominicus 9, 239
domnani 359 (1)
domnicellus 37
domnicus 235
domnina 37
domnizare 33
domnulus 235
domnus 235
domus 12; (**masc. and fem.**) 346 (1); (**2d decl.**) 355 (1)

donec 11
dont 70
donum (**masc.**) 349
dormio 224
dormito 309
dormitorium 37
dormo 416
dorsus 347
dossum 291
dou 397
Double Consonants 161–4, 247, 328
  Double = Single 162–3, 247
  Double > Single 161, 328
  Single > Double 164, 328
Double Forms 158
Double Negation 75
Double Prefixes 30
doucet 37 (-ittus)
doussa 376
drachma 144
drappus 16
d'rectus 229
Dreux 151
drieto 292
dub(i)tare 231
ducalis 39
ducatus 37 (-ta)
duce = duc 412
ductus 440
dui 167, 378
dukissa 37
dulcior (noun) 18
dulcor 18, 37
dume(c)ta 266
dunc 40
d'unde 70, 393
duo 378
duos 138
durare 229 (5)
Duration 99
duricia 276
Durocasses 151
duxi 429

e 165, 177, 196–9, etc.
  accented 165, 196–9

ē 196–8
ĕ 177, 199
η 182
ε 183
ē > i 196–8
e unacc. > i 229 (2)
e > y 224
e prefixed to s + cons. 230
eé > e 225
eu 214
ié > e 225
unaccented 219, 228, 229 (2), 232, 243, 244
ē > e 165
ĕ > e 165
η 182
ε 183
e- 28
-e 40
 -e > -æ 174, 244
 -e > -i 244, 364
-η 38
-ea 421
eacit = jacet 224
eam = jam 224
-ebam: see -ea
ebbi 411
ecca 24
eccam 24
eccas 24
ecce- 24, 65
ecce ego 65
ecce hic 24, 65
ecce ille 24, 65
ecce iste 24, 65
ecce nunc 65
ecce tu 65
eccillam 24
eccillud 24
eccillum 24
eccistam 24
ec(c)lesia 146, 162, 182, 328
eccos 24
eccu- 24, 65
eccu' 'ic 326
eccu' ille 24, 65
eccu' iste 24, 65, 326

eccum 24, 62, 65
eccu' sic 24
e contra 47
ecus 226
ededident 426
edere 13
edificai 424
-edo > -ido 197
edus = hædus 210
eé > e 225
effigia 355 (2)
effondrer 356 (2)
effrenis 376
eglesia 256
egloge 330
e(g)o 60, 73, 263, 385
ego-met-ipse 66
ει 190
-ei 411
-εία 146
eiius 271
-ειν 36
eio = ejus 298
-εῖον 146
ejus 170, 298
elementum 231
elephantus 38
elex = ilex 200 (2)
elifanti (pl.) 368
elimentum 231
-elis > -ilis 197
Elision 157, 242
-elius > -ilius 197
-ellus 37, 42
elmo 343
elud = illud 201
-elus > -ellus 42
emere 12
encaustum 149
Enclitics 156
-enda 37 (-anda)
Endings: Personal 442–50
enim 11
-ens 39 (-ans)
-e(n)simus 311
-e(n)sis 39, 311
-ent > -eunt 416, 449
-ent > -unt 449

-entia 37 (-antia)
-enus > -inus 42
eo = ego 73, 385
eo quod 82, 110
eoru 309
episcopalis 39
epistula 144
equus 12
equus = æquus 210
-er > -re 245
-er 39 (-arius)
érable 43
-ere (perf.) 450
-ere > -ire 197
eredes 251
-ĕrem 346 (3)
eremus 150
eres 251
ergī. 14
ergo 11, 14
ericius 42
erigere 31, 429
-erium 37
erminomata 191
ero 411
-ero 39 (-arius)
ersi 429
erubisco 414
-ĕrunt 450
ervum > erum 226
ervus (3d decl.) 356 (2)
-es > -i 443
-es = -is 174, 244, 365–6, 444
es- = ex- exs- 230, 255
-ης 38
Esaram 233
-escere 34, 35, 197, 413–4
eschernir 341
eschine 341
esclate 343
-esco > -isco 197 414
escupare 255
es(i)mus 419 (1)
-esimus > -isimus 197
esmes 419 (1)
espiar 343
espier 343

INDEX. 199

espiritum 230
esquena 341
esquiver 343
essagium 255
esse 112-4, 126 (2), 419 (1)
  esse = essere 419
  esse = sedere 402
-esse 161
-essem 161
essere = esse 419
es(t) 285
estatio 230
estau 397
estaun 397
Estephanus 230
estou 397
estribar 341
esum 419 (1)
-et = -it 244, 444
et at ubi 49
et . . . et 84
Ethiopia 188
etiam 11, 14, 277
etsi 14
et sic 47
-etus 437
eu 214
ev 190
Eugeneti 359 (2)
-eum 37
eunuchizare 19
Eurus 191
-eus 39
Euua 344
evangelizare 19
-evi > -ei 424
Evidence 5
ex 14, 77, 92, 95
ex- 23, 25
  ex- = es- 230, 255
-ex > -ix 42
exaltare 25
exauguratus 39
excellente (**nom.**) 367
excoriare 25
excussi 429
excussus 441
exeligere 30, 274

exeligit 274
exe(m)plu 306
exiat 224
exient 449
exinde 60
exire 31, 266
exodus 337
expabui 428
expandutus 441
expaventare 35
explendido 230
exquartiare 276
exs- = es- 230
exstinctus 440
exstinxi 429
exsucidus 39
exsucus 23
extensa 37
extimare 255
extra- 27
extrabuccare 27
extranus 42
ex tunc 47
-*ezza* 277

f: see **Labials**
fa 264, 404
fabam 320 (1)
fab(u)la 236
fac 264, 404
faccia 278
face = fac 412
facentem 416
facere 10, 404
facheret 410
faciam 278
facias 224
fac(i)ebam 225, 420
facienda 37
facimus 448
facire 404
facitis 448
factum 266
factus 440
facul 242
fæcit 209
fædus 320 (1)
fæmina 209

fænum 209
fænus 347
fageus 39
failla 324
fait 266
fallii 430
fallire 406
fallitus 441
falsare 34
falsitas 37
familia 42
famis 366
fammi 264
famul 242
famulabus 358
fante 311
faor 324
farcitus 440
fare 404
farsus 440, 440
fascia 10, 275
faselus 334
fasena 320 (1)
fasia = faciat 285
fasiolus 224
fata 266
fatatus 39
fate 404
fatus 347
faula 236, 318
febrarius 226
feced = fecit 282
fec(e)ru(nt) 233
feci 430
fëhu 343
felicla 234
felis 255
fem(i)na 239
feminabus 358
Feminine: see **Gender**
femps 356 (2)
femus (**3d decl.**) 356 (2)
fenire 229 (4)
fenum 209
ferbeo 323
feritus 434
ferre 12
ferro 160

fervere 399
fervura 37
fesit 260
feu 343
fezem 44
fiaba 289 (1)
fiam 419 (2)
fib(u)la 235
ficatum 16, 141
ficit 197
fictus 440
ficus (**masc. and fem.**) 346 (1)
ficus (**2d decl.**) 355 (1)
fidens 311
fiele 160
fiens 356 (2)
fieri 112, 409, 419 (2)
fiero 160
fiet 419 (2)
figel 242
fiios = filios 274
filiabus 358
filias (**nom.**) 357 (1)
filiaster 13
filio(s) 298
filius 155, 274; = filios 244
filix 197
fillio 247
Fimes 86
Final Syllable 240–5
finctus 440
finis (**adj.**) 17
finiscere 35
finxi 429
fio 343
fiorentino 154
fioretto 37 (-ittus)
fiorisce 414
fir- 29
fircum 320 (1)
Firenze 86
Firmus -onis 362
fiscla 234
fistula 234
fistus 197
fixi 429
fixus 441

flaba 289 (1)
flagrare 292
flaonis 324
flator 37
flaus 240, 324
flavor 37
fletus 11
fleuma 268
fleurit 414
fleuve 208 (2)
floralis 292
florecer 414
Florentinus 37
florire 400
florisco 400
flovium 208 (2), 217
fluviorum 224
foces 213
focus 8, 12
fodiri 406
folia 352
follia (**noun**) 18
follicare 33
fons (**fem.**) 346 (4)
fons 356 (2)
fonte 205
fonz 356 (2)
foras 81, 96
forbatre 29
forbire 407
Foreign Words 19; see **Germanic Words** and **Greek Words**
foresia 311
foris 81
foris- 29
forisfacere 29
forismittere 46
formaceus 39
formosus 161
formunsus 208
forsitan 305
forte 40
fortescere 34
fortia 37
fortis 10
  fortis fortis 55
fossato 37 (-ta)

fractus 440
fragellum 289 **(2)**
fragilis 233
fragrantia 37
fra(g)rare 270
Francesco 341
franctus 440
Frankensis 39
Frankiscus 39, 341
Franko 341
franxi 429
frate 295
fratelmo 388
frat(t)re 164
frax(i)nus 239; (**mc.**) 346(1)
fraumenta 268
frecare 201; cf. 256
frenum -us 347
fricatus 435, 440
fricda = frigida 238, 259
frictus 440
frigare 256; cf. 201
frigdaria 219, 231
frigdura 37
Frigia 187
frig(i)dus 166, 200 (1), 233, 238, 259
frigora 351
frigorem 347
frixi 429
frondifer 11
frualitas 263
fructa 351, 361
fructus (**2d decl.**) 355 (1)
frundes 205
frunza 351
frutta 351
fugii 430
fugire 406
fuçitus 439
fūi 431
ful(i)ca 237
fumát 424
fundus (**3d decl.**) 356 (2)
fundutus 441
funtes 205
funus 11
fuore 160

INDEX.

furbjan 407
furma 203
furmica 229 (6)
fusa 351
fusi 429
fusus 441
Future 125-9, 411
  New Fut. 127-9, 411
  Periphrastic Fut. 126
  Pres. for Fut. 126 (1)
Future Perfect 119, 123-4, 410, 423

g: see Gutturals
gy 272
gabata 13, 236
gabta 236
gaita 343
gaite 343
galatus 330
gallina 288
gamba 13, 263, 331
gammarus 330
garba 341
garofulum 149
garum 329
gaudia (sg.) 352
gaudimonium 20
gaudutus 441
gauta 236
gaveola 257
gavia 16
gecchire 343
geisla 341
geiuna = je- 259
geline 288
gelus (2d decl.) 355 (1)
gemellus 13
gemire 406
gemitus 439
gemui 428
gena 13
Gender 345-53
  Fem. and Neut. 351-3
  Masc. and Fem. 346
  Masc. and Neut. 347-50
  Neut.Pl.>Fem.Sg. 352
  Neut.Pron.and Adj. 350

genesis 148, 183
Genitive 88-9, 383
genitores 12
genitus 17
genna 229 (1)
gentilis 17
gentis (adj.) 17
gen(u)arius = jan- 259
genuculum 37, 42
genuflectere 46
genum 355 (1)
Gepte 259
gequir 343
Gerapolis = Hier- 259
gerbe 341
Germanic Consonants 340-4
  b, c, g 341
  ð, þ 342
  h 343
  w 344
Germanic Endings 36
Germanic Words 19, 152, 340-4
Germanissa 37
Gerund 104
Gerundive 105
gesso 187
gesta (sg.) 352
giga 341
giga 341
gigantem 229 (3)
ginocchioni 40
Giovannoni 362
giret 187
girus 187
giscle 341
glacia 355 (2)
Glacus 211 (1)
gladium 347
glanderia 39
glatz 355 (2)
Glaucé -énis 359
Glaucu (nom.) 372
glirem 166
glos(s)a 161, 185
gluria 203
glut(t)ire 162

glut(t)o 163
gnæus 324
gocciare 276
gœrus 187
golosus 228
gonger 329
goule 177
gracilis 233
gracilus 376
grada 351
gradus 355 (1)
grandis 12
granditia 37
graphium 145
grassetto 37 (-ittus)
grassus 257
gratis = cratis 257
gravare 34
gravior 377
grece 210
Greek Accent 143-50
  Oxytones 144
  Paroxytones 145-6
  Proparoxytones 147-50
Greek Consonants 327-39
  β, γ, δ 329
  κ, π, τ 330-1
  θ, φ, χ 332-4
  Liquids 335
  Nasals 336
  σ, ξ 337
  ζ 338-9
Greek Endings 36, 38, 146
Greek Vowels 180-93
  Diphthongs 188-93
  Single Vowels 180-7
Greek Words 19, 36, 38, 143-50, 180-93, 327-39
greü 40
grevior 377
grevis 195 (4)
grex (fem.) 346 (4)
grossior 377
grotta 187
gruis (nom.) 367
grunnio 281
guarire 344
guarnire 36, 407

guatare 343
gubernamentum 37
gubernare 36, 330
guerra 344
guidare 36, 398
guiderdone 342
guisa 344
gulo 37
gumma -i -is 38, 186, 330
gustus (2d decl.) 355 (1)
guttur (masc.) 347
Gutturals 253–70
  c > c' 258, 260–1
  c > g 256–7
  c, g before back vowels 263
  c, g before cons. 265–70
  c, g final 264
  ct 266
  g > g' 258–9, 261
  g intervocalic 263
  gm 268
  gn 172 (2), 269
  gr intervocalic 270
  gy 272
  k 253
  nct 267
  Palatalization 258–62
  qu 254
  sc > sc' 260
  x 255, 266
gylosus 228
gyrus 187

h 249–52
  h > k 252
habam = fabam 320 (1)
habe = ave 318
habe(b)am 421
habeo 273
habere 10, 121–4, 127–30, 239, 273, 285, 400, 401, 421, 438, 449
haber 242
habe(t) 285
nabeunt 416, 449
habibat 400
habire 400

hab(i)tus 239
hábuerat 137
habutus 438
hache 343
hacherece 39
hædus 320 (1)
hamula 235
hanca 343
hanche 343
hant 401
hao 401
hapja 19, 343
haram 251
hardir 343
hardjan 343
harena 320 (1)
haribergum 19
has 401
hat 401
hatire 36
hatjan 36
haud 11
haunitha 342
haunjan 19
haunt 401
havite 400
haz 355 (2)
hegit 251
hëlm 343
helme 343
hepatia 19
here 219, 244
heredes (sg.) 367
heremum 251
Hiatus 136–8, 222–7
hibernus 13
hic 63–4, 67–8
hic ipse 64
hiem(p)s 13, 297
hiens = iens 251
hilerus 233
hinsidias 251
hircum 320 (1)
his- = is- ins- 230
hispatii = spatii 230
historia 146
ho 40
hoc 63, 163, 350

hocsies **277**
hodie 272
hodio 251
hom(i)nes 232, **235**
homni (pl.) 368
homo 10, 71
honera 251
honor 346 (2)
honte 342
hora 12, 185
hordeum 272
horrescere 11
hortesia 311
hospitale 12
hossa 251
hostium 251
Hûgo Hûgon = Húgo Hugónem 152, 362
huile 274
humerus 12
humiliare 34
Huon 152, 362

i 165, 200–1, etc.
  accented 200–1
    ĭ 200
    ī 201
    i̯ > e 201
    e > i 201
    ĭ > i̯ 165, 200
    ī > e 201
    ĭ > i̯ > e 165, 201
  i (cons.) 222
  i > y 224
  –î > –e 224
  ι (Greek) 184
  –ι (Greek) 38
  ié > e 225
  ii > i 227
  prefixed to s + cons. 230
  unaccented 219, 221, 228, 229 (3)(4), 240, 243, 244
    in hiatus 222, 224–5, 227
    ĭ > e 229 (4)
    ĭ > a 229 (3)
–ia 37, 146
–ĭa 37, 146

INDEX.

-iamus 224
-iare 33, 34
-ibilis 39
-ibo 125
-ic 251
-ica 37
-icare 33, 34, 35
-icca 37
-iccus 37
-icem 42, 346 (3)
-iceus 37, 39, 42
-icius 37, 39, 42
icse 313
-iculare 35
-iculus 42
-icus 39
idem 61, 309
id ipsum 62, 350
idolum 150, 190
-idus 39
-i(d)yare 339
ié > e 225
-iebam > -ebam 225; >
 -ibam 420
-ie(n)s 311
Ienubam 259
-*ier* 39
-*iere* 39
-ies > -ia 335 (2)
iesta = gesta 259, 352
ifer 311
iferi 311
iferos 306, 311
ifimo 311
ifra 311
-*igia* 277
igitur 11, 14
ignire 33
ignis 12
ignotus 310
-igo 37
ii **unaccented** > i 227, 423
-ilis 39
-ilius 42
illac 140
illæ **(dat.)** 390
illæi 390
illæjus 390

ille 10, 61–8, 389–92
illei 390
ille ipse 64
illejus 390
illi = ille 390
illic 140
illo **(dat.)** 390
illorum = suus 387
illud > illum 282, 350
illui 390
illujus 390
illum = illud 282, 350
illurum 390
-illus > -ellus 42
im = in 310
imaginarius 39
imbecillis 376
immudavit 256
Imperative 115–6, 412
impinguare 25
impinxi 429
implicat 139
implire 400
-ímus > -ímus 447–8
in 86, 92, 95, 96, 97
in- 23, 25
in + s > is 310
inanimatus 23
in ante 47, 48
incendiderit 426
Inchoative Verbs 400, 413–5
inclausus 139
incohare 250
in contra 47, 48
incudo 42, 370
incuminem 42
incus 42
-íncus 37
inde 60, 71, 384
inde fugere 46
Indefinite Article 57
Indefinite Pronouns: see
 Pronouns
Indicative
 Conditional 130, 411
 for Imperative 116, 412
 for Subjunctive 117

Future 125–9, 411
Future Perfect 119, 123–4, 410
Imperfect 120, 420–1
Perfect 121–4, 422–31
Pluperfect 123–4, 410, 432
Present 120, 273, 397, 401, 403–5, 415, 416–9
indicibilis 39
induruit 224
-inem 346 (3)
infa(n)s 10, 311
i(n)fans 171
infantiliter 40
i(n)feri 171, 219
infernus 13
Infinitive
 as Noun 111
 Conjugations 396–407
 dicere 406
 esse 419
 facere 404
 for Clause 111
 for Imperative 116
 for Subjunctive 111, 117
 for Supine and Gerund 103, 104
 habere 400
 Passive 109
 Perfect 109
 with habere 125–9, 411
 posse 403
 Present Active 102, 109
 velle 403
 with Accusative 82, 110
inflare 31
Inflections
 Forms 345–450
 Use 85–130
infra- 27
infraponere 27
infri 219
infurcare 25
-ing 37
ingenium 9
ingens 259
in giro 48

INDEX.

-ingus 37 (-incus)
in hodie 47
Initial Syllable 228-30
inlatus 32
in mane 47
in medio 48
innoce(n)ti 306
innocus 226
in odio 43
inprobus 32
inquid 282
in quo ante 254
-inquus 37 (-incus)
ins- = is- 230
in semel 47
insiememente 41
insola 232
instruo = struo 230
ins(u)la 171, 233, 284
intcitamento 260
inte(g)rum 270
Interamico 307
Interanniensis 307
Interrogatives: see Pronouns
Intertonic Vowel 231
intra 96
intra- 27
intratenere 27
intravidere 46
intre 245
intro(r)sus 291
intus in 49
-inus 37, 42
-īnus 39
-io > -o 416
ipsa mente 41
ipse 61-8, 390-2
ipse ille 64
ipse ipse 64
ipsejus 390
ipsimus 66
ipsud 390
ipsujus 390
ipsus 390
iraisser 413
irascere 413
ire 126 (5), 405
-ire 33, 34

is 62-4, 67-8
is- = ins- his- 230
-is = -es 244, 365-6, 444
-*is* 38
-iscere 34, 35
Ischia 284
ischola 230
ischolasticus 230
-isco for -esco 197, 414
iscripta 230
-iscus 39
is ipse 64
ismaragdus 230
isperabi 230
ispose 230
-issa 37
-issare 33
isse 313
-isse 161
-issem 161
-issimus 166
istare 230
istatuam 230
iste 63-8, 390-2
iste hic 64
iste ille 64
iste ipse 64
istudio 230
it = id 282
-it = -et 244, 444
ita 11
Italia 224
Italic Tribes 1, 2
-itare 34, 35
-itas 37
-īte > -íte 448
-iter 40
-itia 37, 277
-ities 37
-Itis > -ítis 448
-ittus 37
-itudo 37
-ítus 42 (2), 436, 438, 440, 441
-ítus 435, 438-9
-ium 37
-iunt > -unt 416
-ius 39

-iva 37
iventa 311
-ivi > -ii > -i 423
-ivit > -iut -iit > - it 423
-ivum 37
-ivus 39
-ix 42
-izare 33, 34, 339
-ιζειν 33
izophilus 333

j 271
jacente(m) 309
jacis 244
Jacobus 150, 329
Jacomus 329
jagante 229 (3)
jaiant 229 (3)
jajunus 229 (1)
jambe 263
-jan 36
janarius 226
jaquir 343
jauzei 426
jëhan 343
jehir 343
jejunus 229, 229 (1)
jeniperus 229 (5)
jenua 229 (1)
jenuarius 229 (1)
jeune 208 (2)
jiniperus 229 (5)
Joanneni 359 (1)
Joannentis 359 (2)
Joannis 244
jocus 12
jovenis 208 (2), 217
jovis 367
jubari 322
jubem(m)us 163
jubenis 318
jubentutis 318, 322
jubere 11
Judaizare 19
judicat 424
judicius 347
judico 239
judigsium 278

INDEX. 205

juglus 233
Julianenis 359
Julianeta 37 (-ittus)
Julitta 37 (-ittus)
juncxi 305
juniperus 229 (5)
junxi 429
Jup(p)iter 163
jurātorĭŭ 39
juria 272
jur(i)go 219
jusso 355 (1)
justicia 276
justitia 276, 277
justius 277
juv(e)nis 235
juventa 356 (3)
juvente 318
juxta 81, 96

k 246, 253
kadamitatem 289 (3)
kanditos = candidus 330
karessemo 201
Karica 37 (-icca)
kaukoulato = cal- 288
kleme(n)s 311
kozous = conjux 311, 339
kumate 298
ky = qui 187, 223

l: see Liquids
  ly 274
la = illa 392
Labials
  Assimilation 313
  b 315–9
    initial 316
    intervocalic 318
  by, py, vy 273, 319
  f 320–1
  Fall of Vowel after Labial 235–6
  Influence on Vowels 217
  p 312–4
  u 326
  v 322–5
    after liquid 323

  intervocalic 324
  Voicing 314
laborait = -avit 424
laceus 254
lacte 367
lactem 347
lacus (2d decl.) 355 (1)
ladro 372
ladrone 372
lætiscere 34
lambros 331
lamna 235
lampada 356 (3)
lampa(s) 38, 144, 335
lancia 224
la(n)terna 306
lanutus 42
lapsus 315
laqueum 347 ; cf. 254
lardum 237
Latinization 1, 2
latrone (nom.) 367
lat(t)rones 164
lattucæ 266
Lauriatus 224
lausenga 37 (-ing)
lauzi 443
Lazis = Ladiis 339
lealis 263
lebat 318
lebis 318
lebra 256
lectio 9
lectus -um 347
lectus (p.p.) 440
legare 201
leges 259
legit 259
legui 428
leniit 423
lenticula 42
lentis (nom.) 367
leo 38
leticia 276
levare 34
leviarius 39
levior 377
levitus 435, 439

lexi 428, 429
Liaison 133, 159
liamen 263
libe(n)s 311
liberio 298
libertas (nom. pl.) 357 (1)
libraria 37
ligare 201, 263
ligna (sg.) 352
lignum –us 172 (2), 347
liminare 37
linguas (nom.) 357
liniamenta 224
Linking 133, 159
lintium 224
Liquids
  Assimilation 293
  Dissimilation 292
  Fall of Vowel after Liquid 237
  Fall of Vowel before Liquid 233–4
  l 287–9
  ly 274
  Metathesis 294
  r 290–6
  rs 291
  ry 296
lit(t)era 163
lit(t)us 163
Livitta 37 (-ittus)
ll > l 161
llave 288
Locative 86
locun 305
locuplens 311
locuplex 255
lodi 443
loir 166
longa mente 41
longe 40
longior 377
longius 377
longum tempus 13
loquella 42
loreola 213
Lost Words 11–4
lotus 213

INDEX.

luce (dat.) 244
lucĕre 399
lucire 400
lucor 37
lucto 355 (1)
lucus = locus 205
ludus 12
lugĕre 399
lugire 400
luminem 347
lunæ dies 89
luoghi -ora 349
lŭrdus 207 (1)
luridus 166, 207 (1)
luxi 429
luxuria 355 (2)
ly 274

m: see **Nasals**
ma = mea 388
-μα 38
machina 144
machinari 9
macra 376
madias = majas 272
madio = majo 272
madrema 388
maestati 259
maester 259
magias = majas 272
magida = 38, 145
ma(g)is 56, 71, 74, 84, 157, 259
ma(g)ister 259
magnisonans 44
magnus 12
Maia 188, 222
Maiiam 222
mais = magis 157, 259
major 170, 377
mala mente 41
male 40
male habitus 44
malicia 276
malleus 274
mal(l)o 161
malus malus 55
mam(m)a 16, 359

mam(m)anis 359
mammula 13
manducare 13
mane 13
man(i)ca 239
manică 37 (-icca)
maniplus 42, 233
manos 355 (1)
mansi 429
mansio 12
mansorius 39
mansus 441
manuaria 18
manuplus 42
manus (**masc. and fem.**) 346 (1)
manu tenere 46
Maps: pp. x, xi
Marcianus 278
Marculus 284
mare (**fem.**) 349
marem 347
mares = -is 244
mari -e 364
marinarius 39
maris (**masc. and fem.**) 347, 349
markensis 39
marmor (**fem.**) 353; cf. 347, 369
ma(r)mor 292; cf. 347, 353
marmora 351
marmorem 347, 369
marrir 407
marrjan 407
Marsianesses 277
Marsuas 187
Marsyas 187
mas = magis 157
mascel 242
Masculine: see Gender
masc(u)lus 234
masma = maxima 238
massa 338
mate(r) 295
materia 355 (2)
matrona(s) 298
mat(t)rona 164

matutinus 13
maurus 336
maxime 56
maximus 56, 220, 238, 297
maxumus 220
Meanings of Words 7-10
Change of Meaning 8-10
mecu 309
Medea 190
Medentius 338
media 272
medianus 39
medicus 239
medio die 43
medio loco 43
medius 272
meletrix 292
melior 377
melius 56, 377
melum 195 (5)
membras 352
memoramus (**perf.**) 424
-men 37
mendatium 276
me(n)sa 311
mense(m) 309
mensi (**pl.**) 368
me(n)sis 171, 198, 201, 311
me(n)sor 311
mensorium 37
menta 184
-mente 41
mente habere 46
mentire 409
-mentum 37
mentus 347
menus 201
mercatus (2d decl.) 355 (1)
meretis 232
meridies 281 (2)
mer(i)to 237
mers = merx 255
Messac 277
messui 428
messura 37
met- 24, 66

INDEX.

Metathesis 245, 255, 289 (1), 294
Metiacus 277
metipse 24, 66
metipsimus 66
metitus 441
meuble 204 (1)
meus = mi 87
mextum = mæstum 255
mezzo 272
mi = meus -a 87, 387
mi = mihi 250, 385
miaulare 17
michi 252
mienta 184
migat = micat 256
mihe 244
milex 255
mille 161, 381
millefolium 38
mil(l)ia 161
mimoriæ 229 (2)
minester 201
ministeri(i) 89, 227
mi(ni)sterium 231
minist(r)orum 292
minor 377
minsis 198, 201
minus 201, 377
minus- 29, 245
  > mis- 245
minus credere 29
minus est 29
minus pretiare 46
minutus 10
mirabilia 37, 229 (4), 231
mis = meis 388
mis- 245
miscere 399
misculare 35
misera 376
mis(s)i 161, 163, 429
missorium 37
mis(s)us 441
mistus 440
mixticius 39
mobilis 204 (1), 217

moc 428
modernus 18
modo modo 40
moere = mov- 324
Mœsia 187
molui 428
molutus 439
monarchia 37
monasterium 182
-monia 37
monibam 420
moniti = mu- 228
-monium 37
mo(n)strare 311
monumento = -um 244
Mood 115-9
morbu(s) 298
mordĕre 399
morire 406
moriri 406
Morphology 345-450
morsi 429
morsus 441
mortificare 46
mortu(u)s 226
mossus 438, 440, 441
motto 187
movi 428
movit 244
movita 37; cf. 438, 439
movitus 438, 439; cf. 37
movutus 438, 440
muc(c)us 163
mueble 204 (1)
mul'erem 225
mulier 9, 136
mulieris 136
mullus 187
mulsi 429
multum 74
multus 71
muntu = multum 289 (2)
mur 206
murare 229 (5)
muri -a 349
muritta 37 (-ittus)
murta 187
mutare 229 (5)

Mute + Liquid 132, 160
mut(t)ire 162
myrta 187
Mysia 187
mysterium 182, 187

n: see Nasals
n + fricative 171, 311
ny 274
nacui 428
nam 11
narratus 37 (-ta)
Nasals 303-11
  Final or + Cons. 304-6
    -m falls 309
    -n falls 310
  mn 307
  n + fricative 171, 311
  ny 274
nasco 255
nascutus 438
nasum -us 347
natatorium 37
nativitas 37
natus 13, 438
naucella 13
naufragus 325
nautat 236
navicella 37
navitat 236
ne 14, 75, 83, 229 (2)
Nebitta 37 (-ittus)
nebula 235
necare 9
necator 37
necatus 435, 440
necavi 428
nec ente 71
nec unus 71
ne ente 71
negare 263
negat 256
Negation 75
negliencia 259
nemo 71
neofiti 334
nepoti(s) 298
ne'ps'unus 71

nepta 37
neptia 37
neptilla 13
Nerba 317, 323
nerbo 323
nerf 323
Neroua 322
nervia 349
nervus 323, 349
Neuter: see Gender
ni = ne 229 (2)
nichil 251
niepos 177
ni(g)rum 270
nihil 71, 250, 251
nil 250
nimpæ 332
nise 229 (4)
nitidus 238
nittus 238
nivicare 18, 33
nobe 318
nobilis 11
nobis 318, 385
nocĕre 399
nocui 223, 328
noembrios 324
noembris 324
noicius 324
nolo 161
nome 336
nomem 305
nomes = nomina 369
Nominative 97, 100, 373, 383
  Absolute 97
non 75, 203
nona(i)nta 380
nonna 16
nonnita 37 (-ittus)
nonnitus 37 (-ittus)
nonnus 16
noptiæ 207 (2)
nora 208 (3)
Normannice 40
norus 208 (3)
notrire 229 (5)
noii 40

Nouns 345–73
  see **Declension and Gender**
nous 177, 324
nova(i)nta 380
novellus 13
novius 207 (2)
noxeus 224
ns 171, 311
nubis 366
nulli (**gen.**) 395
nullus 71, 395
num 83
Numerals 57–8, 378–82
  Accent 142
nummus 328
nun = non 203
nunc 12
nuncius 276
nuncquam 305
nunqua(m) 305, 306, 309
nupsi 297
nutrire 166, 229 (5)
nutritio 37
nutritura 37
ny 274
nynfis 306

o 165, 167, 177, 197, 202–5, etc.
  accented 202–5
  ō 202–4
    ō > ǫ 197, 203
    ǫu > ou 167
  ǫ > u 202
  ǫ > ou 203
  ŏ 165, 205
    ŏ > ǫ 205
  ǫ > uo 177
  o for au 212–3
  oi > œ > e 192, 215
  oó > o 225
  ou > ǫu 167
  unaccented 219, 228, 229 (6), 243, 244
  uó > o 225
-o 37, 40
o (Greek) 186

ω (Greek) 185
ob 14, 79
ob– 28
obdormire 28
obferre 32
obliscor 324
oblitare 34
obprimere 32
observasione 277
oc 251
occansio 311
occidere 212
occubavit 256
occu(m)bas 306
occurire 406
–occus 37
ocio 276
ocium 276
octa(gi)nta 380
oc(u)lus 219, 234
odedere 426
Odissia 187
œ 215
  œ for æ and e 215
offeret 406
offerire 406
offersi 429
offertus 435, 440
offla 235
oi > œ > e 192, 215
οι (Greek) 192
ola 213
oleo 274
oleum 38, 274
oli 274
oli(m) 309
olio 274
omnes = –is 244
omnimodus 44
omnis 12, 71
omo 251
–omus 446
on 71
–on 36
–ον 38
–ων 38
–ones 40
–oneus 39

INDEX.

-onius 39
-*ons* 446
-o(n)sus 311
onus 11
ọ́ó > o 225
operare 409
ophekion = officium 334
opprobare 28
-or 37, 42
  feminine 346 (2)
  -or > -re 245
  -or > -ura 42
ora = hora 251
oracionem 276
orata = aur- 212
oratia = Hor- 251
oratorium 37
orbus 9
Order of Words 50-3
Ordinal Numerals 382
-orem 346 (3)
oricla 212, 229 (7)
oridium 339
-orium 37
-orius 39
orma 186, 337
ornatura 37
orphanus 186
ortaret 432
ortus = hor- 251
orum = aurum 212
orzo 272
os (masc.) 349
-*os* (Greek) 38
Oscan 2
-osco > -usco 197, 202-3
ossiculum 42
ossuculum 42
ossulum 37
ossum 356 (3)
ostensio 37
ostensor 37
ostentare 34
ostia = hos- 251
ostium 202
ostrum = aus- 212
ot = aut 213, 229 (7)
ote = aut 213, 229 (7)

otia 277
otobris 266
otogentos 266
-ottus 37
ου **(Greek)** 193
ọụ > ọu 167
Ouiouia = Vibia 318, 322
oum 167, 324
ovum 167, 217, 324
oze = hodie 272
ozie = hodie 272

p : see **Labials**
paceveci = pacifici 321
pagandum 256
pag̣anus 8, 263
pa(g)e(n)sis 39, 259
palanca 332
palasium 277
Palatalization 258-62, 272-8, 296
Palatals 271-8, 296
  by 273
  c': see **Gutturals**
  cy 276, 278
  dy 272
  g': see **Gutturals**
  gy 272
  j 271
  ly 274
  ny 274
  py 273
  ry 296
  scy 275
  ssy 275
  sty 275
  sy 275
  ty 276-7
  vy 273
palatium 277
palleum 224
palma 145
palpebrum 352
palpres 134
pandiderunt 426
pani 364
panneus 39
pantaisar 332

paor 324
papaver (masc.) 347, 369
papilionis (nom.) 367
pap(p)a -us 16
papyrius 39
parabula 144, 236
parabulare 155
paradisus 190
paraula 236, 318
parcui 428
parecer 414
parens 10, 12
parentis (nom.) 367
parentorum 368
pari 364
par(i)etes 136, 225
parietibus 224
Parigi 86, 227
pari mente 41
Paris 86
Parisiis 227
parsi 429
parsus 439, 441
part 160
partenem 416
Participle
  Fut. Active 106
  Fut. Passive 105, 408
  Perfect 102, 108, 434-41
  Present 102, 104, 107, 408
Particles 156-8
particularis 39
partunt 416
parutus 438, 439
pasmer 300
passans 39
passi(m) 309
Passive 112-4, 409
passos 355
paucum tempus 13
paucus 71
paul(l)um 161
Paulus -onis 362
paupera 376
pauperorum 376
pausa 38
pavi 428

pa(v)onem 324
pa(v)orem 324
pavura 42
pavutus 440
paze 260
pectinare 33
pectorem 347
pediculus 42
pedis (nom.) 367
peduclum 234
peduculus 42
pejor 170, 377
pejus 377
pelegrinus 292
pellabor 293
pellicere 293
pellige 293
pello 293
pendutus 441
pe(n)sare 171, 311
pensi 429
pensus 441
Penult 232–9
per 14, 79, 93, 96, 99
per > pel 293
per 160
per– 26
percolopabat 237
perdedit 139, 426
perdita 37 (–ta)
perdonare 26
perdutus 438, 439
pere 160
pere(g)rinus 270
peres = pedes 281 (2)
Perfect 121–4, 410, 422–31
 Strong 427–31
 Weak 422–6
Perfect Participle: see Participle
Perfect Subjunctive 119, 123–4
per giro 48
per girum 48
peria(t) 285
Periphrastic Future 126
perít 423
perlum = præ– 294

perpenna 292
persi 429
pe(r)s(i)ca 239
persona 71
Personal Pronouns: see Pronouns
persus 439, 441
Pesaro 151
pessica 291
pessimus 377
pestio 284
pestulum 284
petít 423
Petrus –onis 362
petto 160
peuma 268
ph: see Greek Consonants
phalanx 181
pharetra 145
phaselus 334
Phasis 181
Phebus 192
phiala 145
philosophia 37
philus 184
phimus 184
Phitonis 332
phitonissæ 332
phoca 185
Phœbus 192
Phonology 131–344
Phyebæ = Phœbe 215
piano 40
pictus 440
pietas 298
pietra 160
pignus 172 (2)
pi(g)ritia 270
Pilipus 332
pinctus 440
pin? 365
pinxi 429
piper 38, 183, 347, 369
piperem 347, 369
pirata 144, 190
Pisaurese 297
Pisaurum 151
pitocco 185

pius 167
placentia 37
plach 154
placuit 223, 326
plagiare 33
plangit 259
plantare 33
planura 37
planxi 429
platea 146, 190
plaudisti 426
pleps 297, 315
plicare 10, 435
plicatus 435
plodere 213
ploja 169, 208 (4), 273
plostrum 212
plotus 212, 213
plovere 169, 208 (4), 217
pluere 169, 208 (4), 217
Pluperfect 118, 123–4, 410
 432, 433
Pluperfect Subjunctive 118, 123, 433
plurigo = pr– 292
plus 56, 74
pluvia 169, 208 (4), 273
poco 40
podium 272
poella 208
pœna 192
poeta 192
poggio 272
polippus 145
pollicare 37
pollulum 213
pols 370
poltre 134
polve 370
polvo 370
polypus 145
pomex 207 (2)
pon(e)re 239
pontevecem 321
pontivicatus 256
pontufex 220
poplex 255
pop(u)lus 10, 235

INDEX.

por 14
porcellus 37
porphyreticum 187
portare 12
posi = posui 428, 429
Position 160–4
positus 238, 439
posmeridianus 285
posse 126 (3), 403 (1)
Possessives: see Pronouns
posso 403 (1)
pos(t) 96, 285
postea 275
pos(t)quam 11, 285
posturus 238
postus 238
Post-Verbal Nouns 21
posueram 285
posuet 244
posui(t) 285
potebam 403 (1)
potebo 403 (1)
poteo 403 (1)
potere 403 (1)
pôteri 410
potestas 356 (3)
potionare 33
potis 17
potius 74
præ 14
præ– 28
præber(e) 242
præcoca 376
præda 209
prædestinare 28
præediscer(e) 242
præfetto 266
prægna(n)s 255, 311
præstare 31
præstavi 422, 430
præstus 376
prandium 272
pranzo 272
pre– 28
prebiter 300
preda 209
Prefixes 21–32

pregnax = prægnans 255; cf. 311
prendere 225, 250
prendiderunt 426
prendo 250
prensi 429
prensio 37
prensus 441
Prepositions 76–81, 85–9
presbyter 148, 300
presbyterum 148
Present 120
for Future 126 (1)
Stems 273, 397, 401, 403–5, 415, 416–9
presentis (nom.) 367
presium 277
pressi 429
pressorium 37
pressura 37
pressus 441
presta 210
presteti 139
prete 300
pretium 277
preveire 300
pride(m) 309
primitius 324
principens 367
pri(n)cipis 306
Prixsilla 255
pro 14, 79, 95
pro– 28
probai 424
Proclitics 156–8
prodis 17
Progne 330
proles 11
prolongare 28
promptulus 39
Pronouns 59–71, 383–95
Demonstrative 61–8
Indefinite 71, 395
Interrogative 69–70, 393–4
Personal 60, 67, 384–6
Possessive 60, 387–8
Relative 69–70, 393–4

Pronunciation 131–344
prophetissa 37
prophetizare 19
propietas 292
propio 292
propter 14, 79, 96
provata 318
provitus 435, 439
proximus 377
psallere 36, 337
ptisana 145
pudicicia 276
pugnus 172 (2)
pulvus 347, 370
punctus 440
puni = poni 203
punidor 39
punxi 429
pupillabus 358
puplu 309
pup(p)a 163
pure 40
puritas 37
purpura 145, 186, 330, 332
purpureticum 187
putator = po– 229 (6)
puteolis 136
puteum 347
putrire 400
putrisco 400
puulva 356 (3)
Pyrrhus 187
pyxis 187

q 246, 252, etc.
qu 223, 226, 254
qu > k, 226, 254
qua 82
quadraginta 142, 380; cf 259
quadra(i)nta 380
qua*d*ro 283
quæsi 426, 429
quæstus 436, 440
qualis 70, 71, 394
quamta 306
quan 305

INDEX.

quando 14, 82, 281
quannu 281
Quantity 159–77, 221
  Development of New Quantity 176–7
  Disappearance of Old Quantity 173–5
  Doubtful Quantity 166
  Length before Consonants 170–2
  Position 160–4
  Unaccented Vowels 174, 221
  Vowels in Hiatus 167–9
  Vowel Length 165–77
  Words from Other Languages 174–5
quantu(m) 309
quantus 12, 71
quare 12, 82
quarranta 142, 259, 380
quase 244
quasi 83, 219, 244
quat(t)or 226, 379
quattordecim 379
quat(t)ro 226, 245, 379
quei 393
quejus 393
que(m) 309
quen 305, 309
querceus 39
quercinus 39
querel(l)a 42
questor 210
questus 210
quetus 225
qui 69, 71, 393
qui = quia 82
qui = ky 187, 223
quia 82, 110, 168
quiæti 209
quicumque 71
quid 350
quidem 11
quiensces 311
quietus 225
quin 11
quinqua(gi)nta 142, 380

quinque 172 (1), 200
Quintrio = Win- 344
quippe 11
quique 71
quiritare 229
quis 69, 71, 350, 393
quisque 71
quisquis 71
quo 73
quo = quod 282
quoad 11
quod 14, 82, 110, 282, 350
quodlubet 220
quomodo 14, 82
  > comodo 226
quoniam 14, 82, 110
quooperta = co- 254
quoque 11
quot 12, 71
quot = quod 282
quum > cum 226

r: see Liquids
  rs > ss 291
rabies 319
radius 272
rænante = reg- 269
raggio 272
rama (pl.) 361
ramenc 37 (-incus)
rancura 42
ranucula 42
rap(i)dus 239
rasi 429
rasio = ratio 277
ratio 277
razzo 272
re- 23, 25
recapitulare 25
recípit 139
recolli(g)endo 259
Recomposition 31, 32, 139
rectus 440
recubitus 37 (-ta)
reculons 40
reddedi 31, 139
redempsi 429
redemti 313

redít 423
redivit = -bit 318
refusare 17
re(g)alis 263
re(g)ina 259
regis = -es 244
regnancte 267
regnum 172 (2)
Relatives: see Pronouns
reli(n)quat 306
relinque = -it 285
remasit 311
Remidium 272
remissa 37 (-ta)
renégat 139
renum = reg- 269
Repetition 40, 55, 74
replenus 23
repositorium 37
reprehensus 250
requærere 25, 139
requærit 139
requebit 225
res 10, 71, 355 (2)
  res nata 13, 71
respondĕre 399, 449
responduntur 449
responsi 429
restitueram 285
restivus 39
resurge(n)s 311
retenere 31, 139
retenet 139
retere = reddere 286
retina 17
retro 81
retro- 28
retro(r)sum 291
retundus 229 (6)
reuuardent 344
reve(r)sus 291
reversus sum = reverti 410
revolutio 37
rexi 297, 429
rhetor 335
rhetorissare 33
richesse 341
rictu = rectum 198

INDEX.

ridēre 399
rideri 409
riges = re- 198
rigna 198
rîkitia 341
Rimini 86
ripidus 39
riqueza 341
risi 429
risus 441
rius 241, 324
rivaticus = rip- 314
rivocaverit 229 (2)
roborem 347
robur 9, 347
rogavo = -bo 318
ro(g)itus 259, 435
Romance Territory : p. xi
Roman Empire : p. x
Romanice 40
Romanu (**nom.**) 372
–pos 38
rosi 429
rosum = ros 356 (3)
rosus 441
roubôn 36, 341, 398
rs > ss 291
rubare 36, 341, 398
rubeus 319
rugiada 356 (3)
rura 351
ru(r)sum 291
russum 291
rutare 34

s : see **Sibilants**
 final s in 1st pers. pl.
  445
 initial s + cons. 230
 scy, ssy, sty, sy 275
 sa = ipsa 392
 –sa 37 (–ta)
sabbatizare 19
sablum 235
sacra 376
sacramentum 231
sacrista –anis 359
sacristano 359

sacritus = διάκριτος 272
sæculum (**masc.**) 349
sæpes sepes sæps 209, 367
sæpia 182
saginæ 42
Sagitta 37 (–ittus)
sagma 19, 268; (**fem.**) 349
Saguntum 338
saïne 42
saint 267
sălbatec 229 (3)
salbum 317
salii 422, 428
salitus 436, 440
salivi 428
salma 268
salsi 428, 429
salsus 440, 441
saltem 11
salticulare 35
salvage 229 (3)
salvatico 229 (3)
salvaticus 229 (3)
sanctissimus 377
san(c)tus 172 (1), 267
sandal 330
sanguem 370
sanh 267
sapcha 272
sapēre 402
sapiam 272
sapidus 39
sapienti (**pl.**) 368
sappia 272
sapui 426, 428
satis 74
sauma 268
scabia 355 (2)
scæna 182, 210
scalciare = excalceare 230
scandalizare 19
scaplas 234
Sca(u)rus 211 (1)
scena 182
schema 19
schernire 341
schiatta 343
schietto 343

schioppo 284
sclitib. (stlis) 284
scloppus 284
scopulus 38
scoriare = excor- 230
scriba –anis 359
scripit 312 (1)
scripsi 315, 429
scriptum 315
scri(p)tus 313, 440
scrivano 359
scultor 313
se = si 229 (4)
se = *è* 419 (1)
sead = sit 419 (2)
sebe = sibi 201
secatus 435, 440
secula 200 (3)
secu(n)do 306
secuntur 254
sed 11, 14
sed = *se* 229 (4)
sedano 335
sed(e)cim 239
sedere = esse 402, 419
seditur 399
sedui 428
sedutus 441
segnai = signavi 424
segolo 200 (3)
sei 419 (1)
sel 160
selinum 150
sem 419 (1)
Semelé 359
semita 239
semo 419 (1)
semper semper 74
sempre 245
semul 201, 201 (2)
senape 184
senatus (2d decl.) 355 (1)
sene = sine 201
senex 12
senper 306
senta = semita 239
sentam 416
sententem 416

senti 298
sentia 421
sentii 428, 429
sentitus 436, 441
sentor 37
separare seperare 231, 233
sepelitus 436, 440
sepes 209
sepia 146, 182
seppia 182
sepsies 277
septa(gi)nta 380
septe(m) 309
septrum 260
septuazinta 339
septum 209
sepulchrum 251
sequere 406
sequire 406
serbare 323
serbat 323
serbus 317
Serios = Sergius 272
serore = so- 229 (7)
serpentinus 37
serra = sera 247
serutinus 16
servare 323
servicium 276
servire 323
servisium 277
servitium 276, 277
servitudo 37
ses = es 419 (1)
šes̆ 419 (1)
sest = est 419 (1)
set = est 419 (1)
set = sed 282
seta 209
setaceus 39
setis = estis 419 (1)
settembres 313
seus = suus 387
si 14, 83, 229 (4)
si = sibi 385
siam 419 (2)
siamus 419 (2)
sibe 219, 244

sibi 201, 219, 221, 244, 385
sibī 219, 244, 385
Sibilants 297–302, etc.
 final s 298, 445
 initial s + cons. 230
 scy, ssy, sty, sy, 275
 ss > s 161
 z: see Greek Consonants
sic 264
Sicilianus 39
sidibus = se- 198
siede 419 (1)
siem 419 (2)
siete 419 (1)
siffatto 264
siffler 318 (2)
sifilus 318 (2)
signum –us 172 (2), 347
sigricius = secretius 256
silevit 422, 428
simus 220, 419 (1)
sinapis –e –i 38, 150, 184, 337
sinatus 228
sine 95, 201
sinexter 201 (3)
–sio 37
sirena 356 (3)
sis = si vis 324
sive 11
skëna 347
skërnôn 341
skiuhan 343
slahta 343
slëht 343
soaru 295
soave 224
sobreus 224
socera 37
soc(e)rum 232, 233
soef 224
sofferire 406
sol 13
solacium 276
sola mente 41
solatium 276
solbere 317

solbit 323
solia 224
soliculus 13, 18
sol(i)dus 237
solingo 37 (–incus)
solo (dat.) 395
solsi 429
soltus 438, 439, 440
soluit 224
solus 395
solutus 438
solvitus 438, 439
soma 268
somos 419 (1)
sona = zona 338
sonatus 435
sons 419 (1)
sophia 146
–sor 37
sorcerus = sortiarius 39
 (–arius)
sordidius 377
sorex 42, 213
soricem 42, 213
–sorium 37
–sorius 39
soro(r) 295
sous = suus 167, 387
sozer 154
spacium 276
spallere 337
spandere = exp- 230
Spania 230
Spanus 230
sparsi 429
sparsus 441
spasmus 144
spat(h)a 332
spat(u)la 12, 38, 234
speca = spica 200 (3)
speclarait = -avit 424
spectante = exp- 230
spëhon 343
spelunca 329
spene 355 (2)
speni from spes 355 (2)
speramus = –avimus 424
sperantia 37

INDEX. 215

spes 355 (2)
spiritus (**2d decl.**) 355 (1)
splorator = exp- 230
spoliatur = -or 244
spo(n)sus 171
spontaneus 39
squarciare 276
ss > s 161
staacio 276
stablarius 231
stagnum (**masc.**) 349
stahu 397
stais 397
stait 397
stantia = inst- 230
stao 397
stare 397
stasio 277
statio 277
status 438
staŭ 397
staunt 397
stegola 200 (3)
stel(l)a 163
Stephanus 183
steti 426, 428, 430
stetti 426
stetui 426, 428, 430
steva 200 (3)
stilla = stella 198
stingo 226
-stinxi 429
stipes = stips 367
stirpis (**nom.**) 367
stlataris 284
stlis 284
stloppus 284
storax 187
stren(n)a 163
stren(n)uor 164
Stress : see Accent
strîban 341
strictus 440
strinctus 440
strinxi 429
strofa 334
stropa 334
stroppus 186

strucere 417
structus 440
struere 417
strugere 417
strumentum = inst- 230
struxi 429
stupescere 35
stup(p)a 163
suabitati 318
suadel(l)a 42
suavis 224
Suavitta 37 (-ittus)
sub- 26
subaudire 26
subcludere 26
subcumbere 32
Subjunctive 117-9
 for Imper. 116
 for Indic. 117
 Imperfect 118
 Perfect 119, 410
 Plup. = Imperf. 118
 Pres. 397, 403, 405, 415, 419 (2)
sublimus 376
submonsus 439, 441
subornatris 255
subplantare 32
subsannare 26
Substitution of Words 13
subterranus 42
subtus 81
suc(c)us 163
suceroni 362
sud = sub 315
sufferit 406
suffertus 435, 440
Suffixes 33-42
 Change of Suffix 42
 for Adj. 39
 for Adv. 40, 41
 for Nouns 37, 38
 for Verbs 33-6
 Greek Endings 36, 38
suis (**nom.**) 367
sulphurem 347, 369
sumpsi 298
sumptus 308

sumus 220, 419 (1)
suora 295
suos 138
super 80, 90, 96
super- 26
superabundare 26
superfacere 26
superstitis (**nom.**) 367
Supine 103
sup(p)ra 164
sup(p)remis 164
supra- 26
suprafacere 26
supre 245
-sura 37
Surd > Sonant : see Voicing
sursi 429
su(r)sum 291
surtus 440
sus = suus 226, 388
-sus 37, 441
sus(s)um 291
sutis 419 (1)
suus 60, 387-8
sy = ty 277
sycomum 141
sycotum 141
Syllabication 131-3
symphonia 146, 332
Syncope 219, 229, 231-9
Synonyms 12
Syntax 50-130

t : see **Dentals**
ty 276-7
-ta 37
tab(u)la 236
tactus 440
talentum 149, 330
talis 71
tamen 11, 14, 84
tan 306
tanctus 440
tanger(e) 242
tantu(m) 309
tantus 71
tanxi 429
tapinus 144

tapis 182
tapit 182
tap(p)ete 162
tarde 40
tarir 342, 407
-tas 37
tasso 342, 343
tata 16; -anis 359
Tatius 277
tatus 16
taula 236, 318
taurellus 37
taxi 429
telebra = ter- 292
tempaccio 39
tempesta 356 (3)
templus 347
tempo 298
tempus 13
tenit 244
ten(n)uis 164
Tense 120-30
tensi 429
tensura 13
tensus 441
ténueram 137
tenui 428
tenutus 438, 440
Teodor 332
-ter 40
tercius 276
Terentio = -us 298
tergĕre 399
tergum -us 347
termen 356 (3)
terminaciones 276
terra(m) 309
tersi 429
tersus 441
-της 38
testa 13
tetrus 376
texui 428
texutus 440
thahso 342, 343
tharrjan 342, 407
theios 333
thensaurus 311

Theophilus 333
thesaurizare 19
thesaurus -um 189, 347
thrēscan 342
ti = tibi 385
-tiacum 277
tibe 244
tibī 221, 244, 385
-tim 40
timbre 187, 331
timor (**fem.**) 346 (2)
timoratus 39
timpurĭ 369
tinctus 440
tingo 226
tinguere 226
tins < census 260
tinxi 429
-tio 37
Titius 277
Tivoli 86
toll(e)re 239
tollitus 435, 439
tolsi 428, 429
tolui 428
tomolus = tumu- 208
tonatus 435
tondĕre 399
tonica = tu- 208
tonsus 441
-tor 37
torcĕre 399
torco 226, 399
toreomatum 191
-torium 37
-torius 39
torma = tu- 208
tornus 186
torqu(e)o 226, 399
torsi 428
tortus 440
tot 71
tot 204 (2)
toto (**dat.**) 395
tot(t)us 12, 71, 163, 204 (2), 395
totum (**adv.**) 74
tous = tuus 387

tra- 26, 299
trabucare 26
tracere 417
tractatus 9
tractus 440
tradedit 31, 139
traducir 299
traduire 299
Tragani = Traj- 259
tragere 417
trahere 417
trans- 26, 299
transannare 26
tra(ns)duco 299
tra(ns)jicio 299
tra(ns)luceo 299
tra(ns)mitto 299
transplantare 26
tra(ns)pono 299
tra(ns)tulo 299
tra(ns)veho 299
traps 315
trasporre 299
travis (**nom.**) 367
traxi 429
trebus 201
trei = tres 379
trei 298
treis 177
tremulat 235
trepaliare 33
trepalium 16
tres 379
trescar 342
trib(u)la 235, 352
tribuna(l) 242, 289
Trícasses 151
trienta 259
trí(g)inta 142, 259, 380
trinitas 37
trinta 380
tris = tres 198
tristus 376
triumphaut 241, 325, 424
-trix 37
trobaire 37 (-tor)
Troge = -jæ 259
Troja 170

INDEX. 217

Troyes 151
tructa 38, 185
trutina 187
tu 60
tucti 204 (2)
-tudo 37
tuit 204 (2)
tulĕrunt 450
-tulus > -clus 234
tum = tuum 226, 388
tumum 187
tuos 138
-tura 37
turrensis 39
turri -e 364
-tus 37 (-ta), 440
Tuscanus 39
tutto 204 (2)
tuttus 204 (2)
tuus 226, 387–8
ty 276–7
  ty > cy 277
  ty > sy 277

u 165, 206–8, etc.
  accented 206–8
    ū 206–7
    ū > u 165, 206
    ŭ 208
    ŭ > u̯ > o̯ 165, 208
  u cons. 222, 326
  ü 178, 187, 192, 206, 220
  ui 216
  unaccented 219, 228, 229 (5), 243, 244
  in hiatus 222–6
    uo > o 226
    uu > u 226
    uó > o 225
    uu > u 226
ubi 73
-uc(c)us 37 (-icca)
-uculare 35
-uculus 42
-udo > -umen 42
ü 178, 187, 192, 206, 220
-ugo 37 (-ago)
ui 216

-ula 37 (-ulus)
Ulixes 187
ultra 166
-ulus 37, 39
  > -ellus 42
-um 40
Unaccented Vowels: see Vowels
unde 10, 70, 73, 84, 393
undecim 166, 379
-undus 39
ungo 226
unguere 226
unicornis 44
unigenitus 44
unire 34
uno (**dat.**) 429
-unt = -ent 449
unus 10, 57, 71, 298, 378, 395
  unu(s) 298
unxi 429
uó > o 225
uo **unacc.** > o 226
uobit = obiit 177
-ura 37, 42
Uranus 193
urbis (**nom.**) 367
urbs 12, 297, 315, 367
-ŭrem 346 (3)
urps 297, 315
usare 34
Use of Cases 85–100
Use of Inflections 85–130
Use of Words 54–84
usque hodie 47
ustium 202
ut 11, 14, 82, 111
-uta 37 (-ta)
utrum 11, 14, 83
-utus 39, 42, 438, 440, 441
uu **unacc.** > u 226
uuadius 344
-uus > -itus 42
uxo(r) 295
uxore (**abl.**) 244

v: see Labials
vacuus 42 195 (6), 223

vadere 126 (5), 405
vadum 344 ; -us 347
valde 237
valia(t) 224, 285
Valinca 37 (-incus)
vallensis 39
valneas = ba- 316
vanitare 34
vaqua = vacua 223
vaqui = vacui 223
vastare 344
vasus -um 347, 356 (3)
vea = via 201
vecere = veh- 417
vecinus 229 (4)
veclus 234, 284
vedea 421
veďere 283
vef 226
vegere = veh- 417
ve(he)mens 250
vehere 417
vel 11
velle 126 (3), 403
vendita 37 (-ta)
vendutus 438
vene = bene 316
veni 428, 430
veninum 42
venire 126 (5)
venitus 436, 438, 440
venui 428, 430
venuta 37 (-ta)
venutus 436, 438, 440
ver 13
verbex = vervex 323
Verb Forms
  Inflection: see Conjugation
  Use 72, 101–30
Verbs: see Verb Forms
verbus 347, 349
verecundia 231
verecunnus 281
vernac(u)lųs 234
vernum tempus 13
ve(r)sus 291
vertragus 19

vervex 323
ves(s)ica 162
vestibat 420
vetatus 435
vet(e)ranus 219, 231
vettovaglia 154
vetulus 12, 13, 234, 284
vetus 13
veyo = video 272-3
vezem 445
vezzo 278
-vi = -vui 428
via 167, 201
viaticum 8, 239
vibi = bibi 318
vibit = bibit 316
victore (nom.) 367
victualia 18, 37
victurias 203
vic(u)lus 234, 284
videderunt 426
video 272-3, 416
videre 72, 272-3, 283, 416, 428, 430, 438, 441
videunt 416
vidi 428, 430
vido = video 416
vidui = vidi 428, 430
vidutus 438, 441
viduus 226
vieni 177
vig(i)lat 259
vi(gi)nti 142, 259, 380
vilescere 34
villa 10, 12, 358
villabus 358
Vincentzus 277
vincisti 426
vinctus 440
vincui 428
vincutus 440
vindemiator 224
vindico 239
vindimia 197
vindo = ve- 197
vinia = -ea 224
vinsi 428, 429
vinti 380

vinus 347
virginem 233
vir(i)diaria 237
vir(i)dis 237
vir(i)dura 18, 37
viror 37
virtus 10
viscui = vixi 428, 429
visit = vixit 255; cf. 285, 428
vistus 441
visus 441
vitellus 37
vitium 278
vitricus 13
vit(u)lus 234
vius = vivus 324
vivacius 377
vixcit = vixit 255; cf. 285, 428
vixi 255, 285, 428, 429
vixi(t) 285; cf. 255, 428
vixutus 440
vobīs 385; cf. 318
Vocabulary 6-49
vocatio = vac- 195 (6)
Vocative 87
vocitus = vacuus 42, 195 (6)
vocitus = vocatus 435, 439
vocuus = vac- 195 (6)
Voice 112-4
Voicing 256-7, 286, 297, 314, 321
volatilia 37
volemus 403 (2)
volere = velle 403 (2)
voles 403 (2)
volestis 403 (2)
volimus 403 (2)
volon 39 (-undus)
volsi 429
voltus 438, 439, 440
voluntate (nom.) 367
volutus 438
volvitus 438, 439
voster 199 (1), 387
vovis = vobis 318; cf. 385
Vowels 136-8, 165-245
Accented 194-218

Clerical Pronun. 218
Diphthongs 209-16
Influence of Labials 217
Single Vowels 194-208
before gn 172 (2)
before j 170
before n + fricative 171
before nk 172 (1)
Breaking 177
Celtic Vowels 179
Close and Open 165
Differentiation 165
German Vowels 179
Greek Vowels 180-93
in hiatus 136-8, 167-9
in words borrowed by other languages 174-5
Latin Vowels 178
Position 160-4
Quantity 165-77, 221
Unaccented 219-45
Final Syl. 240-5
in hiatus 222-7
Init. Syl. 228-30
Intert. Syl. 231
Penult 232-9
Quantity 221
Vulgar Latin 3, 4
Vulgar Words 15, 19
vulnus (masc.) 349

w (Ger.) 344
w (Latin) 224
Waddo 344
wadum 344
wahta 343
walde 344
Wandali 344
warjan 344
warnjan 36, 407
wastare 344
watan 19, 344
wërra 19, 344
werrarius 39
werrizare 33
wiðarlōn 342

Wintrio 344
wîsa 344
witan 36, 398
Word Order 50-3
wost- 344

x 246, 255, 266

y (Greek) 187
y (Latin) 224
ymnus 251

z 246
zabul(l)us = dia- 339
zacones = dia- 339
zaconus = dia- 272, 339
zagante 229 (3)
zampogna 332
zanuari = ja- 339
zebus = die- 339
Zefurus 187
zelosus 339
zerax = hierax 339

zes = dies 272
Zesu = Jesu 272, 339
zeta = diæta 339
zie = die 272
zins 260
zio 333
ziziper 312 (1)
Zodorus = Theo- 277
Zogenes = Dio- 272
zosum = deorsum 339
Zouleia = Julia 272, 339

www.ingramcontent.com/pod-product-compliance
Lightning Source LLC
Chambersburg PA
CBHW020850090426
42736CB00008B/315